The Society for Psychical Research
1882–1982

A HISTORY

The Society for Psychical Research
1882–1982

A HISTORY

Renée Haynes

MACDONALD & CO
LONDON & SYDNEY

©1982 by Renée Haynes
First published in Great Britain in 1982 by
Macdonald & Co (Publishers) Ltd
London
Maxwell House
74 Worship Street
London EC2A 2EN

ISBN 0 356 07875 2

Filmset, printed and bound in Great Britain by
Hazell Watson & Viney Ltd, Aylesbury, Bucks

Contents

Acknowledgements

The author and publishers would like to thank the Society for Psychical Research for permission to quote from its *Journal* and *Proceedings*. These quotations and all others are also acknowledged in the text.

Much gratitude is also due to the Society's Secretary, Eleanor O'Keeffe, for her constant generous help with detailed references and small essential items of information, and its Librarian, Nicholas Clark-Lowes. I should moreover like to thank my kind typist Miss Caroline Clayson for coping with my handwriting and with my afterthoughts so patiently and efficiently over the last five years.

Thanks, too, to all the people who have talked over the themes of this book with me – and are not responsible for the use I have made of their remarks. I remember with love Rosalind Heywood, constructive, sympathetic but by no means always in agreement in our happy discussions.

Foreword

Though Jane Austen said that history should always be written by a partial, passionate and prejudiced historian, it could reasonably be felt that these are not really the qualities needed to deal with the records and the development of a century-old learned Society. Still, no one is without them; and the historian can best discount their influence on what he has written by stating what they are. After that, to adapt the legal maxim a little, *Caveat lector*; let the reader beware.

I shall try, therefore, to make plain — as far as I am conscious of them — just where my own partialities, prejudices and passions lie. They are all in favour of careful objective observation, all against dismissing reported events as impossible 'because they cannot happen'; a very common practice among distinguished persons who have been trained to exclude 'irrelevant' considerations from their reasoning, to cultivate a kind of tunnel vision that can only follow the headlights of the intellectual car they are driving along a road mapped out in accordance with preconceived ideas. That

> 'Geographers on pathless downs
> Put elephants for want of towns'

is rightly to be condemned; but it is wrong to lump in with them those earlier cartographers who inscribed on certain regions 'Here be dragons' (giant lizards, as at Komodo? the skeletons of prehistoric saurians?), inscriptions which ought surely to inspire the explorer to go and see for himself.

The habit of rejecting the unfamiliar, disguising intellectual sloth as a strict desire for truth has of course a very long history indeed. To look back no more than a century or so: in the era of philosophic rationalism − or rationalization − Hume rejected first-hand accounts of what would now be called psychosomatic cures at the Cemetery of Saint-Médard because, he said, these were miracles, and the laws of nature showed that miracles could not happen. In the early Victorian age experts who wanted to dismiss the fact that hypnosis could inhibit awareness of pain argued that a patient under hypnotic anaesthesia had shown no sign of discomfort while his leg was being sawn off, quite simply *because he had been paid not to scream*. Later on, as Brian Inglis has shown in his delightful *Natural and Supernatural*,[1] French experts argued, when the telephone was first demonstrated to them, that the demonstrator had had a ventriloquist hidden under the table.

I am also, personally, more disposed to accept the evidence for paranormal events given by ordinary reputable well-balanced eye witnesses, by anthropologists, by historians and by lawyers accustomed to weighing testimony than that yielded by prolonged large-scale experiments and evaluated by statistical methods, useful as these procedures can be. This is not only because I am what is disdainfully labelled in some circles 'an Arts type', and because my own mind is not a mathematical one and my own inclination is to agree with Disraeli's remarks as to 'Lies, Damned Lies, and Statistics' (to which one might now add Computers, whose results can be so successfully fiddled by experts such as the gentleman who was discovered by the merest accident a year or two ago to have transferred, ingeniously and painlessly, sums from various bank accounts to his own).

My preference for spontaneous cases arises also from a conviction that paranormal faculties are best studied in the context of ecology − the natural setting of time and place and interacting circumstance in which they arise − rather than in the laboratory; and that if they are also to be examined in scientific terms, such terms should be those of the life sciences, such as biology and physiology, rather than those of physics. This is because they emerge in living beings, and the more highly organized those beings are, the more they will vary,

1. London, 1977.

not only in themselves, but in their reactions to different backgrounds and people. This is why it is so difficult to produce the 'replicable experiments' so often demanded. Humans are individuals, conscious selves, each one of them unique; and it is useless to assume that they can be treated as units of awareness all equally endowed – or not endowed – with paranormal faculties all working at the same rate in the same way, so that if you only test enough of them you will get exactly the same results wherever, and whenever, and by whomsoever the tests are carried out. There are, inevitably, too many variables.

Nevertheless I am sure that quantitative experiments can contribute much to psychical research – those with the plethysmograph, described in chapter 8, have certainly done so – so long as they are carried out by people who keep in mind that 'the time, the place and the loved one' may produce one result where a different time and place and person may well produce another. A laboratory at ten in the morning, with a detached and unfamiliar figure operating incomprehensible machinery is not always good at evoking faculties rooted in the process of keeping alive as an individual or as a species, and in primordial emotions.

'Partiality, prejudice and passion' probably have much to do with what I have called[1] – by analogy with the pain threshold which varies so much from one individual to another – the Boggle Threshold; the level above which the mind boggles when faced by some new fact or report or idea. That of the academic is usually fairly low: that of various Californian sects tends to be pretty high. My own boggle threshold is fairly high, calmly acceptant, where reports of telepathy, precognition and poltergeist outbreaks are concerned, since all of them have been observed so often and in so many parts of the world throughout the centuries (and probably because I have personally come across all three). It drops sharply, however, when presented with concepts such as ectoplasm, materialization and reincarnation, and reacts with violence to the use of esoteric language, whether of the respectable, highly technical variety best known as Computerisch – all too often used as a status symbol – or of the sort concerned with 'vibes', higher planes and undefined 'auras'. (I once met a woman who was flying to the west coast of America to have her 'torn aura' repaired by some guru expert in invisible mending,

---

1. Cf *Encounter*, August/September 1980.

and longed to know if it were going to be darned, patched or glued, and what with.)

This second kind of idiom, the language neither of science, nor of intuition, nor of every day, is apt to expand into such totally meaningless sentences as 'Pure consciousness is the essence of pure nature and manifests itself as infinite correlation blocking out negative thought'. If you go to a fair you can see how a very small dollop of pink sugar can bubble in the vendor's machine into a vast fluff of candy floss – and taste how a mouthful reduces itself to no more than a faint metallic tang on the palate. This particular idiom is best compared to curried candy floss. I have mentioned it because I am allergic to it and probably unfair to those who use it.

I have tried to write a history of the Society's work and achievements rather than of its members themselves and their interactions, explosive as these have sometimes been. All this must be taken as part of the nature of things in an association of sharp and lively minds from different backgrounds. The Society has always included scientists of various disciplines, philosophers, writers and painters, technicians and business men, clerics, doctors of medicine (and other subjects), the tough-minded, the tender-minded and the open-minded, detached observers and zealots for this or that point of view. Man is a political animal, and every human group must contain people sympathetic or unsympathetic to one another, people conditioned to work in different ways, people painfully aware of how fast academic attitudes may degenerate into pedantry, how soon acceptance may decay into credulity, people who even think in different modalities, as that distinguished member not long dead, Dr W. Grey Walter, Head of Research at the Burden Neurological Institute at Bristol, pointed out in his *Eddington Memorial Lecture* for 1968[1]. This should be read by all who have to deal with ferocious arguments and fundamental misunderstandings past or present. He pointed out that some people think – as he did himself – in terms of sensory imagery, colour, shape, texture for instance, while others (many of them scientists, as Galton pointed out long ago) think in an almost entirely abstract way.

Those at either end of a very broad spectrum may wholly fail to grasp one another's modes and sequences of thought. Those in the middle, so to speak, who are able to use both are specifically taught,

---

1. Cambridge University Press, 1969.

if they choose to do scientific work, to use the abstract mode alone and, often implicitly, to despise the rest.

Grey Walter pleaded that each group should be induced to recognize the other's way of thinking as perfectly valid and urged to learn it, as an alternative language of the mind. The importance of his argument for theologians and philosophers, iconoclasts and devotees, mathematicians and writers, is obvious. It is equally important in the work of the Society for Psychical Research. This is not incidentally highly centralized and monolithic, but is carried out by individuals or small groups. I have tried to concentrate on that work itself rather than on the different ways of approach to it; but they need to be recognized. Moreover, it is not only members of what used to be called the Two Cultures who are liable to disagree with one another. Personal, social, ethical and political differences, different culture patterns, and above all different and unquestioned assumptions will provoke misunderstanding. And those of different faiths or none – Agnostics and Atheists, Buddhists, Christians, Jews, Muslims, Spiritualists, Theosophists, Unitarians and so down the alphabet possibly to Zenists and Zoroastrians – will consciously or unconsciously relate their findings to their beliefs; sometimes to the enrichment of both, sometimes to the impoverishment of one or the other, especially if an easy and misleading reductionism is involved. On the whole, though, there can be a stimulus to thought, and to new modes of understanding perennial ideas. It must always be remembered however that no research of any kind can be a religion; certainly not psychical research. It is an exploration, a continual attempt to consider the workings of the psi function and what it implies about the complex nature of reality in general and about the interaction of mind and body in particular.

Last of all: I am conscious all the time of how much I have had to omit, to sketch briefly rather than to explore in depth, to indicate rather than to discuss. I can only plead in mitigation that this book could have taken ten years to write and ten volumes to print. Even so, there have been times when the process seemed like trying to reduce the primeval soup whence life on earth evolved into a packet of Oxo cubes. I have tried to indicate my own preferences so that you may make allowances for them.

RENEÉ HAYNES.

The Society: Aims and Structure; Ends and Means

The Society for Psychical Research was founded in 1882, largely by a group of scientists and philosophers connected with Trinity College, Cambridge. Its aims, as succinctly set out in every number of the Journal, are 'to examine without prejudice or prepossession and in a scientific spirit those faculties of man, real or supposed, which appear to be inexplicable in terms of any generally recognized hypotheses'. It does not hold or express corporate views.

Its Articles of Association, formally adopted in 1895, and signed by Henry Sidgwick, W. F. Barrett, FRS, F. W. H. Myers and others, declare that among its functions are to investigate psychical phenomena, including hypnotism, somnambulism and thought transference; to help students and enquirers; to establish or help to establish similar Societies in Britain and overseas; to run reading rooms and laboratories; and to hold discussion meetings and lectures. Constitutional and administrative procedures were also set up.

The Society was reconstituted in 1955 in accordance with the provisions of the Companies Act of 1948. Its Council was to consist of eighteen members elected at an Annual General Meeting. Six of these retire (after three years' service) every year but may stand for re-election. The Council may co-opt up to twelve members, each for one year.

It elects new members of the Society, provided that they can furnish two references each. This is done by ballot if there is any difference of opinion.

The Council also elects – or re-elects – a President every year. He (or a Vice-President) acts as Chairman at each Annual General Meeting within his term of office. He is *ex-officio* a member of all the Committees annually appointed by Council to handle various aspects of the Society's work.

There were many such Committees in early days, but their number has declined of late, and their function has in many cases shifted towards discussion and advice. Among the most important at present is the Research Grants Committee which examines applications for money to finance various research projects, some at universities, some in the field. The Library Committee has the continuing responsibility of dealing with a large and important collection of archives – letters, pamphlets, periodicals from many parts of the world – and books ancient and modern. It also buys new works. A Management Committee, consisting of some of the Society's officers, makes recommendations on administrative matters to Council for approval.

The Society's first volume of *Proceedings*, published in January 1883, contained its Constitution and Rules and put on record that 'membership does not imply any particular view of the phenomena under investigation' nor any belief in 'physical forces other than those recognized by Physical Science'.

The *Journal*, first published in 1884, was available only to members until 1949. Until 1981 it was edited by members with a general interest in the Society's range of studies; but it is now to be run by a series of distinguished academics, the first of whom is Dr John Beloff, of the University of Edinburgh. It appears three times a year.

Proceedings are not very often issued today, as the cost of printing is so high, but an informal News Letter is now being published.

The Society also produces many pamphlets, leaflets, cassettes of lectures given at its monthly meetings and the text of the Myers Memorial Lectures which have been delivered at irregular intervals since 1942; irregular again because the fund set up to establish them has to cover the costs of printing. Pre-eminent among the lecturers have been G. N. M. Tyrrell (whose study of *Apparitions* is now available as a fully fledged book which has been translated into several languages), C. D. Broad, Gabriel Marcel the French philosopher, Garth Moore, Emilio Servadio the Italian psychiatrist, Robert Thouless and W. Grey Walter.

Though the Perrott-Warrick Studentship in psychical research set up in memory of F. W. H. Myers at Trinity College, Cambridge is completely independent of the Society, it has been held by a number of its members (see Appendix I).

One of them, Celia Green, served for a time as Research Officer to the Society, a post which has appeared and disappeared as financial fortunes fluctuated. Dr E. J. Dingwall devoted his remarkable energies to it for a period in the nineteen-twenties; Dr Woolley resigned from it in 1931, and Dr – now Professor – Donald West, later a President, held the post until a full-time worker in the field could no longer be financed. He then devoted much energy to unpaid part-time work. It is now sadly clear that this work must depend on volunteers.

The Society has co-operated with many others, notably in America, France, Germany and Holland (and in its early days with societies in Russia). In our own country its members are beginning to succeed in establishing psychical research as a subject suitable for study at university level. Thus, at the Psychology Department of the University of Edinburgh Dr John Beloff (a former President) will supervise a self-funded candidate working on a post-graduate thesis on some parapsychological topic for a PhD or Master's degree. The Psychology Department of the University of Surrey, at Guildford, offers a course in parapsychology as part of its General Studies programme; the Instructor is Dr Susan Blackmore. And the Department of Teaching Studies at the Polytechnic of North London runs an optional course in parapsychology for students reading for a Bachelor of Education degree. Mrs Anita Gregory, the Instructor, will also give general guidance on the subject.

The Society's Golden Jubilee and its Centenary have both coincided with times of economic stress. On each occasion there have been proposals to change its nature in the interests of its own survival. In 1931 efforts to boost membership by 'becoming a propagandist body' or by trying 'to attract publicity by sensational methods' were rejected by its governing body as 'disastrous in the long run'. In a similar struggle today the same principle looks likely to be victorious. What is the good of keeping a name alive if it no longer represents the same continuing identity, the same integrity of theory and practice in the search for truth?

I

Mechanism and Meaning

The nineteenth century saw the growth among intellectuals in this country of a certain Noble Gloom, at first heartfelt and spontaneous; then cultivated and finally fashionable. It had its roots, I believe, in the conscious or unconscious acceptance of an analogy between living processes and the mechanical triumphs of the industrial revolution. This probably began with Descartes' contention that animals were automata. Then together with the rise and development of technology — spinning jennies, factories, railways — there arose and developed a habit of regarding the whole universe as a vast complex machine. One theologian indeed compared it to a watch invented and set going by the Creator. Darwin's theory of evolution did not only contradict the beliefs of those Christians who accepted a literal interpretation of the Book of Genesis and a cosmic timetable based on Archbishop Usshers's ingenious calculation that the world had been created in 4004 BC at 4 o'clock in the afternoon. It argued that everything had come into being by way of lucky or unlucky chance; that the universal machine had neither designer, nor mechanic, nor purpose; and that even human awareness of its existence was a meaningless by-product of its workings. Consciousness was an epiphenomenon, thought was as it were the sweat of the brain.

Present day analogies with radio, television and theoretical physics have enabled us to admit to our minds a whole host of new ideas, a 'light shot' pattern of thought. This makes it hard to understand from hindsight why the mechanistic view was so easily accepted, not only by physical scientists, engineers and technicians but also by

I

writers and scholars and philosophers, though these of course may have remembered Lucretius' 'fortuitous concourse of atoms'. But so it was, and Victorian prose and poetry alike echo its thudding impact; witness Carlyle[1] on a 'Universe all void of Life, of Purpose, of Volition, even of Hostility . . . one huge immeasurable Steam engine rolling on in dead indifference', and the girl in Meredith's poem looking with despair at the clear night sky ('the stars', she whispered, 'blindly run'), and the conversation of that brilliant young classical scholar F. W. H. Myers with George Eliot in a Cambridge garden when 'she . . . taking as her text the three words . . . God, Immortality, Duty, pronounced with terrible earnestness how inconceivable was the *first*, how unbelievable the *second* and yet how peremptory and absolute the *third*'.

Presently there erupted into public knowledge, apparently from outside the realm of automatic physical causation, the early 'phenomena of Spiritualism'; the spontaneous unaccountable movements of objects, the inexplicable 'voices' heard by sensitives and the rapped out 'messages' that seemed to make sense and to indicate purpose. All this had originated in America in 1848 with what would now be labelled an outbreak of poltergeist activity in a house at Hydesville, near Rochester, New York, into which a Mr and Mrs Fox had just moved with two of their daughters, Margaret who was fifteen and Kate who was twelve. There were rappings, bangings and noises like furniture being dragged around the floor; all were assumed to be the work of a ghost. The girls asked this ghost to answer their questions by way of a code of rappings, whence they worked out that it was the spirit of a pedlar who had been buried in the now waterlogged cellar. A committee of local people investigated what went on, and found that the noises (which continued) could not be traced to any normal physical cause; and presently Margaret and Kate were giving impressive seances in New York City, with their elder, married sister Leah as impresario. These were well reported, and soon other individuals and groups all over the country were producing similar phenomena, supplemented by the playing of musical instruments such as accordions and guitars. Much of this brought in money, and was quite certainly associated with ingenious frauds perpetrated not only by those public entertainers who had climbed onto the profitable

---

1. Thomas Carlyle, *Sartor Resartus*, Book II, chap 7.

ghostly bandwagon, but also, it would seem, by mediums whose curious powers were for one reason or another at a low ebb and had to be eked out so that the show could go on. There were also, however, 'home circles' run on an amateur basis, without any financial complications; and these too apparently got interesting results.

Stories of haunted houses, apparitions, premonitory 'warnings', fortune-telling and so on had long been dismissed officially as 'fooleries', the products of fancy, superstition, madness or deceit; but the new well publicized movement was harder to write off, largely perhaps because of those do-it-yourself techniques. Here were no hearsay anecdotes, growing as they passed from mouth to mouth, but happenings apparently perceived on the spot by several people at once.

The trouble was that they were all attributed to the activities of spirits, an explanation that made it very much harder for many to accept the facts. Some investigators found the first so impossible that they tended to reject the second. One of these was T. H. Huxley, whose wide ranging intellectual curiosity had led him to have several sittings with the American medium Mrs Hayden, wife of a New England newspaper proprietor. One of the first of her kind to visit this country, she arrived as early as 1852, and impressed both the archaeologist Lord Dunraven and the mathematician Augustus de Morgan, who was 'perfectly satisfied that something or someone was reading my thoughts'.[1] Unfortunately Huxley's reactions to her do not seem to have been preserved, though he rejected an invitation, in 1869, from the two year old Dialectical Society to join a Committee to investigate Spiritualism. Its report, in 1871, recognized the occurrence of physical phenomena, and it may have been this that induced him to sit, in 1874, with another medium, Charles Williams. With him were F. W. H. Myers, Charles Darwin's son George (a Fellow of the Royal Society) and the latter's maternal uncle, Hensleigh Wedgwood, a man of great moral probity who had resigned from a well-paid post rather than act against his conscience. A clear and carefully observed account of the seance occurs in

---

1. Brian Inglis, *Natural and Supernatural*, London, 1977.

Huxley's *Life and Letters*[1] and further fascinating details are to be found in his correspondence,[2] including a remark by George Darwin that unless he had seen it for himself he 'could not have believed in the evidence of anyone with such perfect *bona fides* as my uncle being so worthless', and a similar comment by Charles Darwin. There are also some letters to and from Wedgwood himself; an exchange of views about some very unconvincing 'spirit photographs' (showing the tophatted Wedgwood flanked by flat looking transparent figures, rather like clothes on hangers) and how they could have been produced by normal means, and a note of a seance in 1879 in which a triply sealed envelope is said to have been transported by a (celestial) messenger to a medium named Bastian in the United States, who had been instructed to write at once revealing its contents. This was to take a fortnight; the speed of its return, and its American stamp and postmark were to guarantee that all was genuine. (There was of course no air mail in those days.) Unfortunately neither a follow-up nor a reply is to be found.

It is not surprising that neither Huxley nor Charles Darwin was a member of the Conference held on January 5, 1882 at 38 Great Russell Street, then the headquarters of the British National Spiritualist Alliance, to discuss the foundation of a 'Society for Psychological Research'. There is some difference of opinion as to where the final initiative came from. It is generally thought to have originated with the group of scientists and scholars at Trinity College, Cambridge, who had long been studying and discussing the subject; but Dr Fraser Nicoll claims that the idea began with a conversation between 'two Spiritualists', a journalist named Dawson Rogers and the physicist William Barrett who had already done some experimental work in Ireland with what were then called 'Mesmerism' and 'thought transference' and had read a paper on psychical phenomena to the British Association in 1876 (a paper whose publication was vetoed).

It would be interesting to know exactly what was meant by 'Spiritualist' in the 1880s. It seems unlikely that the movement had then become a fully organized religious cult, as it is now, with its

---

1. Leonard Huxley, *Life and Letters of Thomas Henry Huxley*, Vol II, pp 143–149, London, 1903.

2. Now in the Archives of Imperial College, London.

own churches, since several other men Dr Nicoll so labels were Christian – one was in holy orders – and two were Theosophists. Perhaps the term implied no more than a firm belief in the immortality of the soul and in the possibility of getting into touch with the spirits of the dead through amateur or professional mediums. It certainly does not seem to have meant much more with Barrett, who wrote in 1887[1] that though he was convinced that 'the simple phenomena of Spiritualism', such as raps and the inexplicable movement of objects, did occur, he did not 'believe that an extra-mundane intelligence' was at work in them; but that 'mind, occasionally and unconsciously, can exert a direct influence on lifeless matter'; an idea very much alive today.

The ever reliable Mrs Sidgwick, writing Professor Sir William Barrett's obituary in 1926[2] calls him '*the* Founder of the Society' and describes his coming to Cambridge in the autumn of 1881, and reviving the enthusiasm of the group there (which had become somewhat discouraged) by 'reading to us a large budget of cases, experimental and spontaneous, collected by himself . . . pointing to what we should now call telepathy. The formation of a Society was under consideration that autumn and winter, and Professor Barrett . . . was engaged in stirring up interest in various quarters.' One of these was indeed Dawson Rogers, of the British National Association of Spiritualists.

A Committee was nominated by the Conference to carry out its Resolution to found the Society. Its chairman was Professor Barrett himself and among its members were Edmund Gurney, Stainton Moses (once a clergyman, then a schoolmaster), F. W. H. Myers, Dawson Rogers, Henry Sidgwick and the persevering Hensleigh Wedgwood, at whose house in Queen Anne Street the first meeting was held. There was also one woman, Mary Boole, widow of the mathematician. After six months however the minutes record that 'finding she remains the only lady on the Council' (into which the Committee had developed) 'Mrs Boole expressed the wish to resign. Under the circumstances, the Council concludes to accept her resignation with regret'. What could 'the circumstances' have been? Were they simply the result of some embarrassing female modesty?

---

1. SPR *Proceedings*, Vol 4, April 1887.
2. SPR *Proceedings*, Vol 35, 1926.

Did she feel overruled by all those deep male voices, without a chance to speak? Was there some irreconcilable disagreement between personalities or principles? Did she think, as Mrs Henry Sidgwick later seems to have thought for a while, that the pursuit of psychical research might damage the cause of feminism (both unpopular subjects tinged with a certain sense of impropriety)? We shall never know; but the fact that she could put forward being 'the only lady on Council' as a reason for resigning, and that Council should have accepted it instead of co-opting another woman to serve with her, casts a gaslit gleam on the general atmosphere of the period.

The Committee firmly rejected a motion to include the loaded word *occult* in the title of the Society, and settled on its present name. Henry Sidgwick was invited to become its first President. After some consideration, and rather reluctantly, he agreed. Gurney and Myers, who had both been his pupils, held back until his decision was known, then finally committed themselves to membership. Perhaps they were alarmed at the possibility of Hensleigh Wedgwood's taking over. A mixture of moral integrity and intellectual credulity could have had alarming consequences for a scientific society. It looks as if the Constitution and Rules published in the first number of *Proceedings* in 1883 had been framed with such possibilities in mind. They expressly state that 'membership of the Society does not imply the acceptance of any particular explanation of the phenomena investigated, nor any belief as to the operation in the Physical world of forces other than those recognized by Physical Science'. The statement still printed at the front of every issue of the Society's *Journal* echoes the same determination to stay open minded. It runs, in a fine leisured Victorian prose, 'The purpose of the Society for Psychical Research, which was founded in 1882, is to examine without prejudice or prepossession and in a scientific spirit, those faculties of man, real or supposed, which appear to be inexplicable on any generally recognized hypothesis. The Society does not hold or express any corporate views. Any opinions expressed in its publications are, therefore, those of the authors alone.'

It is worthwhile to look in a little detail at the matrix of Cambridge men so deeply involved in the foundation of the Society, a group of friends who had long been interested in its subject matter, and who influenced its development for many decades. They shared the same cultural background, they took the same values for granted, and they were closely linked not only by their academic studies and by their intellectual and aesthetic values, but also by their family connexions. Some eugenist of the future might well study the extraordinary preponderance among them of Balfours (and of crypto-Balfours in the female line); clearheaded philosophers, mathematicians and scientists who were not too deeply conditioned by their studies to recognize that things did happen which could not be explained in any terms known to them.

Most influential of all, then, was Professor Henry Sidgwick, on whose decision to accept the first Presidency of the Society so many other decisions depended. He was a man of diamond-cut integrity. He went up to Trinity College, Cambridge, as an impoverished undergraduate of seventeen and was made a Fellow when he was twenty-one, in 1859. That year saw the publication of *The Origin of Species*; and he was so much shaken by the way in which evolutionary theory contradicted 'the Christian religion as then taught in England', that, after ten years of interior struggle he resigned his Fellowship, since it could only be held by '*bona fide* members of the Church of England', and he could call himself one no longer. His College then made him a Lecturer in Moral Sciences, for which there were no theological conditions; some years later he became a Praelector in Moral and Political Philosophy, and later still Knightbridge Professor.

As an undergraduate he had joined the Ghost Club, one of whose founders had been his future brother-in-law, E. W. Benson, who ended up as Archbishop of Canterbury; and he had spent much time in investigating ghost stories. In 1860 he had his first sitting with a medium, whom he thought a 'complete humbug' apart from the puzzling fact that she seemed to have levitated a table. Four years later he sat with a friend, a Mr Cowell, who had produced by automatic writing what purported to be messages from a spirit communicator. Though this entity could not provide any satisfactory evidence of who he was – or had been – both Cowell and Sidgwick heard 'inexplicable raps', which bothered the latter considerably. He wrote on one occasion to Frederic Myers 'as for spirit rapping . . . I believe there is something in it, don't know what, have tried hard to discover, and find that I always paralyse the phenomena. My taste is strongly affected by the obvious humbug mixed up with it, which at the same time my reason does not over estimate.' How many learned, accurate and open-minded psychical research workers have echoed this state of mind over the last century!

As has been noted, his pupils included Arthur Balfour (philosopher and Prime Minister), Edward Gurney and F. W. H. Myers; all felt, as the last wrote in his obituary, 'like the companions of Socrates' in working with this man, initially seen as cold, "righteous" and reserved, but who later revealed himself as 'sympathetic, benign and wise'. He had moreover, as another SPR member, that harsh character Frank Podmore, pointed out 'the rare power of holding judgment in suspense instead of plunging comfortably down to a conclusion and sticking to it; a power lacking in Podmore himself, who adhered first to out-and-out Spiritualism, and then swung over to out-and-out scepticism.

Revisiting Trinity in December 1869 – the year in which Sidgwick resigned his fellowship – Myers asked,[1] on 'a starlight walk with him . . . whether he thought that when Tradition, Intuition, Metaphysic had failed to solve the riddle of the Universe, there was still a chance that from any observable phenomena – ghosts, spirits, whatsoever there might be – some valid knowledge might be drawn as to a World Unseen'. 'We caught together', he continued, 'the distant hope that Science might in our own age make sufficient progress to open the spiritual gateway which she had been thought to close.' Three years later Sidgwick wrote to him, hoping that 'the English mind, with its uncompromising matter of factness might put the final question to the Universe with a cold passionate determination to be answered which *must* come to something'. Meanwhile he went on working; at his University post; at urging onwards a project for the higher education of women; and in various forms of psychical research. He was much interested in the early work of William Crookes with D. D. Home in the 1870s, Crookes with his almost despairing cry under attack, 'I never said it was possible, I said it was true!' In 1874 he joined with Arthur Balfour, Frederic Myers and Lord Rayleigh in further work, and in 1875 visited 'the slate-writing medium Dr Slade' and found his effects 'spurious'. In April 1876 he was married by E. W. Benson to Eleanor Balfour, then thirty years old, sister of Arthur. She too was passionately interested in women's education (in fact she had

---

1. Cf F. W. H. Myers' Obituary of Sidgwick, SPR *Proceedings*, Vol XV, 1900–1.

collaborated with Sidgwick in raising money for bursaries to be used in this way in Cambridge); and she too was passionately interested in psychical research, possibly through her friends the Lytteltons, connexions of the Tennants at whose house in Grosvenor Square stodgy Mrs Humphry Ward[1] described 'the exquisite set known as the "Souls" . . . dancing or thought-reading or making music as it pleased them'. Miss Balfour also went to family seances in Carlton Gardens with Lord Rayleigh, who was her brother-in-law and had coached her as a girl in her favourite subject, mathematics. She was, says her biographer Ethel Sidgwick,[2] 'elated by the idea "that notwithstanding the very inconclusive . . . phenomena . . . we might possibly be communicating with beings from another world".' Lord Rayleigh remained non-committal; though later on he went so far as to say, 'To my mind telepathy with the dead would present comparatively little difficulty when it was admitted as regards the living'. One may compare this with a remark of hers in a lecture at Cambridge long afterwards in 1912, 'if telepathy is a fact, and if the process is psychical, not physical, the way to supposing that discarnate minds can communicate with ours seems to some extent cleared'; though she continued with characteristic caution that the possibilities of telepathy among the living were so wide that 'they must be excluded before we can be sure that a further hypothesis is necessary'.[3]

The Sidgwicks were childless, but this 'marriage of true minds' was fruitful in psychical research throughout its course, and long after Henry Sidgwick's death in 1900. During much of his lifetime his wife did a prodigious amount of work; she began by devoting the autumn of 1876 to collecting ghost stories – but remained rather in the background, partly because she was so deeply involved in their other great common interest, the establishment of Newnham College. She became its treasurer and Vice Principal in 1880, when they both went to live in one of its buildings, North Hall. Here are some contemporary memories,[4] in this rather different setting, of the couple who were to influence so deeply the pattern and the course of psychical research until the survivor's death in 1937; and

1. Enid Huws Jones; *Mrs Humphry Ward*, London, 1873.
2. Ethel Sidgwick, *Mrs Henry Sidgwick*, London, 1938.
3. Ibid.
4. Ann Philips (ed), *Newnham Anthology*, Cambridge University Press, 1979.

even afterwards. An American woman, one A. Willcox, recalls Professor Sidgwick's brilliant conversation at High Table 'like a mountain stream, full and sparkling' but leaves to another the acid comment that he *had* to talk brilliantly, to distract attention from the food. Some of his wife's students were devoted to her, some regarded her with apprehension. She 'had no small talk', 'discouraged personal chit-chat' and, said Miss Clough, whom she succeeded as Principal in 1892, 'could not quite imagine anyone's not being guided by pure reason, and so did not always allow for "feelings".' There was indeed an occasion when she was told someone thought she had 'meant' (i.e. implied) something unsaid. This elicited the firm statement, 'It must always be understood that I never "mean" anything.'

She was essentially a mathematician; though, like Bertrand Russell, a mathematician of that rare sort who can express meaning lucidly and intelligibly in words as well as in figures. Her biographer[1] noted that 'after one of the most cruel sorrows of her life' (perhaps the mountaineering death of her distinguished biologist brother Francis in 1882) 'she confessed that to work out a problem in mathematics relieved her heart more than any condolences'. Alice Johnson, a friend who was demonstrator in charge of the Balfour Laboratory at Newnham, and later worked with her at the Society for Psychical Research, remarked perceptively that 'I imagine the abstract nature of mathematics seemed to her especially adapted to a disembodied existence'. Alas for the innumerate!

Cool, detached, reasonable, lucid, scrupulously just and accurate in the pursuit of objective truth, the standards of the Sidgwicks and their friends have deeply influenced the Society. There have of course been certain disadvantages. One of them was that Mrs Sidgwick's temperamental difficulty in imagining 'any one's not being guided by pure reason' and in 'allowing for feelings' has sometimes been regarded as a rule for everyone engaged in psychical research (even though she did observe, as a puzzling datum, that mediums needed to be 'humoured').

An innate lack, or an acquired repression, of warmth and sympathy may be useful for the mathematician, the physicist, the astronomer; but it is the reverse for those who deal with human

---

1. Ethel Sidgwick, ibid.

individuals. In parapsychology in particular it will defeat its own ends, by way of what is now called 'experimenter effect'. Sensitives who produce psi phenomena are by definition likely to produce the commonest of them all, telepathy, which will soon make them aware that they are being envisaged not primarily as living selves, but as mechanisms, as laboratory rats, or worst of all as potential or actual frauds. This awareness is likely to inhibit or even to paralyse their paranormal abilities. It does not, by the way, depend on the expression or the manner or the body language of the experimenter himself. It can work at a distance, as happened in a project set up some years ago by the late G. W. Fisk, in which individuals all over England were to 'guess' three times a day at the position of the hands on a cardboard clock in his study. A cheerful, outgoing man (like the most genial sort of schoolmaster), he obtained results considerably above chance until − unknown to his guinea pigs − another, shyer experimenter took over some of the work for a while; during this period the results dropped to the average to be expected on probability.

It is fairly rare for an experimenter to combine the warmth and enthusiasm needed to elicit paranormal activities with the ability to examine and evaluate the results of his work in a statistical form. For much of the time there must be an interaction between two types of mind. Co-operation is essential, even though at their worst moments the groups may envisage one another as Cold Fish − and Patronizing Cold Fish at that − on the one hand, and Hot Swallowers on the other − and co-operation there has always been, though not without ups and downs.

To return, though, to the 1880s. The newly formed Society's First Circular to members − who were clearly assumed to be energetic − dealt with its general work. It appealed for help in experiments with 'thought reading, or, as we should prefer to call it, thought transference' (an oddly mechanistic image) and suggested the use of playing cards, numbers, coloured discs, geometrical figures, patterns and tunes (the application of the calculus of probabilities to results was not discussed till 1885). Precautions were outlined, silence was advised and it was suggested that researchers should observe whether it was especially productive to carry out experiments between two people only. They were asked to note the nature of the impression received, whether visual or 'audile'; whether some 'agents' (i.e.

those trying to transmit the impression) were more successful than others; whether percipients belonging to some especial family or group were more successful than others in receiving impressions; whether the health of agent or percipient seemed to affect results; whether there was a 'sensitive stage' of a particular length, and if so what that length was, and whether the faculty, whatever it be, improved with practice. They were also to look for evidence of 'Reichenbach effects', and the seeing of 'luminosities' (a seeing which rather suggests that certain individuals share the capacities of bees and some apes to perceive ultra violet light).

Members were also asked to collect evidence for clairvoyance, and for 'physical phenomena of the kind commonly called spiritualistic'. Here untrained investigators were warned against working with paid mediums and encouraged to collect from amateur ones and 'home circles' evidence as to 'lights, raps, voices, the unexplained movement of objects etc' and also to collect general information about 'the so-called dowsing rod'. Haunted houses should be examined before reports were made, and both local legends, and normal explanations of the phenomena observed should be investigated. All information must be kept confidential in these cases, as the selling value of the house might otherwise be affected. Finally, reports of dreams, coincidences, second sight and apparitions were needed, both at first hand and in references in biographies and foreign work.

Perhaps it was because of the 'references in biographies' that the group dealing with this last mixed bag of data was called 'The Literary Committee'. Headed by Edmund Gurney in London and Frederic Myers in Cambridge, it was one of the most vigorous and fruitful of them all, and did an enormous amount of work in verifying and checking evidence, and interviewing witnesses all over the country. The others, except for Professor Barrett's 'Committee on Thought Transference in Dublin', were London based. It was these which dealt with Mesmerism (Frank Podmore), Reichenbach Experiments (W. H. Coffin), Physical Phenomena (F. S. Hughes) and Apparitions and Haunted Houses (E. R. Pease).

Among the earliest members and associates of the Society were Leslie Stephen (father of Virginia Woolf, Vanessa Bell, and Bloomsburyana in general), John Addington Symonds the litterateur, Alfred Tennyson, William James, John Ruskin, W. E. Gladstone, the painters Frederick Leighton and G. F. Watts, and Mark Twain (duly disguised as S. L. Clemens) who probably wanted to join the Society because of the strange precognitive dream he had had about seeing his brother dead and lying with red flowers on his breast in an unusual kind of coffin, a dream startlingly fulfilled. There was also Lewis Carroll in his public *persona* as the clerical mathematician, the Reverend C. L. Dodgson, who was writing as early as December 4, 1882 to his friend Langton Clarke[1] 'That trickery will *not* do as a complete explanation of all the phenomena of table rapping, thought reading etc. I am more and more convinced. At the same time I see no need as yet for believing that disembodied spirits have anything to do with it. I have just read a small pamphlet, the first report of the "Psychical Society" on "Thought Reading". The evidence, which seems to have been most carefully taken, excludes the possibility that "unconscious guidance by pressure" (Carpenter's explanation) will account for all the phenomena. All seems to point to the existence of a natural force, allied to electricity and nerve force by which brain can act on brain. I think we are close to the day when this shall be classified among the known natural forces and its laws tabulated . . . and when the scientific sceptics who always shut their eyes . . . to any evidence that seems to point away from materialism will have to accept it as a proved fact in nature . . . or will find the Report published by Trübner for two shillings very interesting, all the more so that "thought reading" is a phenomenon on which any domestic circle can experiment for themselves; it needs no professional "medium".'

This is a fine detached assessment from C. L. Dodgson, despite the curious assumption that the 'natural force allied to electricity' could not be reconciled with materialism. Lewis Carroll, however, seems to have had some direct awareness of telepathy; witness his remark in *Alice Through the Looking Glass* about 'people thinking in chorus'.

It is said that physicists regard some of his writing as oddly foreshadowing some of their findings today; notably in the images of the Red Queen, who had to keep running to stay where she was, and the White Queen, whose memory worked both backwards and forwards in time, and who screamed piercingly before accidentally

---

1. L. C. Morton Cohen and R. Lancelyn Green, ed, *Letters of Lewis Carroll*, 2 vols, London, 1979.

pricking herself with her brooch. Psychical researchers too may be interested in this precognitive lady, and in Carroll's remarks in *Sylvie and Bruno* as to 'the best time for seeing fairies'. These tie up nicely with various modern studies of dissociation and 'altered states of consciousness'. 'It must be a *very* hot day . . . and you must be just a *little* sleepy – but not too sleepy to keep your eyes open, mind. Well, and you ought to feel just a little eerie; if you don't know what it means, I'm afraid I can hardly explain it . . . And the last rule is, that the crickets (grasshoppers) shouldn't be chirping.' Warmth: relaxed awareness: something given and accepted; uninterrupted quiet; what better conditions could there be for some sort of extrasensory perception? This passage appeared in *Aunt Judy's Magazine* for Christmas 1867. When the serial came to be published at greater length in book form many years afterwards Carroll[1] suggested that there were three worlds: our own; Outland, a curious burlesque of this; and Fairyland. In a state of trance humans unseen by those they observed, could perceive people and events in Outland (which sounds like a sort of collective unconscious); but in an 'eerie' state they might actually share in what went on in Fairyland, while still remaining aware of their own world. Fairies might take on human form, and time might go into reverse or stand stock still. Though the words Fairies and Fairyland have a tinsel ring today, they were still numinous to Carroll, a century ago; and it is plain that the Father of English surrealism, as French writers have called him, knew from within some of the odder experiences later to be explored by parapsychology.

1. Cf Ann Clark's *Life of Lewis Carroll*, London, 1979.

2

Problems for Investigation

B efore getting down to a detailed survey of the Society's work, it could be useful to look at a few of the subjects to be tackled; at the landscape – or jungle – of beliefs, opinions, unarguable assumptions, inflamed feelings and social complexities within which it had to labour; and at the continual effort to frame theories into which findings could be fitted.

Although many of its early members were – like Frederic Myers – passionately anxious to confute the dogmatic materialism of contemporary intellectuals, and to establish evidence that conscious human personality survives bodily death, the task actually set before them was 'to examine without prejudice or prepossession, and in a scientific spirit, those faculties of man, real or supposed, which appear to be inexplicable under any generally recognized hypothesis'.

Among these faculties were several which have since been accepted in theory or in practice or both, very largely as the result of the Society's work – or rather of those of its members, acting individually or in groups, since it has no collective opinions. Thus hypnosis, once extremely suspect, has been very carefully investigated, has become respectable, and is used for various medical purposes including the treatment of skin diseases,[1] psychotherapy and anaesthesia, shedding light, *en passant* on some very remarkable features of the unconscious mind; as when a patient anaesthetized in this way for an appendicitis operation suddenly screamed in the middle of it 'because the arc

---

1. Cf Stephen Black, *Mind and Body*, London, 1969.

lights were burning her shoulder'.[1] The psyche had obeyed instructions not to admit to consciousness any pain in the abdomen; but no
one had said anything about shoulders. I owe this fascinating piece
of information to the well-known Italian psychiatrist Dr Emilio
Servadio, who has long been an overseas member of the SPR. An
English member, Eric Wookey, was one of the founders in 1952 of
the British Society for Medical and Dental Hypnosis, its first
Chairman, and later its President.

Again, dowsing – used in practice for hundreds of years but long
despised in scientific theory – is well on the way to being explained
in terms of what Charles Richet[2] called 'rhabdic force', some
influence arising from the ground; an influence to be traced, in
modern Russian parlance,[3] by 'bio-physical methods', or, in current
English terms, through the sensitivity of certain people to small
variations in the earth's electromagnetic field brought about by the
presence underground of running water or of mineral deposits. It
looks indeed as if the two 'sensors' involved in stimulating the
dowser's muscles to react with such startling violence – the forked
twig or rod can twist like an independent living creature in his
hands – had now been discovered by Professor Z. V. Harvalik,[4]
formerly Professor of Physics at the University of Arkansas, and later
an adviser to the US Army. He maintains that they are to be found
respectively in the head, near the pituitary and pineal glands, and
in the adrenal glands, just above the kidneys. If these are sheltered
from electromagnetic activity the dowser cannot function. This
fascinating discovery does not of course account for the well-
documented phenomenon of map dowsing, in which the diviner uses
a small pendulum over a map of the area to be searched for water or
minerals, and notes the way in which it swings. It looks as though
the two methods were related to one another after the manner of
sensory and extra sensory perception; as if the psyche were stimulated
by some form of psi – possibly clairvoyance – to produce a reaction
in the muscles rather than in the image-making faculty, a veridical

---

1. Personal communication.
2. Charles Richet (SPR President, 1905) in *Thirty Years of Psychical Research*
(English translation), London, 1923.
3. Cf Francis Hitchings, *Pendulum, the Psi Connection*, London, 1978. He also
mentions the work of Harvalik: for which see
4. Christopher Bird, *Divining*, London, 1980.

hallucination expressed in unconscious movement instead of conscious 'sight' or 'hearing'. Of course the SPR was not the only group to investigate all this; but many of its individual members – whose motto might well be Galileo's *Eppur se muove* – have continued to direct attention to the fact that dowsing works in practice, whatever the explanation may be, or however impossible to understand. This began as early as 1884 when the second volume of *Proceedings* carefully reported various unsuccessful experiments with dowsers carried out by scientists, and various successful projects with dowsers carried out on a business footing by architects, builders and land owners.

The early researchers had first of all – and again and again and again – to establish to their own satisfaction, and to convince other people, that 'phenomena inexplicable in ordinary terms' did in fact occur. Among these 'ordinary terms' of explanation were of course deliberate fraud (including hallucinations induced by suggestion), genuine illusions and delusions, misinterpretations and the bubble-gum proliferations of gossip. These last two, maddeningly enough may hold some core of truth. Thus if someone subject to psychosomatic reactions to stress says that because a witch 'over looked' him itching weals broke out all over his body, he may well be making a perfectly accurate statement, which boils down to the fact that because some old woman he feared cast a malign glance at him a skin rash erupted; but this is not necessarily a psi phenomenon. And reports of something inexplicable that really did happen will change as they pass from mouth to mouth, partly because most people like telling a really good story and tidy up details as they go along, and partly because those concerned may not always hear exactly what is said, and will always and inevitably connect it with their personal preoccupations. The process is a bit like what went on in the old fashioned party game known as Russian scandal (no political innuendoes). In this, the first of a row of people sitting side by side whispers something to his neighbour, who passes it on to his, and so on to the last of them. He repeats aloud what he has heard, the first repeats what he originally said, and the two are usually very different. The process may run something like: 'John Brown's bought a Rolls Royce', 'Joan Brown's made a good choice', 'Joan Brown's marrying Jim Boyce', 'Joan was always one for the boys' . . .

It is not surprising that one of the first preoccupations of many researchers was to rule out — as far as this could be managed — all possibility of fraud. That fraud was widespread and well organized on a commercial basis is shown by a wonderful catalogue (now in the Harry Price Library at University College, London) entitled *Gambols with the Ghosts*, circulated to mediums and conjurers by an American firm at the turn of the century. Among its items are 'luminous materializing Hands and Faces, Luminous materialistic Ghosts' and, at fifty dollars, 'a Full, luminous female form (with face that convinces) which . . . appears gradually, floats about the room, and disappears'. There were also an apparatus for Spirit table and chair lifting; Spirit Bolts and Handcuffs which appeared to — but did not — ensure that the medium could not move; and 'a Holding Test, a small pocket apparatus — easily concealed in the hand when placed on or around a person's arm, remaining there and giving the feeling as though they were being held by the medium's hand. This allows the medium full use of his own arm and hand, which he can replace at any time and move the holder.' This was presumably for dark seances only. There are no less than twelve gadgets for 'slate writing'; a curious marvel produced among others by the famous Victorian Mr Eglinton (who also specialized in strange lights and the movement of small objects). The ingenious method used was exposed in a review[1] by a Russian member, Count Perovsky-Petrovo-Solovevo, of Hereward Carrington's *The Physical Phenomena of Spiritualism, fraudulent and general*.[2] Two slates were examined, set face to face, and marked by the investigator, who then saw them sealed. However, the liquid glue used for this purpose had been mixed with iron filings and powdered chalk; thus, 'when this packet is put under the table the medium tips it, so that the chalk and filings run into a corner, applies a magnet to that corner, and traces a message in mirror writing on the under side of the bottom slate. When the packet is opened there is the message.' Q.E.D.

Carrington — who did in fact believe in the occurrence of inexplicable rappings and object movements — also exposed various other tricks, including some used in 'spirit photography', 'materialization' and 'dematerialization'; here he noted that 'robes of such fine material that they go into a dummy watch, letter, or hollow boot

1. SPR *Proceedings*, 21, 1908–9.
2. Boston, 1907.

heel' were employed, even in 'the famous incident of the dematerialization of Mrs D'Esperance's legs at Helsingfors in 1893', of which
one longs to know more.

At first materializations seem to have been accepted or rejected *as
such* by those interested, who made no attempt at explanation. They
only marvelled; and would even snip pieces from the apparitions'
clothing, noting that the cuts closed up again leaving no sign that
anything had happened (though they did not report whether the
clothes still fitted; perhaps this complication did not occur with
loose flowing skirts). Those who rejected materializations said equally
simply that they were *all* fraudulent. However, they continued to
occur and to be seen not only by devotees but by objective researchers
and an attempt at rationalization began; in 1894 Charles Richet who
was among other things a distinguished French physiologist produced
the concept of 'ectoplasm', 'an unfamiliar form of matter', which he
believed to be exuded by certain mediums, notably the Italian
peasant, Eusapia Paladino. Ectoplasm could be modelled like living
plasticine into various independent forms such as hands and faces
(sometimes complete with turbans). Some took it for granted that
this must be the work of spirits. Richet, a staunch adherent of 19th
century rationalism, prepared to 'admit any possibility rather than
that of an extra-terrene mind' maintained[1] that it was carried out by
the unconscious mind of the medium through a process he called
ideoplasty. This would be a useful name for all those body reactions
that can be produced by suggestion, whether it comes from outside
the mind (as when a hypnotist raises blisters by touching the skin
with a pencil which he says is a red hot poker), or from inside, as in
the instance of those psychosomatic weals produced by the fear of a
witch, or as in the red whip marks that can appear on the back of
someone reliving repressed memories of experience in a concentration
camp.

It was instantly assumed by some mediums that ectoplasm —
unlike such exudations as sweat — had a neural structure of its own,
and was able to feel; in fact that it was connected with the central
nervous system. They maintained that if a light were suddenly
turned on during a dark seance or if some suspicious sitter were to
grab a handful of the stuff, the shock would be extremely painful, or

---

1. Charles Richet, *ibid.*

even physically dangerous, to the medium involved. Ectoplasm could, it was said, be photographed; there is an extremely unappetizing picture of a young woman known as 'Eva C' (who had been found cheating under an earlier pseudonym) dribbling it down her dress. It looks like a rather tatty white beard in aspic that has not quite set. Other photographs, enlarged and projected on a film screen bear a close resemblance to butter-muslin; the weave is unmistakable to anyone who has used it, say to make sour milk into curd cheese. There have also been suggestions that some forms of ectoplasm markedly resembled pieces of white paper (with faces drawn on them) which had been swallowed and regurgitated. To say this is not necessarily to condemn all ectoplasm as bogus. Art follows nature, fake follows fact;[1] and fraudulent devices arose in many instances to reproduce genuine phenomena for which a medium's strange paranormal talents had faded out, temporarily or permanently. Having said this I must acknowledge that my own personal boggle threshold is low where ectoplasm is concerned; at any rate the visible kind. The invisible sort, as tentatively formulated by Sir Oliver Lodge, FRS,[2] who took part with Richet and others in some of the Paladino seances, is easier to accept, and to interpret in contemporary terms. He suggested that she moved various objects, including an escritoire, 'by an invisible ectoplasmic rod, some structure unknown to science, which could transmit force to a distance' and noted that 'there must be some mechanical connexion to make matter move . . . it was as if she had long supernumerary limbs . . . invisible pseudopods'. Though the imagery here is structural, even physiological, it is not incompatible with Professor John Taylor's[3] later theory that such events may be brought about by extra low frequency electrical activity, which has been given the startlingly suitable acronym of ELF.

To detect and to eliminate fraud, then, to prove that investigators were not simply – or elaborately – being diddled was, remains, and

---

1. It has been suggested that ectoplasm is so revolting that it must be genuine – since no one would have invented anything of the kind for public relations purposes.

2. In *Past Years*, London, 1931. Sir Oliver, first and foremost a physicist, was President of the Society for Psychical Research in 1901–3 and again (with Mrs Henry Sidgwick) in 1932.

3. John Taylor, *Supermind*, London, 1975.

must always remain among the first priorities of psychical research. From this sprang the long continued policy of the Society never to work again with a medium once discovered cheating; a policy which probably deprived it of much valuable material, since as has already been noted, some fakes were undoubtedly used to fill in when the faculty for producing the genuine article had dried up. 'The show must go on' is after all a principle practised in most performances which people pay to attend; a principle recognized by the Society in suggesting that it was best if possible to work with amateur mediums rather than with professional ones.

This is perhaps the moment to examine a class-conscious grievance, painful as a boil, which is sometimes brought forward today – that the young Society was 'snobbish' in its assumptions, its theories and its practices, because its early members, almost all drawn from the upper middle class, with a strong university flavour, were inclined to trust one another, but to suspect the good faith – and sometimes the intelligence – of people from different social strata. (Regarding 'intelligence', it should be remembered that universal education had only got going in 1870, twelve years before the SPR's foundation in 1882, and that illiteracy and want of general knowledge were still widespread among people born before say 1860.)

The fact is true. The interpretation is not. What was involved was not snobbery, but something quite different. The Society's members came from what might now be called, in sociological jargon, 'an aberrant subculture'. They shared certain ideas, notably that of what they would have called 'a sense of honour', and these ideas inspired certain codes of behaviour. They had been conditioned to believe that it was essential to be truthful, honest and loyal; that it was not only wrong but (even more shaming) 'not done', say, to read other people's letters, to cheat at games, to fake evidence in academic work. They realized moreover that this code was not universally accepted, and were therefore cautious in their dealings with those who did not necessarily hold to it, and might be tempted to cheat for money, or for power, or for self-inflation; or who, even more misleadingly, might not even realize that courses of action which seemed perfectly natural to them were condemned. (For a neutral instance of such differences in traditions of honourable behaviour one need only look at the fact that whereas English schoolchildren have long been firmly discouraged by their teachers from informing

against one another, French school children used to be *invited* to do
so.) So it was not snobbery but ordinary commonsense that led
members to trust one another — after all, most of them were
colleagues, or relations or both, personally known for many years —
but to withhold confidence from people who could not necessarily be
expected to share their own standards; to withhold it at any rate
until their *bona fides* and common sense had been tested.

Every psychical researcher was, and is, bound to try to disentangle
fact both from fantasy (which had in turn to be distinguished from
the use of tinsel verbiage because the speaker knew no other way of
expressing himself) and from deliberate fraud. But it was unfortunate
— though perhaps inevitable — that to do so aroused such strong
feelings among investigated and investigators alike. The former were
injured because their honesty seemed to be doubted, the latter were
frustrated because there seemed so often to be grounds for such
doubt.

The desire to discover and to establish truth grows very sour when
it is repeatedly thwarted; sour and explosive. Hence outbreaks in
many academic disciplines of a disease old enough to have a Latin
name, which needs no explanation: *furor scholasticus*. It is particularly
prevalent in parapsychology because students of this subject have *two*
targets for their anger. They do not only tend to blame one another
in a fine scholarly way for inaccuracy, misrepresentation, pointless
methods of 'busywork', and general wrongheadedness. They need to
be cautious about the human subjects with whom they deal; no trusty
mathematical symbols or innocent molecules or guileless guinea pigs
these, but beings capable of variation, error, and wilful, planned
deceit. Caution can all too easily harden into suspicion, and suspicion
into moral indignation. This, though sometimes valuable, needs
careful watching, since it is so often accompanied by a lethal mixture
of superiority and self-righteousness, which can turn what should be
an impartial enquiry into a ferocious inquisition based on the
principle that everyone concerned in the case being examined must
be considered guilty of deception unless or until he is proved innocent
(a reversal of the principles of English law). Any subsequent report
of such an enquiry tends to be a Case for the Prosecution rather than
an unbiased statement of the facts.

Such feelings are understandable enough. It is maddening for
people who have worked long and hard to find out what really

happened to discover how much what looked like objective statements were coloured by the preconceived ideas of those who made them, and how easily they could be contaminated by imagination or mistake. It was more maddening still to detect deliberate intent to deceive, particularly where this had been successful for a while. Nobody likes to be fooled, and it is rare to find such an example of calm as Everard Feilding who, well aware of what he called 'the mass of occult twaddle with which our experience is so abundantly blighted'[1] remarked after carrying out much 'futile or inconclusive work' of his own, 'Well, we've learned more about the psychology of mediums',[2] and combined investigation with laughter. Thus when Research Officer to the Society,[3] he took the precaution of carrying with him some pink baby ribbon and a pair of scissors, just in case they might come in useful, on a visit to a 'physical' medium he did not trust. He arrived early, was shown into the room where the seance was to be held, and was asked to wait. While waiting, he looked behind the curtains, attached to which he found some prawns. He instantly provided each with an elegant pink sash; and so adorned they later appeared as 'psychic apports from the seaside'. History does not relate either whether they had been boiled or what the medium, or the other sitters thought.

On an occasion when he was charged with flippancy he replied that it was the only way to 'preserve one's sanity in dealing with this kind of subject'; and it certainly preserved him from the extraordinary bitterness which has long been one of the occupational diseases of psychical research workers, whether they are investigating spontaneous events – hauntings, poltergeist outbreaks and so on – testing the claims of mediums, or carrying out large scale experiments, whose results can be compared statistically with those that could have been achieved by chance.

It should be noted that Feilding's 'flippancy' was certainly not combined with superficiality. He carried out a great deal of hard, persevering and sometimes boring work with various mediums. His careful method of evaluating results appears very clearly in an article he contributed to the *Dublin Review* in the second quarter of 1925.

---

1. Reviewing a book in SPR *Proceedings*, 18, 1903–4.
2. E. N. Bennett, in his obituary of Feilding, SPR *Proceedings*, 44, 1936–7.
3. Rosalind Heywood, *The Sixth Sense*, London, 1959.

'It is only', he wrote, 'by the patient accumulation of facts, disregarding sources of error which experience gradually indicates, that ultimately a probability can be built up which . . . becomes *so* probable as to exclude any other reasonable conclusion.' He was himself convinced in the end 'of the . . . existence of some force not generally recognized, which was able to impress itself upon, or to create the appearance of, matter'.[1]

These brief glances at the nature of the Society's work, with its perennial problems, personal and practical, must give place to a more detailed account of its various branches which remain of course as closely interlinked as the branches and roots of baobab trees, however painstaking the attempt to separate them out; though this may be a little easier now that we have a sort of telescopic hindsight extending over a hundred long full years. A century ago the field was an almost pathless wilderness to be observed and explored and mapped out at ground level.

In compensation, many of the pioneers had an advantage now almost extinct — a combination of youth, leisure, energy, and financial security. They could pursue whatever subjects interested them most, since they were not obliged to seek for or live on research grants (which, invaluable as they are, must in the nature of things depend to some extent on the views and priorities of those who make them). Some had private incomes, adequate or meagre; others could combine investigation with the work of their university posts (a state of things which still survives to some extent). Alternatively, they did not have to engage in psychical research as something to be carried on only after working hours spent in earning a living, some hobby to be pursued in a free time eroded by unavoidable household activities such as cooking, cleaning and do-it-yourself repairs from painting and papering to washering taps and mending fuses.

Shocking as all this may seem from a sociological point of view today, it made for independence, flexibility, energy and liberty in research work; a liberty to 'do one's own thing' which was specialist rather than elitist.

---

1. E. N. Bennett, ibid.

3

Apparitions and Phantasms – the Ground Work

From the very beginning the subject matter – and the member-ship – of the various committees overlapped. Thus, 'Thought Reading' (or 'Thought Transference') was obviously connected with 'mesmerism', as it had been shown to occur most vividly in induced hypnotic trance, and with 'Apparitions'. Apparitions them-selves could not well be investigated without reference to 'Haunted Houses' – and all alike were involved with the instances of 'dreams, coincidences and second sight' to be collected from a variety of sources by the Literary Committee, which proved the most lively of them all, however much its duties may have sounded like those of people collecting pieces of material for a rag bag.

The first issue of the Society's *Proceedings* in 1882 contained no less than three reports by the Committee dealing with Thought Trans-ference (much of the experimental work was concerned with the paranormal reproduction of drawings, a method that has survived the test of time and was recently used to investigate Uri Geller's extrasensory powers). There were also one from the Committee on Haunted Houses, which noted sadly that 'ghosts seem to be no respecters of persons, and no amount of scientific watchfulness will make them come "to order",' two from the Committee on Mesmerism and a particularly fruitful one from the Literary Committee, based on the answers received to a questionnaire circulated to members of the Society and to advertisements in the Press.

This last paper also appeared in the enterprising *Fortnightly Review*. It was written by the secretaries of the Committee, Edmund Gurney and F. W. H. Myers (who were also energetic members of the Committees on Mesmerism and on Thought Transference). They observe deprecatingly that 'its pages are more likely to provoke sleep than to banish it'; since, though the 'overwhelming quantity of recorded evidence' is striking, accounts themselves can become tedious precisely because they turn out to have so many features in common, features which of course make them much easier to classify, and even to assess. There is also the matter of triviality, of the comparative unimportance of certain incidents; among them a scientific draughtsman's sudden impression 'in his mind's eye' at ten o'clock one morning of 'a little wicker basket containing 5 eggs' of which two were very long, with clean yellowish shells, and one was round, white and smudged with dirt. He was working at home, and at lunch time was startled to recognize the two long yellowish eggs standing in egg cups on the table. He told his wife what had happened and she fetched the remaining three, still in the little basket just as he had 'seen' them some hours before; she said her mother had sent them down for him that morning. Later he discovered that the older lady had finished packing the basketful just at the time when he had visualized it. Equally impressive in its unimportance is the account of the apparition of a man who was unwell and could not get to work that day being seen by two of his colleagues who did not know of his absence. They took it for granted that he was really with them, and were only a little puzzled that he did not talk or smile. They were even more puzzled when he returned next morning. These two incidents in fact stand out as especially interesting and significant precisely because they *are* so trivial. They carry no emotional charge, give no scope for drama. No one would make an exciting story about either.

There are of course many startling cases too; Bishop Wilberforce's awareness that his son's foot had been crushed in an accident at sea, for instance; a boy's impression of his brother's illness; a mother's direct knowledge of a child's death far away; and the apparition of an old wet-nurse first to her nursling's wife, and then to their five-year-old daughter and *her* nurse. It is interesting to note that the wife's first reaction was to 'dose both' (and possibly herself?). In the same way, a man who reported to the Committee on Haunted Houses that having seen an apparition at the end of a brightly lit passage outside his room, he had returned to bed and 'resolved to take a dose of physic in the morning'. Is this a recurrence of the idea that evil spirits can literally be purged away; an idea most vividly exemplified in the attempt to dislodge the Devils of Loudun by administering enemas to those afflicted?

For the modern reader of this First Report, who has not been wearied as the writers were by the laborious highly concentrated work of accumulating, checking, classifying and beginning to interpret the records, this paper is anything but soporific. It is fascinating both in itself, and for the fact that it lays down invaluable guide lines for future work. It also coined the term Telepathy (not to mention Telaesthesia, which has long since faded out); deprecated the use of the word 'supernatural' to indicate paranormal phenomena; and noted that psychical research in the 1880s was 'in the position of zoology . . . in Aristotle's day. Aristotle had no scientific treatise to consult, he was obliged to go down to the fishmarket' to see what was there, and listen to what the sailors told him. But 'the source of zoology could not have been upbuilt without his omnivorous curiosity'.

The writers' own 'omnivorous curiosity' was working overtime in those early years. Further reports followed the first. The second, in 1883, notes that over 10,000 letters have been written in collecting and verifying evidence. Observing (already!) that 'our Society claims to have proved the reality . . . of the transmission of thoughts, feelings and images from one mind to another by no recognized channel of sense' it suggests that these impressions ought to be called phantasms rather than phantoms, because they can be auditory, tactile and purely mental, as well as visual. The Committee 'would like a regular census of death-dreams and hallucinations' and information as to how many people in England have had them. A careful distinction is made between '*veridical* hallucinations, which do in fact coincide with some crisis in the life of the person concerned', and other purely subjective kinds.

There followed an attempt to rough out *A Theory of Apparitions*. These (like 'phantasms') included, as well as things 'seen', shared experiences ranging from the emotional to the physical as when a Cambridge undergraduate was overcome by a sense of extreme illness, cold and misery from 8 to 11 one evening when, though he knew nothing about it, his twin brother lay dying miles away at home. There were inexplicable impulses to do something, as when a foreman at work felt forced to return to his house and arrived to find his wife had been run over, had been carried indoors, and was calling for him. There were 'transfers of ideas', as in the case of a youth who always 'knew' when his elder brother, who lived some way off, was going to pay one of his unannounced and irregular visits to the family business at which he was working. And so on.

It is interesting to see even at this early stage, a careful note that when the writers use the word 'force' they do not mean physical force; and that this, and other analogies for whatever is at work in telepathy *are* only analogies, whether cast in the form of 'Mr Knowles' "brainwaves" ' (remarkably precognitive of Mr Knowles, as the electrical activities of the brain were not discovered until 1929) or based on 'Dr Maudsley's concept of luminiferous ether' or anything else.

The Fourth Report, published in 1883–4 – they were working at high speed – reiterates the idea that apparitions of all kinds are 'impressions transferred by telepathy' through the unconscious mind, and suggests that the positive results of small experiments in say 'tasting ginger, or reproducing diagrams' may be related to crisis apparitions in the same sort of way as 'the sparks on Puss's back' are related to lightning. It explores the curious different modes in which such apparitions are perceived, whether as figures, complete in every detail, seemingly present in a room; or in hypnogogic imagery – those vivid pictures some people see as in a private cinema show within their eyelids *before* they fall asleep – or as a reflection in a window pane, or even on a white curtain, as it were the sheet for a magic lantern show (rather than on a television screen today, as they were usually 'stills').

There is also a tentative discussion of 'collective percipience', which cites the odd story of how young Philip Weld, away at school at St Edmund's, Ware, was drowned in a boating accident, and was 'seen' at the same time by his father and sister, walking together at home. He looked well and happy, and a young man in a black robe was with him; but both of those who saw him were sure that he had died. At the funeral his father looked in vain among the priests present for the young man (they knew that Philip had been the only one to die). Some four months later he and his daughter were at

Chipping in Lancashire and paid a courtesy call on the parish priest, whom they did not know. They had to wait a few minutes before he was free, looked at the pictures on the wall and suddenly recognized in a print that carried no inscription the face of Philip's companion. Asked later who it was, their host said it was the young Polish Jesuit, St Stanislaus Kostka. They had never before seen a portrait of him, though they knew Philip had in fact been devoted to his memory. The implications of this narrative are not all fully discussed.

A year later Mrs Sidgwick published in the third volume of *Proceedings* (1885) a factual, astringent and fascinating survey of *Phantasms of the Dead*. It will be remembered that she had herself spent many months earlier on in collecting ghost stories for the Society, which must have amassed and checked on a considerable quantity by the time she began to write this study, since she notes that *only* 370 of the large number in its possession would be examined, as the rest were for various reasons much less valuable. In her usual methodical way she sets out many explanations in normal terms of what is said to have happened. Deliberate hoaxing is the first; she sets it aside as rare, and says it could only be relevant to six of her cases. Exaggeration is another. The risk of this has been minimized by accepting only first-hand accounts (she does not seem to have allowed for the distorting, tidying or dramatizing effects of long term memory). A third explanation is that the whole thing was an illusion; the observer had simply misinterpreted what was going on. She remarks here that short-sighted people – who see everything in a blurred way in any case – are especially prone to visual illusions, like the Shakespearean character who noted 'how easy doth a bush become a bear'. Drifting fog and changing lights, too, may well suggest the movement of a ghostly figure in indeterminate robes. These possibilities were particularly likely in the 1880s when 'peasoup' fogs unpredictably thickened and thinned and swirled not only in London streets but inside London houses; and short-sighted women were often reluctant to 'disfigure' themselves with spectacles (or if they were not, their parents were on their behalf. Charlotte M. Yonge fans will remember vividly poor Ethel May's unavailing efforts to be allowed a pair.) Illusion can also misinterpret normal sounds; apparent knockings, footsteps, whisperings, the rustle of a dress may be caused by the pattering or scratching of rats or mice, or, in terraced houses, by what is happening on the other side of a party wall. (This still goes on, it is interesting to note, in the present premises of the SPR, where the sound of footsteps is transmitted along the beams from next door.) Last of all Mrs Sidgwick remarks that a living being may sometimes be mistaken for a ghost. This happened to me during World War II, trying to get a lift some ten miles home from work during the blackout. I used to stand in a country main road, shining a torch onto my left hand (which wore a red ski glove) and making the hitch-hiker's sign. But cars and lorries, most helpful by daylight, refused to stop after dark, and indeed even seemed to accelerate. In the end I returned to wait an hour for the regular bus to go slowly lurching homeward through mud, rain or snow.

It was two months before the explanation came to me. Someone said at a local party, 'You're interested in ghost stories. Did you know there's a very well authenticated one of a luminous red hand being seen in mid-air, evening after evening, on a particular stretch of the Witney road?' I authenticated it still further!

Mrs Sidgwick accounts for collective visions by telepathy between the original perceiver and the bystanders. She makes the obvious but very necessary point that though one can check whether hallucinatory visions of living or dying people are veridical (that is, that they relate to some objective happening – accident, illness, danger – to the person seen) this cannot usually be done with hallucinatory visions of those already dead, known, or indeed unknown, like the figure of the spectral housemaid seen at different times and by different people on the stairs of a house in Hyde Park Place. (This did not worry the perceivers because they took for granted that it was a real *live* housemaid. Only when the various reports began to be checked did anyone realize that no such person would have been there at the relevant times.)

Nevertheless, the few outstanding cases she examines include one or two which, even though they cannot be checked, might just possibly be accepted as evidence for some sort of contact with the dead. In one of these the Warden of an orphanage sees the figure of a dead mother visiting her child, who sees her too and is overjoyed and comforted. In another a man supposed to have killed himself appears to a friend and tells him what really happened; and his explanation is checked and verified. In a third, and fourth, percipients recognize the photograph of a phantom seen earlier on. (Cases of this still happen today. I know of one myself.)

She also studies reports of houses in England, southern Europe, and India, in which 'haunts' are unexpectedly encountered from time to time by different tenants who know nothing of the possibility. Here again, she makes some general observations; that modern houses can be haunted, just as much as old ones; that in only one instance known to the SPR did a haunting happen annually on a given date; that there is little evidence to connect most appearances with tragedy; that no special kind of light is needed for seeing them, they have been observed by daylight, by artificial light, by the light of a dying fire and, in the dark, by a light emanating from themselves. They appear and disappear in different ways. They emerge out of nothing and fade away into it. Or they come in, gliding or walking or running, by the door, and go out in the same way. Or they leave by entering another room, from which there is no exit, and which is empty when explored. Various theories are discussed, among them one that leads directly to philosophy. It is that an apparition 'occupies space' and would be 'in' a room whether an observer were there to see it or not. The Oxford Limerick comes dancing into the mind:

> There was a young man who said 'God
> Must think it remarkably odd
> When He sees that this tree
> Continues to be
> When there's no one about in the quad'.

Mrs Sidgwick does not go into this particular problem in any detail, though it seems to have puzzled generations of philosophers. Even in our own time Professor H. H. Price[1] has discussed the matter with great care, suggesting that the apparition may occupy what he calls 'inner space', which I take to be the mind's own picture of the haunted room itself, a picture complete with the furniture, the carpet, the windows which are in fact to be seen there by all who actually visit the place, whether or no they perceive the 'ghost'.

---

1. President of the Society for Psychical Research, 1939–41.

She does however ask a question which seems to have puzzled enquirers almost as much; why are apparitions seen in clothes? It is hard, nowadays, to understand both the question and the puzzle; though they probably arose in connexion with what are now called 'out of the body experiences', then sometimes interpreted in terms of 'an astral' – or 'etheric' – body, a rarefied duplicate of the physical one, a 'meta-organism capable of projection at a distance in space'.[1] This, in F. W. H. Myers' words would 'imply the existence of a meta-coat and meta trousers' . . .[2]

Without this curious concept, little difficulty arises. If an apparition is to be seen as anything but a conventional horror – a skeleton, or the 'raw head and bloody bones' of folk-lore – it should surely be recognizable. Except in nudist colonies living persons are seldom seen in public without clothes, clothes which inevitably reflect some of the spectators' ideas about them, and some of their own tastes, preferences and ideas about themselves. Though butchers in striped blue aprons, farm labourers in smock frocks, navvies in corduroys tied at the knee with string are figures from the past, surgeons and laboratory workers still wear white clothes, most clerics have their collars back to front, and blue denims conscientiously frayed at the hem have long symbolized youth's self-identification with the proletariat; while, more individually, the flamboyant Mr X likes purple and gold, quiet Miss Y prefers beige, and Messrs This That and the Other preen themselves in exotic T-shirts, multi-coloured hair or scarlet and white plimsolls. How should an apparition *not* be clothed if it is to be recognized as human at all, and even more if it is to be recognized as one particular human? Whether the apparition perceived carries the image the perceiver associates with the person represented, or the image that person has of himself, *some* image there must surely be (even if the whole affair is 'all in the mind' as is sometimes said in disparagement).

Mrs Sidgwick examines the theory that an apparition is a spirit trying to communicate a message, asks why this should happen in a haunted house (to which the only logical response would seem to be 'why not')[3] and suggests that once a 'ghost' has been seen in a

---

1. W. H. Salter, SPR *Proceedings* 52, October 1958.

2. F. W. H. Myers, SPR *Proceedings* IV, 1887.

3. The question was many years later discussed by W. H. Carington, whose work is examined later.

certain place it is likely to be seen there again. Whether this is to be considered the result of talk and expectation, or of the shock it produces – as if it were an echo perpetually reinforced by each hearer – is not quite clear. She dismisses as 'improbable' the idea that 'some physical influence in the actual building itself' is at work; a suggestion perhaps more acceptable now that analogies from film and video tape are available.

Her final summary is strictly scientific and inconclusive; a matter of classification and discussion. It distinguishes carefully between phantasms of the living seen at the actual time of some great crisis (whether of danger, accident or the process of dying) and phantasms of the dead seen some twelve hours or more after they have drawn their last breath. Of this second group she notes that single appearances are recorded months and years after death, but with little evidence as to whence, or how, or why they come and that there are many cases in which these cannot be sorted out from subjective hallucinations. She notes, too, that there is often good evidence of hauntings in particular houses, but nothing to connect them with the known dead or with any intelligent purpose, nothing on which to found anything but 'tentative hypotheses'; and she does not do even that.

She also remarks that hallucinations should not be considered as 'evidence of anything seriously amiss with the brain'; this remains valuable today, when people who 'see ghosts' or have inexplicable experiences are still apt to say nothing about them for fear of being considered insane, or, worse, of being so.

I have gone into these Reports in some detail partly because they are so clear, so detailed and so well informed, partly because so many of their conclusions are still valid, and partly because they led up to the Society's first full-scale study, that pioneering work *Phantasms of the Living*,[1] published by Gurney, Myers and Podmore a year later, after a full discussion in Council. As in the Report of 1883, phantasms included all sorts of impressions – of touch and of hearing, not to mention what are now called 'hunches' – as well as those that came in a visual form.

This work originally appeared in two large unwieldy volumes. Mrs Sidgwick, who produced an abridged edition in 1918, recorded

---

1. London, 1886.

that she had cut out a note on witchcraft by Gurney, and another by Myers on 'a suggested method of psychical interaction', whether because they were out of date or because there had been a change in fashion is not clear. She had also reduced from 700 to 186 the number of instances cited 'where there is reason to suppose that the mind of one human being has affected that of another without speech uttered, or word written, or sign made'. Some were historical, and there was no way of checking the evidence for them with living witnesses; though Andrew Lang carefully examined a number of them in his book on *Dreams and Ghosts* in 1897, and found that several were well established by contemporary letters and documents. One was Lord Brougham's totally unexpected vision on December 19, 1799 of a university friend with whom he had made a pact that the first to die should try to appear to the other. He had not met him for years – he had gone to India – and seldom thought of him. Brougham, travelling about Sweden, was relaxing in a hot bath after a cold and exhausting journey when he suddenly 'saw' his friend sitting on the chair where he had put his clothes, and 'calmly looking at him'. He nearly fainted with the shock, but recorded what had happened as soon as possible. Shortly after returning to Edinburgh, where he was living, he received a letter from another friend in India telling him that the man had died there on that date.

Some incidents were probably cut for reasons of space, since those retained typified the patterns tediously repeated in a mass of others; tediously to the readers, though obviously not to the people involved.[1] Reports of experimental work later called into question were also cut. In this connexion the later edition examines the doubts cast in 1908 on the results of a series of tests when one of the two young men who had taken part in them 'confessed' to fraud; a 'confession' promptly and stoutly denied by the other! Plainly these results could no longer be used as reliable evidence.

There is a survey of various individual attempts to make telepathic suggestions at a distance; notably those in which a conscious agent tries to get something through to a percipient who has no idea that any such experiment is to be made. (I was myself such a percipient and much frightened when, alone one evening in a house in Gloucestershire except for a very old invalid lady who was fast asleep,

---

1. For further discussion see Chapter 9 on Fact, Fraud and *Furor Scholasticus*.

I 'heard' my name being called again and again, and thought I was going mad. It proved some days later to have been an experiment on the part of my friend the late Penelope Balogh, formerly Penelope Gatty, who was then in a part of London some five miles from where I normally lived with my family. She telephoned to ask whether I had noticed anything unusual on the evening in question, and was much gratified to hear that I had indeed. (With a deplorable absence of scientific spirit I myself was distinctly cross – though relieved.)

Even more alarming must have been the sudden successful telepathic appearances recorded of gentlemanly wraiths in ladies' bedrooms at midnight. There is also a fascinating account by one H. M. Weserman in *Magnetismus und die Allgemeine Weltsprache* of 1822 of his attempts to transfer mental images to sleeping friends at distances varying from one furlong to nine miles. Sadly, however, this is dismissed as 'too old to be useful'; possibly because Herr Weserman was dead and could not be questioned (but had he left no records?) and possibly because of the common human propensity to believe that all ancient testimony must be suspect, and only one's own generation can be trusted.

Frederic Myers' energetic introduction to *Phantasms of the Living* surveys some of the background against which research had been carried out. There had been heated accusations of 'bringing theology into science, and science into theology'; both, it appears, major crimes in the eyes of minor experts on either side, who felt that each field should be placarded *Trespassers will be Prosecuted*, and that Man Traps and Spring Guns should be set for poachers. Undeterred, he reiterates that the authors' researches were essentially non-religious, even though they *were* interested in the Irvingites and their 'gift of tongues', and in the clairvoyant experiences of Swedenborg; that they were unlikely to yield convincing proof of the validity of any specialized form of religion; and that they had a non-committal attitude in the matter of human survival after death. His fellow authors agreed that the whole range of telepathy between the living needed to be explored before taking on this subject, and meanwhile 'extraneous theorizing' was deprecated.

Like Edmund Gurney, Myers was deeply interested in hypnotism. He had himself carried out hypnotic experiments, and had also 'through the kindness of Drs Charcot . . . and Liébault witnessed typical experiments at the Salpetrière in Paris, at the Hôpital Civil in Nancy etc. . . . . and satisfied myself in other ways that the cases vouched for by' various French doctors including Bernheim and Rochet 'had been recorded with candour and accuracy'. He saw hypnosis as 'a handle that turns the mechanism of our being, a mode of shifting the threshold of consciousness . . . by inhibiting normal perception' and so producing 'a temporary freedom from preoccupation with accustomed stimuli', a freedom in which 'man's mind may reveal . . . capacities of which his conscious self is not aware'. Modern do-it-yourself methods of producing 'altered states of consciousness' form an interesting contrast with this, in that they are much more concerned with a sustained personal determination to follow out instructions than with a simple yielding of the will and the attention to the hypnotist. The Ganzfeld technique for instance depends on the volunteer's perseverance in his decision to carry on throughout periods of boredom, anxiety and frustration as he lies completely relaxed in semi-darkness with half a ping-pong ball over each eye, and 'white noise' like the rushing of a waterfall being played to occupy his hearing.

Myers reiterates – as the earlier reports did – that 'telepathy is a fact in Nature'.[1] This has been shown, he argues, by large numbers of different experiments with different people, experiments not only with words and drawings and diagrams, but with taste, with smell and even with the awareness of mildly painful stimulation (oddly enough this seems sometimes to have been felt on the opposite side of the percipient, who experienced in his right arm the sensation of a pinch on the agent's left – a phenomenon observed as early as 1885 by Malcolm Guthrie, who noted that this happened in 'thought transference experiments', with 'impressions both of vision and sensation'.[2] Telepathy has also been shown to exist by the mass of carefully investigated testimony that phantasms of people undergoing some crisis are unexpectedly perceived by their friends and relations with a frequency that chance cannot explain. There is, in fact, overwhelming evidence of the 'supersensory action of one mind on another'. (Yet even now, when Myers' contention is quite widely

---

1. F. W. H. Myers: SPR *Proceedings* IV, 1887.
2. 'Thought Transference Experiments', Malcolm Guthrie, JP, SPR *Proceedings* III, 1885.

accepted, it gives one a shock – like treading on a non-existent stair – to recognize an instance of telepathy.)

Edmund Gurney wrote the remainder of the work (Podmore was involved with collecting and verifying the material; an enormous task). Gurney, as deeply interested in hypnosis as Myers was, began his narrative by discussing the results of the French hypnotists at Nancy, notably Liébault, and went on to Professor Barrett's findings that 'thought-transference' could be achieved without *either* hypnosis *or* 'physical contact'. (The theory of 'unconscious muscular pressure' had been worked to death to explain what was known as 'the will-ing game' in which an object was hidden, someone previously outside the room came in, took the hand of a player in the know, and found the hidden thing with inexplicable speed. This theory was sometimes evoked on other occasions.) He mentions collusion and the use of codes among certain experimental subjects. In this connexion the later edition examines some of Professor Barrett's work with the young Creery sisters. It looks as if their powers had diminished as they grew older. Paranormal abilities often seem to be at their peak in childhood and early adolescence, and to fade out as the years go by. There was probably also some question of what Dr J. B. Rhine half a century later pinpointed as 'the decline effect'. Something of the kind had already been noted by the observant Malcolm Guthrie[1] as occurring in himself as 'transmitter' of impressions, rather than in the would-be receivers. This, however, was no more than an individual experience, and may well have arisen from quite different causes. In the decline effect in general (which I should ascribe largely to boredom with prolonged repetitive tests) the brilliant statistical effects at first achieved by a subject successfully guessing card after card after card, fall to the average and stay there. Disappointing as this is, it does at any rate serve to show that practice does not make perfect this form of extrasensory perception. Interestingly enough, it was *after* such a failure had begun to show itself in the Creery girls that they were caught devising and using tricks. This of course cast a retrospective mildew on their earlier achievements.

Gurney's classification of phenomena for the most part follows that of the earlier papers, though there are some interesting discussions of 'shared dreams' (still being collected and examined – a number

---

1. Op. cit.

were reported at the SPR Conference at Brighton in 1980) and of the telepathically shared experience of pain, as exemplified in the well-known case of Mrs Arthur Severn, whose husband went sailing early one morning, while she stayed in bed. She was suddenly awoken by what felt like an agonizing blow on the mouth, at the same moment as her husband, at sea, had been struck by the tiller. A very intriguing chapter deals with 'Transient Hallucinations of the Sane' and 'the general opinion that they are due to disease, morbid excitement, or at least to indigestion'. This opinion still recurs from time to time. Andrew Lang noted in his *Dreams and Ghosts* (1897) that that staunch rationalist Edward Clodd 'ascribed crystal vision to a disordered liver', and added that 'if no more were needed, I could scry famously'. Even in our own day J. B. S. Haldane explained in this way an experience of entering his study and 'seeing' himself sitting in his own chair at his own desk.

That there might be some foundation for this theory – and for the practice of antighost dosing – appeared in Sir Henry Head's Goulstonian Lectures of 1901, later published in book form as *Certain Mental Changes that Accompany Visceral Disease*. He pointed out that 'reflected visceral pain' did indeed sometimes produce hallucinations and cited a number of cases. J. G. Piddington, who reviewed it with great care,[1] compared these with typical instances in the *Census*, and found some fascinating contrasts. Figures seen in visceral hallucinations, for instance, usually appeared at dusk or in darkness; were black-and-white; were for the most part 'draped, wrapped in a shawl or sheet'; had 'misty or invisible faces'; and produced terror. Psychical hallucinations on the other hand often appeared in daylight or bright lamplight, were seen in full colour, wore ordinary clothes and had clear cut features. They did not necessarily inspire fear.

Though Gurney's firm remark that 'lobster salad may lead to nightmares, but not to hallucinations' may not be totally accurate, it should be remembered that he was careful to note that many other causes – such as anxiety or expectation – might well do so. All the same, he says that in 489 cases he has himself examined, only 24 of the people concerned were 'in abnormal states', and once more calls upon telepathy as the most reasonable explanation of what went on.

---

1. SPR *Proceedings* 19, 1905–7.

It must have been a sort of telepathic ricochet, so to speak, that produced the instance in which a children's black nurse in Barbados 'saw' her employer's brother standing beside her at the time of his sudden unexpected death in Tobago. The woman herself was completely unaware of it. Several such incidents of proxy telepathy have since been recorded and investigated. Sometimes — as here, and as in a similar happening in India with a children's ayah — the percipient has been of a different race from the person most concerned. This may imply either that western people have a greater resistance to extrasensory perception or that — as Prospero Lambertini insisted in the 18th century — the faculty appears most vividly in the uneducated. There may even be some correlation, at any rate in Europe, with the rhesus-negative type of blood, since the groups in which this is most common — Basque, Breton, Cornish, Highland Scots, Irish, Welsh — are those traditionally most prone to extrasensory perception.

Gurney discusses theories of coincidence, and the mathematical arguments for and against using it as an explanation for telepathy. The statistical approach to the data of psychical research was of course nothing new, and he quotes Charles Richet's contemporary essay, 'Le Suggestion Mental et la Calcul des Probabilités' in the *Revue Philosophique* for 1884. That he does not mention F. Y. Edgeworth's independent paper on this theme in the Society's *Proceedings* for 1885 is probably because it appeared too late for reference.

As with earlier work, the authors of *Phantasms of the Living* draw few conclusions and stress the fact that this detailed study will not interest readers with a taste for thrills. And again, they ask for more cases to be written down as soon as possible after they occur, checked and sent to the Society.

It is plain that they had international contacts. The Society gained still more in 1889 when Frederic Myers and Henry Sidgwick attended the first International Congress of Experimental Psychology in Paris. Charles Richet was the Secretary, and the President was Jean-Paul Charcot, whose work with mentally disturbed patients at the Salpetrière had already convinced the young Sigmund Freud that neurosis and hysteria could not all be ascribed to purely physiological causes, and that some bodily illnesses were brought about by the workings of the mind. Even more interesting, from the point of view of psychical research, was Charcot's experimental work in inducing telepathy under hypnosis.

Sadly, Edmund Gurney,[1] who would have been fascinated, was not there. Many Victorians as a matter of course used dangerous chemicals such as ether, morphine and opium to relieve pain (my own great-great-grandmother's recipe book contains a powerful home brew of laudanum, nutmeg and warm brandy and water for 'a complaint in the bowels'). Gurney was accustomed to deaden the pain of his agonizing bouts of neuralgia by inhaling the fumes of chloroform from a small sponge kept in a hair oil bottle. One night in 1888 he died of it. Perhaps it should be said that some sixty years afterwards several ingenious persons have taken it upon themselves to reinterpret this event and have tried to suggest that he committed suicide. It seems more sensible to rely on the evidence of a reliable doctor given on oath at the time than on elaborate theories spun from hearsay and unjustifiable inference two generations later.

Psychologists from all over Europe went to the Congress. Francis Galton was one of the English members; there were representatives from Russia and Latin America, and William James came from the United States. His study, *The Principles of Psychology*, was to appear the following year. (He was to pay tribute to Myers' services to psychology in the obituary he wrote for the Society's *Proceedings* in 1901.)[2]

In the end, the Society was asked to carry out a Census of Hallucinations. This was done by the members of a Committee headed by Henry Sidgwick; among them were Mrs Sidgwick, Alice Johnson, F. W. H. Myers, his brother and Frank Podmore. Following up many of the suggestions made in *Phantasms of the Living* they — in the spirit of the earlier one issued to members of the Society — compiled a carefully thought out questionnaire, beginning, 'Have you ever, when believing yourself to be completely awake, had a vivid impression of seeing or being touched by a living or inanimate object, or of hearing a voice; which impression, so far as you could discover, was not due to any external physical cause?' 410 people — 223 women and 187 men, all over twenty-one distributed this and

1. It is interesting that Myers, writing his obituary, should have said that the SPR had 'the establishment of thought-transference . . . as its primary aim'. It is all too often assumed that it was founded to prove survival.

2. SPR *Proceedings* 17, Part 42, 1901.

collected the replies. The addresses and occupations of those answered were recorded. Most, though not all, belonged to the professional classes. Those who said Yes – 7·8% of the men concerned and 12% of the women – were asked to answer a list of other questions. They were invited to give their nationalities; to state exactly what they had seen, heard, or felt; the place, date and hour of the experience; how old they had been when it happened; what they were doing at the time; their physical health, their emotional preoccupations; whether they had been alone; whether they had had such an experience more than once; and so on.

The enquiry lasted from the spring of 1889 until the spring of 1892, and its results were tabulated and discussed in great detail in the Committee's report, which was published in the Society's *Proceedings* for 1894. It begins by noting that before enquiries can be made as to how telepathy works one has to establish that it does in fact take place. To do this it is necessary both to collect and authenticate as much evidence as possible for spontaneous cases and to carry out experimental work, trying to transmit from mind to mind not only diagrams and the like, but ideas and impressions. (The question of achieving complete repeatability in *mass* experiments had not yet come over the horizon, trailing some way behind it the additional query as to whether in the long run 'the nature of the beast' would make this as impossible as an attempt to test that ancient adage, 'If you hold up a guinea pig by its tail its eyes will drop out'.)

People from many parts of the world answered the long questionnaire. That the largest national groups were Brazilian (12·1%), British (9·4%) and Russian (15·9%) probably reflects the local collectors' enthusiasm as much as national characteristics. The total age range ran from three years old to eighty, and the highest proportion of experiences came, rather surprisingly, from people between twenty and thirty. (One might have expected it to occur more among adolescents; but of course adolescence happens earlier now than it did in those days.)

There are notes on how hallucinations develop. I was particularly interested to find that they sometimes began with the sighting of a cloud; since a hairdresser, knowing my interest in the subject, asked me not to laugh if she told me of one she had had walking along a cliff path. I promised, and she said she had seen a small cloud rapidly approaching across the sea; as it came nearer, its core solidified into what looked like a seafaring man. It came within a few feet of her and disappeared as suddenly as it had come. I said, 'Weren't you frightened?' and she replied with earthy commonsense, 'No. I knew a thing like that couldn't rape me anyhow.'

Sometimes hallucinations begin, says the Report, with a glow of light. Sometimes they are just *there*, and are only known to be hallucinations because they unaccountably vanish. Those who perceive them may feel, as they do so, sensations of intense cold, 'electrical thrills', prickling in the scalp, or faintness. Certain families seemed prone to such experiences; whether for physiological reasons or because tradition makes it easier to accept or 'register' them does not appear.

They occurred most often in states of relaxation, sometimes in fatigue, sometimes in anxiety but very seldom in active grief; and usually to people who were alone at the time. The finding about anxiety is odd, since it usually inhibits extra-sensory perception possibly because, as a form of fear, it causes blood sugar to increase, makes the body ready for instant action, and concentrates attention on immediate happenings: will the taxi heard approaching pass the door and disgorge the late comer; are those heavy footsteps those of a policeman coming to report some appalling accident? It could be of course that the hallucinations that happened when the perceiver was worried were purely subjective, and not veridical.

The effects of expectancy, ordinary suggestion – as at some Spiritualist meetings – and hypnotic suggestion are discussed, and there is a long careful statistical argument as to the number of veridical hallucinations that could be expected to happen by chance coincidence. This is finally assessed as one in nineteen hundred, whereas the number registered in the Census was one in forty-three. It should be noted that cases involving 'a sense of presence' or hallucinations of smell were not admitted. Nor were those in which the perceiver was ill, or concussed. Nor was any kind of second hand information. All had to come from the healthy horse's mouth.

There are a few odd collective hallucinations, including some shared by animals; dogs shrinking away, or howling, ponies trembling and so on (these curiously enough are dismissed as 'unimportant'). Among the purely human incidents is one in which two girls each 'saw' in church one afternoon their sister, who had been in the rectory library all the time; and another in which two perceivers had simultaneous hallucinations, but in different modes. This surely links up with the curious events reported of the day when Goethe lay dying, and every visitor to the house 'heard' music somewhere, but each heard a different kind; a quartet, an organ, a choral chant, a piano, even a concertina.

There are some precognitive incidents; five cases of people seeing their 'doubles'; and a good many instances in which apparitions of the dying were 'seen' within twelve hours of actual death. The period of twelve hours was thought important because, though the impression might well have been received at the moment of departure, it could have failed to arouse attention during a busy day's work, and only emerged into consciousness when this was over. This argument would tell against the idea that the apparitions were 'spirits'.

Nevertheless the authors conclude that 'between deaths and the apparitions of dying persons a connexion exists which is not due to chance alone'; and very cautiously hazard the suggestion that if telepathic communication with the living has a non-physical cause, this shows that the mind is independent of the brain, and thus makes more probable the idea of communication with the dead.

4

Apparitions and Phantasms – Developments

Fashions in ideas change almost as surprisingly and quite as radically as fashions in clothes. During the first decades of the twentieth century, the Society's intense interest in apparitions and phantasms diminished, to be outshone by interest in the psychology, the data, and the implications of mediumship, which was studied at very great length from the standpoints of various schools of psychology, in connexion with cases of multiple personality, and most urgently of all in relation to the question of personal immortality.

Of course, the SPR continued to collect and verify individual experiences, though with the utmost caution, sometimes even distaste, as if they were rather improper, unhygienic, in need of a disinfectant bath. Thus, though a manuscript book of the first notes concerning the curious experience of two Oxford dons at Versailles in 1902 was lodged in its archives soon after it had happened, the matter was treated with distrust rather than interest, since the authors, not being trained psychical researchers, had been so indiscreet as to discuss together what they had seen and heard before writing down their recollections.

Their joint experience, finally published in book form in 1911 as *An Adventure* was very severely reviewed in *Proceedings*. After this, the writers, Miss Moberly and Miss Jourdain (the latter well known to generations of undergraduates of St Hugh's College for her flashes of extra sensory perception, which sometimes proved awkward for them) asked for their MS to be returned. Before this was done, Andrew Lang, then President, looked at it himself and said he would go bail for their good faith, though he suspended judgment as to the parapsychological aspect of what had gone on,[1]

The case itself continued to interest people, and to be discussed despite ingenious – and sometimes acrimonious – attempts to discredit the ladies, or to suggest that they had seen no more than a group of people dressed in 18th century clothes for a masquerade organized by the Comte de Montesquiou. The Society however seems to have paid no further attention to it for some thirty years or so. Maybe G. N. M. Tyrrell's admirable study of apparitions[2] in general served to turn the tide. Later Guy Lambert[3] suggested that the ladies had somehow become aware of an unfulfilled project of one Antoine Richard, an early 18th century garden planner with whose sketches and layouts what they saw had corresponded far more closely than with the landscape of either Marie Antoinette's time or that of 1902. As to the figures perceived, he pointed out that before the book's publication two other ladies, Clare Burrows and Lady Hay had reported similar experiences, preceded, as those of *An Adventure* had been, by feelings of heaviness and depression. Andrew MacKenzie researched the case again, with his usual meticulous care, in two books *The Unexplained* (1966) and *Apparitions and Ghosts* (1971). He stressed the fact that apparitions had been reported at Versailles by various people, some of whom he had been able to interview; for instance, by the Crooke family in 1908, by a Mrs Hatton in 1938, by Jack Wilson, a poultry farmer, and his wife in 1949 and by an English solicitor and his wife in 1955. Neither the Crookes nor the Wilsons nor Mrs Hatton had ever heard of *An Adventure*, as far as they could remember, and certainly none of them had read it. In each case the figures seen had seemed quite real until they vanished, either suddenly or by fading, melting into the background. Notable among them was that of a woman 'in a very full skirt' – it sounds

---

1. Cf *Les Fantômes du Trianon*, edited with a new preface by Robert Amadou, Paris, 1978.

2. First delivered as a Myers Memorial Lecture in 1942; amplified and published in book form (*Apparitions*, London, 1943).

3. 'Antoine Richard's Garden', SPR *Journal*, March 1955 and 'Richard's Garden Revisited', SPR *Journal*, 1962.

like an 18th century hooped dress, or a 19th century crinoline – variously described as yellow, or light gold, or cream coloured. Once she was seen as fair – like Marie Antoinette, whose hair was ash blonde – another time she had dark ringlets. Her hat was not always the same, either. Whether the phantom represented more than one person or whether the variations sprang from the different ideas and associations of those who perceived 'her' it is impossible to tell. What was clear, however, was that people of various backgrounds and avocations did from time to time and quite unexpectedly become aware of 'ghosts' at Versailles. (I use the word in its general sense; this is not the time to discuss all that it may imply.)

But to return to the early decades of the twentieth century and its psychical preoccupations: although, as has been noted, Mrs Sidgwick produced in 1918 an abridged edition of *Phantasms of The Living*, not till 1922 did *Proceedings* contain a new paper on such subjects. This, also by Mrs Sidgwick, dealt with cases of 'Telepathy between Living Persons printed in the Journal since . . . 1886'. (At that time, and until 1949 the *Journal* was a kind of house organ for members only, though *Proceedings* were available to the general public.)

This paper was, like all her work, clear, thorough, painstaking and conscientious. The introduction states her belief that telepathy does indeed occur, and that it is sometimes brought startlingly to the attention of the person concerned by being 'seen' in the form of some external hallucination. (This is probably commonest among people who are good visualizers in any case. Others may have the uncomfortable, though less clear-cut awareness of the poet who complained that

> 'Late last night upon the stair
> I saw a man who wasn't there.
> He isn't there again today
> Oh how I wish he'd go away.')

She also records some more spontaneous cases in which, instead of seeing or hearing as it were 'outside' himself what is happening to someone else, a person experiences it from within, as his own; as when a wife felt in her own thumb the sudden searing pain of her distant husband's thumb being crushed. Rider Haggard's famous dream, which showed first a shared and then a separate awareness, is cited. During the evening of Saturday July 9 1904, he dreamed first that he himself was drowning, and then that his black retriever Bob was trying to tell him it was dying. On Sunday the 10th Bob did not turn up for his dinner – nor ever again. He seems to have been a free ranging dog who slept outside the house. On the morning of the 11th two platelayers on the local railway found a dog collar and dog hairs on the track, and as there were no Sunday trains concluded that on the Saturday night some dog must have been struck by an engine and knocked off the line into the stream below. This flowed towards a weir, under which Bob's body was found the following Thursday.

Mrs Sidgwick seems to have outgrown her curious earlier belief that incidents involving animals were unimportant, as she also records an occasion on which the owner of another missing dog had a sudden inexplicable flash of knowledge that it had chased a rat into a neighbouring chimney flue and could not get out; and yet another in which two people saw a phantom cat known in life as Smoky. Other cases cited include that of a priest living in a clergy house who was awakened from sleep by 'a dark figure' (he took it to be a perfectly ordinary solid person) which said there had been an urgent telephone call asking him to go to a sick parishioner who had seemed in no particular danger when visited earlier that day, but was now dying. He scrambled into his clothes and got to the place in time to administer the last sacraments; but found when all was over that there had been no telephone call. Everything had happened so fast that all the attention had been given to trying to save the patient. (Possibly – this took place in 1918 – there had been no telephone in the patient's home, but this is not clear.) World War I, as such, yielded two particularly interesting cases, one of a young airman seen by several others (in the quarters they all shared), shortly after his death in a plane crash miles away; all took it for granted that it was his living self. The other was of a soldier seen by his sister and her child at the time of his death.

For some while after this no large-scale investigations took place, though the results of the earlier ones went on being discussed, notably by Professor Broad. General questions were raised, as when

Lewis Powles enquired in the *Journal* for October 1931 whether
anyone had come across evidence of the phantasm of a blind man,
alive or dead, observing that a man blind from birth obviously could
not project telepathically 'what he thinks or thought his visual aspect
to be'. Mr Powles plainly meant by 'phantasm' no more than
something *seen*, since a blind man must, like everyone else, have
some *feeling* of his own 'body-image', even if it does not include any
such looking-glass impression as sighted people have; and could, if
the matter were indeed one of 'projection', have projected a voice, a
touch, or a general 'sense of presence'. No answers to Mr Powles'
query seem to have come in, and we are left wondering whether any
'projection' of the kind is necessarily involved. That it does
occasionally happen is clear, since veridical 'crisis apparitions' *are*
sometimes 'seen' in the clothes they have on at the relevant time,
clothes which are totally unfamiliar to the perceiver in that particular
connexion; bush shorts, for instance, if the phantasm 'seen' in
England is in fact in some tropical jungle. Possibly such clothes have
been so habitually worn, so completely taken for granted by the
wearer, as to seem as much a part of himself as his skin.

In general, though, it appears more likely that some telepathic
impulse reaching anyone concerned would arouse his own remembered impressions of the originator (an idea put forward by Myers
and later developed by Tyrrell.[1]) Thus for instance if old blind Pew
in *Treasure Island* had consciously – or more likely unconsciously –
set about emitting some signal of the kind, he would not have needed
to form any neat picture of himself to bring to the perceiver's mind
the image of his blue coat, his sightless eyes, his stick relentlessly
tap-tap-tapping nearer and nearer along the road. To ignite a flash
of horrible memory would have been enough.

That no large-scale piece of work was undertaken for so long may
have been due in part to the recession of the 1930s, which hit the
Society hard, and of course to the alarms and excursions of the war
and the stressful peace of the next decade.

Various members, among them Gerald Heard, Lord Charles
Hope, Dame Edith Lyttelton and Sir Oliver Lodge, took part in a
series of broadcasts on psychical research in January 1934. It was
called *Inquiry into the Unknown*, and the cautious but open minded

1. Op. cit.

Professor Broad, the Cambridge philosopher,[1] contributed a final summary. What was said demonstrated the findings, the ideas, the different currents of thought at work in the Society, and brought in some fascinating cases from listeners. Two, published in the *Journal* that summer, illustrated respectively the uses and the disadvantages of telepathy. In one a mother yielded to an odd strong impulse to post immediately some currency to her son in France (whose pocket, though she did not know it, had just been picked of all he had). In the other a man living in Kenya, worried because his sleepwalking wife sometimes left their bungalow and wandered off into the night, took to locking the doors and hiding the keys in various different places. Three times he was defeated by her telepathic dreams that he was telling her their whereabouts (on one occasion, when he had put them in a brass pot full of porcupine quills she dreamed that he added 'mind you don't prick your fingers!'). Walking in her sleep she duly retrieved them and went out as usual. In the end he kept them under the mattress so that she could not get at them without waking him.

In 1947 Mass Observation on behalf of the Society issued to a panel of its members, some 1500 people, a Questionnaire on Hallucinations, with the intention of discovering whether there had been any marked changes since that of the 1890s. It was of course on a very much smaller scale than its predecessor, and seems to have been confined to this country. In the *Journal* for March 1948 Dr Donald West[2] surveyed the results. He noted that 'among the class of people questioned there has been no diminution in the frequency and no substantial change in the character of sporadic hallucinations' since the earlier Census. 9·9% of those who answered the earlier one had had one or more hallucinations, as compared with 14·3% of those recorded in its successor. In both they were reported more often by women than by men; in both, more than half the experiences were 'mainly visual'; and in both, under a third were 'mainly vocal'. (As dreams, *déjà vu* impressions, sudden changes of mood, and the very real but indefinable 'sense of presence' were deliberately excluded, the remainder can only have been hallucinations of touch, smell, taste and temperature.) Oddly enough, no attempt seems to

---

1. SPR President, 1958–60.
2. Later President, 1963–5.

have been made by the organizers to test whether they were in fact veridical (though there was an enquiry as to whether they were *felt* to be so at the time when they happened. Only 2% of those who answered said yes.)

Sporadic 'haunts' were carefully investigated, though not always reported; often because they were not particularly evidential, often because the people concerned had specifically asked that what happened should be treated in confidence. Two cases described in the *Journal* – with fictitious names etc – during 1948 and 1949 – exemplify the great care taken in this sort of work. In the earlier one Donald West recorded what had been done in the instance of a dance hall said to be subject to bad luck, and haunted by strange noises, the appearance of ghostly faces and the disappearance of various objects. He interviewed a number of witnesses, who gave him exciting though self-contradictory rumours about what went on. One of them occasionally went into trances, boasted of 'psychic powers' and was apt to see – and point out to others – 'faces' in the play of light and shade on the walls and rafters of the place. His psychiatric training inclined him to think that she might 'gain relief from some inner conflict by projecting ghostly visions'. He spent a night on the spot and observed the creaking of the wooden floor, the rattle of doors in the wind and the rhythmic drip of the cistern; but nothing more. Later a disused sewer was found, a runway for rats. This could have accounted at any rate for the disappearance of food.

The following year the November *Journal* contained an equally careful investigation, this time of an office ghost, by Edward Osborn, the Honorary Secretary of the Society (whose professional work was at Chatham House, among the intricacies of international politics). The figure seen, and the footsteps heard were thought to be those of a 'Woman in Brown', believed to have been killed in 1943 by a flying bomb. The head of the department in whose offices the haunt took place was a lady who prided herself on her 'psychic powers', but it was a 'Miss Benson' who worked there who saw the apparition most often, at least a dozen times. Edward Osborn established that it was quite easy to hear footsteps in adjacent offices; gently and sympathetically investigated 'Miss Benson's' own wartime experiences; and concluded that nothing paranormal had taken place.

In any haunt, of course, the very presence of a detached observer with a note book or tape recorder – sometimes indeed with a whole kit of ingenious instruments[1] — must make people slightly self-conscious, and lower the emotional temperature, to the relief of the scared sufferers and the disappointment of the investigator. What still remains to be discussed is whether that emotional temperature encourages paranormal events or only states of mind in which ordinary events are misinterpreted.

It is even more difficult to find out the nature of what has been going on in cases — however capably reported and checked — which have happened only once, or only at sporadic intervals over a long period. One of these[2] was the curious experience of two young women on holiday together at Puys, near Dieppe, in the summer of 1951, who were awoken by sounds which seemed to correspond with those of the great wartime raid on Dieppe some nine years earlier. They began about 4 a.m. and ended, after some variations, about 6.20 a.m. No one else in the hotel heard them, so it looked as if a hallucination was in question; was it veridical, a telepathic sharing, perhaps, of the vivid memories of someone in the town, or had there been access to what might be called by analogy a sort of tape-recording of the past? The writers did not speculate; neither did the percipients, apparently. A Mr Eades wrote to the *Journal* six years later pooh-poohing the story on the grounds that he and his family, camping in the neighbourhood in August 1951 had been awoken by what proved to be the operations of a dredger in Dieppe harbour. G. W. Lambert carried out one of his painstaking investigations, and found out from the Harbour Master's carefully kept records that the dredger had indeed been working on August 4 of that year; it had however begun soon after midnight — 3¾ hours before the 'battle noises' were heard, and stopped at a quarter past eight in the morning, about 2 hours after they had ceased. The idea that the noises were in some way connected with the raid was again attacked a year later by R. J. Hastings, and again defended by Lambert. The whole episode is an admirable example of the inconclusiveness that dogs even the most careful investigations of spontaneous cases, except in instances where a suggestion can definitely be disproved; as

---

1. Cf Appendix II for a description of those devised and used by John Cutten, Hon Secretary, 1968.

2. *Journal*, May/June 1952. 'The Dieppe Raid Case', investigated by G. W. Lambert and Kathleen Gay.

happened when H. J. M. Green demolished[1] – on the evidence of
the GLC's historical Survey of London – the exciting story, supported
by two mediums, that the upper floors of the house at 69 Dean
Street, Soho, occupied by the Gargoyle Club were haunted by Nell
Gwyn, to whom the place had been given by Charles II. He pointed
out that it had not been built till 1732: that there had been no
building at all on the site before 1682; that the one put up after that
had not reached the height of the Gargoyle Club's premises; and that
by the time it was ready for occupation in 1686, Charles II had been
dead for more than a year. It is also worth remembering that among
his last words were, 'Do not let poor Nelly starve'; which would have
been unlikely if she had a largish house of her own to sell if need
arose!

At the request of a meeting of the American Parapsychology
Foundation at Utrecht two years earlier, the Secretary set up a
Conference on Spontaneous Experiences, which duly took place at
Cambridge in July 1955, and resulted in a new enquiry into such
cases being organized in 1956. A questionnaire sent out to members
and their contacts however produced no more than 300 instances.
Then 1300 more poured in as the result of an article in the *Daily
Express* by Mr Chapman Pincher, which had of course reached a very
much wider – and probably very much less inhibited – public. They
arrived at a very awkward time, since the Society was in process of
moving from a spacious house in Tavistock Square, whose long lease
had just run out, to a much smaller freehold property in Adam and
Eve Mews. Mr Salter, Professor Stratton, FRS, then in the last year
of his Presidency, and two experienced members, Mrs Richmond
and Mrs Gay, worked on registering and following up the material;
which was not always easy, as some of those who had sent it in were
not used to writing long letters, and answering sophisticated
enquiries. In 1958 much of the work was taken over by Sir George
Joy, by that time Secretary, and the newly appointed Research
Officer, Celia Green, a brilliant young woman with a degree in
Mathematics, who had joined the Society the previous year. She
organized some of the information obtained (much was too vague for
such treatment) under various headings; the sex of those who reported
experiences (as usual, there were more women than men); their ages,

---

1. *Journal*, December 1970.

which on an average ranged from twenty to sixty (though some of
the reports concerned young children); the relationship, if any,
between the perceivers and those perceived as 'phantasms' (most
common between mothers and sons, with that between wives and
husbands coming next); the percentage of hallucinations which
seemed to be veridical (35·7%); and so on. There were pages of
tables, figures, graphs, analyses; careful gradings in terms of
evidential value; and computer calculations. For the non-mathemat-
ical there was, moreover, an Appendix citing some of the episodes
themselves, which still makes very good reading. The whole report
was produced in the Society's *Proceedings*[1] in November 1960; and its
main firm conclusion was that 'the most important single factor in
the study of spontaneous cases' was 'the state of mind of the person
concerned at the time of the occurrence'.

The report suffered some violent attacks from members of the old
guard who believed that – as had happened with its predecessor –
every instance cited should have been investigated in great depth and
detail. They were still, presumably, taking for granted that the
existence of telepathy and of precognition needed to be proved, and
ignoring the evidence yielded by nearly 80 years of intensive work.
Celia Green replied in the *Journal* to some of their criticisms, saying
she thought the material used 'could provide a picture of the types
of cases involved', making it possible to work out a technique 'for
analysing cases in a form which would lend itself to . . . evaluation
by statistical methods'. She was defended by Professor Gardner
Murphy, who had served as President of the Society in 1949, and
later by Dr Donald West, in his Presidential Address, 'for instituting
a computer tabulation of the relationships between different variables'; a new tool for research.

She opened up other very interesting lines of research by two
papers in the *Journal*. Both were attempts 'to discover what natural
conditions, if any, govern the emergence of extra-sensory perception'.
The first,[2] based on questionnaires (later followed up by tests of
those who replied) in the *Queen* and the *Daily Mirror* respectively,
examined 'The Effect of Birth Order and Family Size' in ESP, and
suggested that the faculty came out more frequently among middle

---

1. *Proceedings*, 53, 1960.
2. SPR *Journal*, December 1965.

class people, where family bonds were tighter. The eldest child tended to produce the highest positive scores in tests (could this be because the eldest child has by definition, been emotionally 'dethroned', and needs to keep in unconscious touch with a busy mother who no longer has time to talk to it as much as before?). The only child, like the youngest child, tended to produce the most 'negative scores'; scores as significantly *below* the average to be expected by chance, as positive scores are significantly *above* it. It seems possible that this may spring from some need for psychological privacy in which to develop alone, some shelter against too much telepathic communication from adoring parents. The other paper, which appeared nine months later, discussed 'Spontaneous Paranormal Experiences in Relation to Sex and Academic Standing'. Slighter than its predecessor – it was based on work with 115 members of Southampton University – it showed two rather surprising results, that science students had had a larger proportion of paranormal experiences than students of the humanities, and that women had had the same proportion as men.

Early in 1967 Celia Green left the Society – a great loss – and set up at Oxford her own Institute of Psychophysical Research, which has published some most interesting work, orientated to the general reader as well as to the mathematical expert. It includes studies of 'Lucid Dreams' and of 'Out of the Body Experiences' – both issued as *Proceedings* of that Institute in 1968 – and of *Apparitions*, a book brought out by Hamish Hamilton. These cite many SPR sources, as well as much material received as the result of press and radio appeals from the Institute itself. All accept the fact that paranormal experiences do occur, and go on from there to examine their patterns, their relationships to the physical world, and their general implications.

Members of the Society continued and continue to investigate and to report individual cases.

One, admirably set out by K. H. Turner of the Doncaster Group for Psychical Study exemplified very clearly the advantages and limitations of scientific enquiry, which can eliminate every imaginable physical cause for parapsychological phenomena without suggesting any alternative origin. This episode, published in the *Journal* for September 1970, took place in a house built about 1925 in a mining area, and peacefully occupied on and off till 1956 when a

Mrs Holt 'saw' a figure bending over her baby's cot. She did not see it again, and continued to live there till 1962. In 1963, after a brief but uneventful intervening tenancy, a Mr and Mrs Brown and their two children moved in, and all went well for another five years. Then came an outbreak of clickings and tappings (which could be heard next door), sensations of cold and the movement of objects, toys, ornaments, chairs. The father of the household 'saw' the figure of a young man, dressed in brown, with a very prominent jaw; and a tough uncle, who had come in to reassure them all, was lying on a bed smoking a cigarette when, with a sudden shock of cold, he felt someone sit heavily down on the side of the bed nearest the door. There was nobody to be seen. The Browns sought refuge elsewhere, and early in May the group paid the first of seven night visits to the place, armed with tape recorders, thermometers, microphones, geological maps, and a device for detecting subterranean tremors. The National Coal Board, to whom the property belonged, was most helpful. But nothing really unaccountable happened, and the investigators finally had to conclude that 'anything of an ostensibly paranormal nature seems to have taken place in the first two or three weeks of April 1968', before they began their researches.

In the next issue of the *Journal*, Andrew MacKenzie and K. M. Goldney reported the results of their discussions with Canon Phillips, D.D. about the account in his book *The Ring of Truth* (1967) of seeing two apparitions of the well-known writer C. S. Lewis. One happened when he was watching television, the other when he was reading in bed. On both occasions he was feeling overworked, mentally exhausted, in a kind of 'greyness of spirit'. On neither had he been thinking of Lewis, whom indeed he had only once met in person, though he knew and admired his work. On that occasion – in Southwark Cathedral – Lewis had been wearing a cassock, which effectively hid his clothes.

The apparition was in 'reddish tweeds', such as (the Canon later discovered) the living man used to wear. It seemed to be aglow with 'health and spirits' and said each time 'it's not so difficult as you think, you know'. Experts comment with interest that apparitions very seldom speak.

A much odder series of events appeared in the *Journal* for September 1972 in Alan Gauld's survey of *The Haunting of Abbey House*, in Cambridge, compiled from notes covering nearly a century which had been collected by Professor Stratton (astronomer-President of the Society 1953–5). From 1860 onwards there had been rumours that there was something strange about the place. More definite reports began in 1908 when a University Lecturer, J. D. Lawson, moved in with his wife and two small children, to be greeted by loud, inexplicable 'bangings'. A little later different members of the family began to 'see' one of the most peculiar phantoms on record, that of 'an animal like a large hare with cropped ears' running about on its hind legs and making a pattering noise. Some thirty appearances were noted during the Lawson's tenancy – they seem to have learned to live with it – and it was 'seen' again in 1920, by the child of a young officer who moved in then; and yet again in 1947, by a small boy from another family. It has been suggested that the wraith represented a dog trained to walk on its hind legs; was the person who trained it the 'nun' much more rarely 'seen'?

Andrew MacKenzie continued to collect, investigate and report interesting cases both in the *Journal* and in book form, and made an especial study of the Cheltenham Haunting first recorded as long ago as 1892[1] by a 'Miss Morton', who was in fact a brilliant young medical student named Rose Despard. It should perhaps be remembered that determination, coolness and detachment were particularly necessary for women attempting to become doctors at this time. The phantasm 'seen' and 'heard' in and around a house in Pittville Circus by a number of independent witnesses was that of a weeping woman in black, believed to represent a melancholy alcoholic who had once lived there. Measures taken to track her if she were a real solid person playing tricks showed that she was not. She glided through trip threads of black cotton, she passed through people who held hands and tried to stop her; a small boy named George Goodall, who grew up to be a solicitor, recollected this happening on the lawn one bright autumn day (he does not seem to have been scared, but took it all as rather fun). What looks like the same haunting has flared up again over the last twenty years in a neighbouring building which had been turned into flats; it was experienced and described by people who knew nothing of the older story.

Like Celia Green and others, Andrew MacKenzie has studied numbers of cases not in the Society's records but derived from the

---

1. SPR *Proceedings*, 1892, 'Record of a Haunted House'.

general public. He and George Zorab, the veteran Dutch researcher, surveyed in the *Journal* of June 1980 an interesting sporadic haunt in a house occupied for thirty years by the same family. It was observed by the parents, one of their daughters and the home help. The latter said nothing about it until her employer made a joking reference to 'our ghost', on which she remarked 'So you do know', and mentioned some of her own experiences. There were apparitions of a young woman dusting a wardrobe, footsteps, the opening and shutting of doors and an apparently physical 'push'. The family accepted what went on and continued to live there. Andrew MacKenzie remarks that, 'Most genuine hauntings, unlike poltergeist cases, are not dramatic', but are nevertheless significant.

There has been a fairly recent revival of interest in what are called out of the body experiences, both as privately known to the person involved and as 'seen' as phantasms by other people. In the first kind the person feels that his identity, his self, his perceiving consciousness is separated from his body, and looks down on it from above, observing with detachment what it does or suffers. It is not always clear whether this observation is as it were direct or in reverse; whether that body is seen the right way round, as its owner might see a photograph of himself, or as he sees his reflection in a looking glass. This sort of experience is usually involuntary — at any rate to begin with — and is liable to happen at a time of stress. In waking life it has been recorded by a clergyman preaching a sermon, by a dentist doing highly concentrated work, and by many racing motorists (who usually regard it as a danger signal that they need a rest). Where it occurs at the moment of an accident, under an anaesthetic, or in a high fever it might be considered purely imaginary, but for the fact that the patient on returning to ordinary consciousness accurately describes events of which he could not normally have been aware.

On some occasions this separate identity seems to go farther afield and to provoke the second kind of out of the body experience, which is so to speak reciprocal. It occurs when the person in this state is 'seen' by somebody else where he believes himself to be. One of the most vivid examples is that of a Mrs Wilmot[1] who, fast asleep in England dreamed in accurate detail that she was visiting her husband

---

1. *Proceedings*, VII 1891–92.

on a ship at sea, and was observed by the rather scandalized occupant of another bunk who enquired rather acidly why a female visitor should have come into their cabin.

It is said that this aptitude can be learned; Richard Sheargold, long a member of the Society has written a good deal about the matter,[1] interpreting it in terms of an 'astral body' separable from the physical one. This, as has already been noted, raises the odd problem of 'astral clothing' and where it comes from. Much interesting experimental work in this field has recently been carried out in the United States; all this has been lucidly and succinctly discussed in a pamphlet by Dr Susan Blackmore, a very capable young English member of the Society for Psychical Research.[2]

Perhaps it should be said that this phenomenon is as it were the mirror image of that of the doppelgänger, where a person suddenly sees from his usual physical point of view, and seemingly with his own eyes, a phantasm of himself. Though many spontaneous instances of this are on record, I know of no experimental work attempting to induce and study this terrifying twinning.

Of late years there has been a decline in the numbers of hauntings and of apparitions reported to the Society (whose help however is often sought in poltergeist outbreaks). Is this because people who are lonely, bored or tired can so easily distract themselves by switching on radio or television? Maybe: but the case of Canon Phillips, and the fact pointed out by various psychologists that the flickering lights of the screen can bring about a slightly hypnotic, dissociated effect (which conduces to extra sensory perception) seem to point the other way. Is it because those who do see such things tend to keep quiet about them; or because the general boggle threshold (the intellectual level of belief beyond which the mind rejects evidence) is too high in this respect; or because of some suspicion lingering from earlier days that reports of the kind, and those who make them, will be received at best with freezing clinical detachment? If this ever was the case it is so no longer; even in the 1920s the President of the day, faced with the quite obviously contrived photographs of 'the Cottingley fairies' (taken by two little

1. Eg Richard Sheargold *The Study and Practice of Astral Projection*, London, 1961 and *The Techniques of Astral Projection*, London, 1964.

2. Susan Blackmore: *Parapsychology and Out of the Body Experiences*, London, 1978.

girls and reproduced under the ægis of Sir Arthur Conan Doyle in the *Strand Magazine*) said gently that children did have fantasies of this kind and that it was perhaps natural that they should make cardboard figures representing them, put them in appropriate places, and take snapshots. Though he did deprecate the publicity given to them, his attitude towards the situation as a whole was both matter-of-fact and understanding.

However one is to explain the fact that fewer cases of phantasms are now reported to the Society, it is to be regretted. It would definitely welcome such reports, especially where they are supported by the evidence of one or more witnesses besides the perceiver. They can be witnesses either to the event itself, or to the perceiver's own statement. It is plain that an account of some particularly vivid impression of an unexpected happening carries much more weight if it is written down as soon as possible after it has taken place, and countersigned either by someone who has shared it, or who has read the statement then and there. The date, the time and the place should be given. Then, if the impression proves to correspond with something that has really occurred, no one can object that hindsight has been at work, as with those maddening after-the-event remarks such as 'I always *did* say something awful would happen to that boy' (or that couple, or that dog . . .).

The Society is also prepared, wherever it is possible, to investigate hauntings, and to do so in confidence (though it does, naturally, like to be free to publish its findings, provided leave to do this can be obtained). The names of places and people can of course be disguised on request. If leave to publish is not given, the records made are kept in its confidential archives.

5

In Touch? The Cross Correspondences

We must now run back up the stairs of time to follow another theme from its first beginnings. Though Spiritualist membership of the Society declined after the first few years, Spiritualist methods of tapping the unconscious mind went on being used, and it seems to have been taken for granted that the more elaborate and time-consuming the method was, the more valuable the results would be; in fact that a message *en code* was much more valuable than a message *en clair*. It has also been suggested that complicated procedures in some curious way put those who employ them at a distance from what 'comes through', so that they are spared the shock of feeling that something within themselves is at work.

The idea of counting psychokinetic raps as a means of communication with their source, whatever this might be, is probably traditional. Joseph Glanvill, FRS, writing of the Drummer of Tedworth poltergeist outbreak in 1661 notes that the energy at work was asked to confirm a statement by knocking five times (which it duly did). And the Fox children at Hydesville in 1848 had a code of one rap for yes and two for no when seeking replies to leading questions.

But complications set in fairly early; notably when a group of successive raps was used to indicate the position of a certain letter in the alphabet, so that ZEALOT for instance would have been spelled out by the carefully counted sounding of 26 – 5 – 1 – 12 – 15 and 20 knocks, separated by brief intervals of silence. The process was still more difficult when table-tilting – very fashionable in the 19th

century – was used. It must have needed considerable concentration
to count how often a table had rocked, even if it were visible, and
more still when the process took place in the dark, and the numbers
of movements had to be memorized as well as observed; even if the
oracle indicated something as simple as 3 – 1 – 20, CAT, as it did
when Mr Pooter[1] had turned off the gas for his *seance* with Mrs James of
Sutton and others, and asked to be given 'the name of the old aunt
Maggy of whom I was thinking'. Brooding over this baffling reply,
he 'suddenly remembered that her second name was Catherine';
which was not necessarily quite as absurd as it appears – and as I
suspect the Grossmiths thought – if it is assumed that telepathy was
at work to provoke unconscious muscular action among the sitters.
As early as 1885 Myers had observed that in telepathy experiments
'ideas latent in the mind' of the transmitter might come through to
the receiver rather than 'ideas which conscious attention is keeping
uppermost'; so that the latter might become vividly aware of the
lamp, the red tablecloth, the curtains of the room where the former
was sitting rather than of the thought upon which he was painfully
concentrating his mind. This certainly happened in the experiments
of Miss Miles and Miss Ramsden[2] in the 1900s, and has been
observed at intervals ever since.

A really lively table of course might get completely out-of-hand,
as happened with the three Miss Macdonalds.[3] Theirs speeded up so
alarmingly that one of them had to jump on it, crinoline and all,
and sit there till it slowed down and stopped at last. To those who
suspect that psi runs in families it is interesting to know that one of
these laughing breathless girls became the mother of Rudyard
Kipling, whose writing contained more than one clairvoyant experience, and of his sister Alice, the 'Mrs Fleming' of the Cross
Correspondences presently to be described.

The ouija board, whose rim was marked with letters of the
alphabet to be indicated by a pointer (or sometimes by a glass
tumbler) provided another way of receiving messages from mysterious
sources. Sitters laid their hands gently upon it, and the pointer
spelled out words letter by letter; later a planchette was used. A

---

1. George and Weedon Grossmith, *The Diary of a Nobody*, London, 1892.
2. SPR *Journal*, March 1906. SPR *Proceedings* Vol 21, 1908–9.
3. *The Three Miss Macdonalds*, London.

planchette is, according to the Concise Oxford Dictionary, 'a small, usually heart-shaped board supported by two castors and a vertical pencil; when a person' (or, one should add persons) 'rests his fingers lightly on the board it is said to move about without conscious volition'. Later the planchette was used on its own, set on a piece of paper on which the pencil wrote. At first this apparatus often produces mere scribbles; but these may later become recognizable words, names, phrases and even sentences; recognizable at any rate to the eye of faith. The name ouija board is now often used as a synonym for planchette, as it was during the 1920s at 'Riseholme' in one of E. F. Benson's gloriously comic Lucia books.[1] Its buyer, stout Daisy Quantock, decides that its first squiggle is to be read as Abfou, 'very Egyptian and antique', and that the subsequent, indecipherable ones must of course be Arabic. An exquisite neighbour, Georgie, joins her, the planchette 'skates about the paper', each operator is reassured to see the other is not deliberately pushing, and later they have a wonderful time together interpreting the resulting script, which is largely in English this time. Abfou expresses all their own feelings, produces some ambiguous messages, 'tells' them to found a local museum and becomes the 'guide' of the neighbourhood. Though all this takes place by way of the planchette, the people who play with it think of it as ouija and suggest 'having a weedj' whenever puzzled, bored or upset. E. F. Benson was a nephew of the redoubtable Eleanor Sidgwick, and a son of that Archbishop who helped to found the Ghost Club; it is obvious that he knew a good deal about the process, and interesting that, while gloriously alive to the humours of the situation and to its sidelights on human emotion, credulousness and far-fetched ingenuity, he allows a genuine and startling bit of precognition to emerge at the end.

Planchette produced a sort of collective automatic writing, whose results Myers once compared to messages conveyed by 'someone maudlin drunk'; it could also be assumed that they were the product of a communal group mind formed by casseroling a number of individual personalities together into a numinous stew. Planchette could of course be operated by one person alone; but this activity lacked co-operative warmth, excitement, 'togetherness'. If the

1. E. F. Benson, *Lucia in London*, London, 1927.

exercise were to be solitary, it was quicker and simpler to carry it out by hand. The automatist took up a pencil – occasionally a pen, but in the days before fountain pens or biros were invented, the constant need to interrupt the flow of writing by dipping it in ink could be tiresome – held its point gently upon a large sheet of paper, and let her muscles act on their own account. (I say 'her' because most of the well-known automatists seem to have been women, partly perhaps because they came from a background in which women had more leisure than men. One of them, for instance, noted that she was always called punctually at 8.15 and that breakfast was brought to her at 8.30. Then her time was her own, except for eating meals and keeping social engagements.) After an interval – longer or shorter according to mood and circumstance – of Abfouvian scribbles the pencil sometimes produced – and produces – letters of the alphabet, readable scraps, names, quotations, sentences coherent or incoherent, and what look like references to the past, the present or the future. In some ways the process itself – which can involve a sense of being 'taken over', writing from someone else's dictation – resembles what happens to a novelist or poet when he really gets going, writes at a gallop for hours together, and later does not recollect what he has written, or recognize the material as his own. Classical poets attributed this to the visits of the Muse. Automatists tend to believe that telepathy is involved, whether with the living or with the dead.

Obviously automatic writing by a single person in solitude is an exercise more for introverts than for extraverts, more likely to attract those accustomed to working alone than those who need the immediate stimulus of company, and the excitement of using a mechanism tinged with magic for them but meaningless to a more analytical mind. So it was that after some frustrating and abortive attempts with a planchette, Mrs Verrall began in March 1901 to write, at first in darkness, with her own hand. Brought up in a sceptical and rather rationalist household, she had read Latin and Greek at Newnham in Mrs Sidgwick's time, and became Lecturer in Classics there. She married in 1882. Her husband, who has also been described as 'fairly sceptical' was a Classical Lecturer and Tutor at Trinity College, Cambridge; she probably knew most of the psychical research group there. Myers indeed was a personal friend. Her first automatic writings were in fluent Latin; a symbol perhaps of the strangeness, the remoteness from the late Victorian world of what was going on. Later on English sentences, and snatches of Greek appeared and continued to appear.

Mrs Verrall herself wrote a fascinating account of her activities.[1] She would yield to an impulse to write, but could not afterwards recollect what she had set down, though this did not usually amount to more than a page. There were one or two 'supposed communicators', including Edmund Gurney, who it will be remembered had died in 1888. There were some instances of what is called *cryptomnesia* – the emergence of memories no longer present in the conscious mind; as when she wrote about a privately printed pamphlet kept in a sealed envelope in a room ultimately identified as Mrs Sidgwick's (and finally found there, though Mrs Sidgwick herself had forgotten all about it). There were examples of telepathy, one with a medium unknown to her, a Mrs Forbes, of whom her script truthfully told her she would later hear through Sir Oliver Lodge. And there was an episode in which her husband tried to transmit to her, telepathically, a classical allusion, known to them both. This is particularly interesting for the fact that though she produced a number of vivid associations with it (illustrating de Bono's theories about 'lateral thinking') the actual words eluded her, as a memory does if you try too hard to recall it.

F. W. H. Myers had suggested during his lifetime 'the formation of a group effort by the dead' to provide evidence for survival; and Alice Johnson notes[2] that he seems to have tried, with Richard Hodgson 'to obtain connexions between the utterances, spoken or written, of different automatists' during the years from 1898 to 1901, when he died. It was after his death that the Cross Correspondences as such began to develop rapidly. These were scripts automatically written – notably by Mrs Verrall herself, who must sorely have missed that brilliant and stimulating personality – which were later found to be interconnected, though produced simultaneously by people in different places, different continents, people who were at first completely unaware of one another's work, even of one another's existence. Some of the scripts did not make sense until they had been set side by side. Others presented identical ideas in different forms.

1. SPR *Proceedings* 20, Part 50, 1906.
2. Automatic writing of Mrs Holland, *Proceedings* 21, 1908–9.

One of the most interesting writers was Kipling's sister, Alice Fleming, writing as 'Mrs Holland' because her family did not approve of such activities. She had begun to produce scripts in 1893, scripts which had yielded at least one strange and moving poem, and had shown awareness of a local legend, not consciously known to her, of a child's burial in a garden. She had 'agonizing headaches' if she refused the impulse to write; it sounds as if, like many sensitives, she had suffered from migraine. In July 1903, after reading Myers' book on *Human Personality*, she got into touch with Alice Johnson, whose portrait is still to be seen at the offices of the Society for Psychical Research, its grimly honest face and set, almost rat-trap mouth suggesting ferocious integrity rather than sympathy or understanding. It will be remembered that she had been a colleague of Mrs Sidgwick's at Newnham (where she had worked as demonstrator in charge of the Balfour Laboratory). She maintained the most rigid scientific standards of evidence, and mercilessly devalued any parapsychological material that was not set out in a way she thought proper. (She was, for instance, one of those who had been extremely sniffy when Miss Jourdain and Miss Moberly of St Hugh's College, Oxford, gave the Society narratives of their strange, spontaneous, partially shared experiences at Versailles.)

In the case of Mrs Holland, however, Miss Johnson proved to be most helpful, as well as most efficient, and her long careful account in *Proceedings*[1] of what proved to be the first of the series of Cross Correspondences is very valuable indeed, not only for its clinical clarity of exposition but for its detailed analysis of all the facts. These cannot always be checked in reports – however punctilious – on later cases, for though their authors had access to all the papers concerned they were not all necessarily at the centre of investigation at the time when each incident was going on (as Alice Johnson was) and the original documents have now been lodged at Trinity College, Cambridge and will not be available for general consultation till near the end of the century. They are said to be full of confidential material not to be made known until the generations of the participants and of their children are dead. Alice Fleming – Mrs Holland – was not a member of the SPR, and had never come across its *Journal* or *Proceedings*. Reading Myers' *Human Personality* seems to

---

1. SPR *Proceedings* 21, 1907–8.

have been her first stimulus to produce in her scripts what looked like material from Myers and Gurney respectively. Oddly enough, 'Myers' seems to have preferred her to write in ink, 'Gurney' in pencil. The handwriting was different in each case, but did not resemble either her own, or those of the supposed originators. It is worth noticing that she seems to have been very doubtful about the provenance of what she had written, and afraid of 'becoming a deceiver, *charlatan malgré moi*'. Miss Johnson, who had a remarkable capacity for keeping her own counsel, firmly told her that though much of what she wrote was obviously inspired by the books, some bits might be evidential; but would not say which they were. However, she was encouraged to continue writing and sending on the results; and this was duly done. It must have taken courage and determination, since her 'communicators' seem to have been excessively disagreeable to her. Myers in his lifetime appears to have been a lovable man, warm and sympathetic, as well as brilliant. Bullying tactics do not seem to fit in with his character. Was it the memory of the unhappy childhood she and her brother had shared (exiled in England with a nagging foster mother, while their parents remained working in India) that made her find these unfamiliar 'personalities' as rude and domineering as some of Lewis Carroll's characters – Humpty Dumpty, the Red Queen, the Ugly Duchess – were to her namesake in Wonderland? They remark that 'you annoy us', they 'chafe at her inattention', describe themselves as 'vexed, or rather, angry', scold her for being 'captious and doubtful'. It is her script that yields the famous remark from 'Myers' that 'I appear to be standing behind a sheet of frosted glass which blurs light and deadens sound, feebly dictating to a reluctant and somewhat obtuse secretary'. 'Obtuse' seems to have been a favourite word: 'you are too sensitive in some ways and far too obtuse in others'. She is also reprimanded for being 'fitful'.

The obtuse and fitful secretary persevered however. The most positive evidence yielded by her writings was of some curious awareness of Mrs Verrall herself, of whom consciously she knew nothing at all. In November 1903 she noted that she had been told to send the script she was then producing to Mrs Verrall at 5 Selwyn Gardens, Cambridge; but she posted it, as usual, to Miss Johnson. The address was indeed that of Mrs Verrall, and could in fact have been found in *Who's Who* though Mrs Holland had no recollection of seeing it there or anywhere else. Moreover, she had never consciously heard of Mrs Verrall. The piece contained a description of a man which fitted Dr Verrall himself, then still alive.

In September 1903 and January 1904 the automatic writings of both women were found by Miss Johnson to contain similar 'messages', stressing the need for co-operation with unspecified 'others'. That April however, the hard-pressed Mrs Fleming left India for a time, and seems to have had a holiday at home. She did not write to Miss Johnson again till February 1905. The latter then suggested that she and 'my friend' (Mrs Verrall, still unnamed) might do automatic writing on the same day each week, and send her the resulting scripts. This was done. There were some blanks, but in March Mrs Verrall wrote about Carpaccio's picture of St Ursula, at which Mrs Fleming had been gazing, and Mrs Fleming again mentioned her name. She also cited the text above the gates of Selwyn College, Cambridge. This – as was pointed out later – contained a small mistake that had always irked Myers. In November 1904 Mrs Fleming was still in England, and Miss Johnson decided to introduce her to Mrs Verrall, after which telepathic impressions appeared more vividly than ever, especially after they had temporarily exchanged rings on the chance that such physical objects might help to increase *rapport* between them. Veridical 'messages' of many kinds seem to have beaten in on Mrs Fleming around this time; about experiments with Eusapia Paladino, about approaching throat trouble in Sir Oliver Lodge, about Richard Hodgson's papers, and about some defective wiring at the house of Everard Feilding. This last script vividly exemplifies the elusive and allusive quality of automatic writing; thus, Feilding was identified by the name of his father (the Earl of) Denbigh, instead of by his own family surname; and the name of the street where he lived is given but not the number. The wiring was however quite definitely defective and urgently needed attention.

Miss Johnson's able survey of this particular case – which came to include one or two other percipients – ends with a discussion of 'a Theory of Cross Correspondences'. She notes that, though it is possible to check the evidence for cases of telepathy between the living, this cannot be done with what looks like telepathy from the dead in any other way but that of cross correspondences, especially where scripts in which apparently meaningless remarks by two writers who do not know one another make sense when they are put together. These, she argues, are evidence of purpose, of 'an active intelligence constantly at work in the present', rather than of 'the temporary passive survival of someone's personal memories' (as it were a collection of tape recordings, to use a modern analogy). She faces the possibility that the script writers may, for some unknown reason, have been telepathically in touch with one another, and that this might have happened through the unconscious agency of Mrs Verrall. But she concludes (like the tough minded Mrs Sidgwick and her brother the philosopher Gerald Balfour) that the Cross Correspondences are in fact evidence for human immortality.

After this particular episode the field of the Cross Correspondences rapidly widened, and many more automatists took part. Mrs Verrall continued until the end of her life in 1916, Mrs Fleming until October 1910, after which her mental health broke down for some years. Perhaps the strain of receiving so many vivid uncoordinated impressions was too much for a creative temperament to bear; one recalls Bergson's theory that the five senses evolved as a kind of protection against a chaotic influx of experience, evolved so that attention could be channelled towards different sources of information, and the perceiver should not be overwhelmed, almost drowned, in floods of irrelevant data.

Others involved, however, remained unscathed. Among them were Mrs Verrall's daughter, Helen, who married W. H. Salter (another graduate of Trinity College, Cambridge and afterwards a long serving Honorary Secretary of the SPR); 'Mrs Willett' (Mrs Coombe Tennant, who did not want her real name to be known until after her death); 'Mrs King', the brilliant Dame Edith Lyttelton, who combined a very active interest in psychical research with a distinguished record of public service (she began automatic writing after her husband's death in July 1913); and 'the Macs', a family of two brothers and three sisters in Glasgow, whose inspiration was set going by reading Alice Johnson's survey. They came from a background unlike that of the other cross correspondents, who had strong university connexions, and were often related to one another by blood, marriage or shared interests. Several were Professors or Tutors in classical subjects, the literature, history and philosophy of ancient Greece and Rome; the majority had some knowledge of classical myths and legends, if only by way of such enchanting books for children as Charles Kingsley's *The Heroes*, or Nathaniel Hawthorne's *Tanglewood Tales*. They had a deep familiarity with the themes and rhythms of the Authorized Version of the Bible, and a tuning fork resonance with English poetry from Shakespeare and Milton to Tennyson and Browning, and occasionally Swinburne (though not much later). It was not simply that they 'spoke the same language' but that it provoked the same echoes in them all; so that, for instance the phrase 'the alien corn' would elicit in each the image of Ruth in tears rather than that of a new sort of breakfast food. There was also of course a negative side to this; association would have precluded any one of them from accepting that splendid line of English poetry written by an Anglophile Spaniard who loved the sea 'My barque is in the bight'.

Such a community of interests certainly contributes to telepathy among the living, as can be seen in Gilbert Murray's experiments in this connexion with his daughters and friends; but it does make much more difficult the task of teasing out how much information in the Cross Correspondences could be attributed to the dead, or indeed to telepathic interaction with them during their lifetime. There was, for instance, the curious Case of the Sevens. In this J. G. Piddington, later a President of the Society, decided to 'leave a letter containing information known to himself alone, and to communicate its contents through a sensitive after his death, before the envelope was opened'. The letter described his secret obsession with the number seven, noting a habit of counting seven steps at a time, looking for allusions to seven in literature, and so on. After this three years went by, years in which Mr Piddington might have died but didn't; then six of the automatists, unknown to one another, began to be preoccupied with sevens. Explanations varied; could it be that he had relaxed control over his thoughts so that they became open to telepathic inspection; could it have been 'Myers' at work?

With hindsight it is possible to wonder whether it was in fact some contemporary preoccupation with the number seven that came through in the scripts. Seven is, of course, a traditionally significant digit in any case. Was there also over those years some discussion in a learned journal about the Seven Wonders of the (ancient) World, or the Seven Sleepers, or the Seven Seals or the white cliffs known as the Seven Sisters, or even of the old saying that 'the seventh son of a seventh son can see further through a millstone than most'? Any such discussion might well have set sevens popping up through the unconscious minds of the automatists like rabbits in some over-populated warren. It would be extraordinarily difficult to trace the possibility now when no one has time or inclination for the practice of picking out bits of each script as it were with stamp tweezers and fitting them together in relation to one another and to various different possible sources in a fragile and rather arbitrary mosaic pattern.

As the number of automatists increased, so did the number of communicators thought to be 'coming through'. As well as those already noted they included Francis Balfour, killed in a mountaineering accident in 1882, Mary Catherine Lyttelton and her sister-in-law Laura, who both died in the mid 1870s, F. W. H. Myers' cousin Annie Marshall, who died in 1886, and Henry Sidgwick himself, who died in 1900. The little Daphne Coombe Tennant, who died eight years later, was the focus of many 'predictions', memories and associations, still being picked over with great ingenuity and scholarly accuracy by G. W. Lambert as late as 1965.[1] They included the identification of various flowers — lotuses, tulips, roses — and references to the death of her mother's cousin in India in 1887.

Most of the communicators seem to have been under the aegis of 'Myers' himself, whose shadowy image from time to time took on the likeness of some demi-god or cult-hero. Not only was he credited with having initiated the Sevens Correspondence, which had nothing to do with him personally, but (as W. H. Salter writes in *Zoar*[2]) there were those who believed that he and his group had practised 'psychic eugenics' and paranormally brought about Mrs Coombe Tennant's recorded longing for another child, a longing that led to the conception of Daphne, whose (predestined?) death before her second birthday prompted her mother's interest in survival, and led to the hindsighted interpretation of yet another set of cross correspondence scripts. (Was this a premonitory echo of the Midwich Cuckoos[3] calling far away in Cloud Cuckoo land before migrating here?)

1. SPR *Proceedings*, Vol 54, August 1965.
2. W. H. Salter, *Zoar*, London, 1961.
3. John Wyndham, *The Midwich Cuckoos*, London, 1957.

The work of interpreting all the Cross Correspondences grew ever more onerous as they multiplied. The references and cross-references in them became so complex, so intertangled that one remembers the girl in the fairy tale who sat crying in despair over the task of separating and sorting out a mass of coloured threads till the dwarf Rumpelstiltskin arrived; struck at them with his wand; and set them jumping into neat heaps. But even he did not have to deal with such extraordinarily tenuous threads, with so many irrelevant flies and fluffs caught in them, spun so freely by so many discursive spiders.

Patient SPR investigators – no Rumpelstiltskins they – attempted this task over many years and from many different angles. Some approached their work after the manner of those trying to solve say *The Times* Cross Word Puzzle, with its anagrams, its quotations, its cryptic allusions to a vast variety of subjects; classics, current events, philosophy, proverbs, old songs, sport. Others looked for symbols; thus, both Lauras and the little Daphne *could* have been indicated by a mention of a laurel; Francis Balfour who had been a marine biologist, was thought to be suggested by allusions to fish, to his name-saint, to seraphs (because Francis of Assisi was known as the Seraphic Doctor) and to mountain climbing. Even the flowers in family coats of arms were drawn into play. This was not so lunatic, nor so arbitrary as may appear; the unconscious mind does seem to work in this curious way, a fact recognized by psychiatrists when they use word-association tests. But a long continued search for symbols can lead to the 'discovery' of hidden meanings in straight-forward sentences, meanings that may or may not be there at all. In this way a long-nosed sufferer from paranoia may come to believe that all references to elephants are intended to insult him; and ardent supporters of the theory that Bacon (or Marlowe, or whoever it may be) wrote the plays of Shakespeare, find mysterious clues implanted in passages that seem to the rest of the world to mean no more than what they say.

Studying the British Cross Correspondences today one comes to sympathize ever more strongly with Gustave Geley's complaint in 1914 that they are extraordinarily complicated and mysterious in contrast with the clear and orderly French cases of the same phenomenon. One can almost applaud the American critics who suggested that some of them were no more than a method of displaying a magnificent and minutely detailed classical erudition; as it were a spread of peacocks' tails embroidered in tiny *petit-point* stitches.

There are said to be some 3,000 scripts in existence, though, as already noted, many of them contain so much confidential material that they are lodged in the safe keeping of Trinity College, Cambridge, till the end of the century. Of all those so far published or discussed, very much the most interesting is the Palm Sunday case, clearly and succinctly set out by Jean Balfour in 1960.[1] In this various automatists who knew none of the facts for some years after their writings on the theme began, kept referring obliquely to Mary Catherine Lyttelton, with whom the shy reserved young Arthur Balfour had been deeply in love at the time of her death of typhoid fever – then still endemic in this country – on Palm Sunday, 1875. He had privately asked that she might be buried with his dead mother's emerald ring on her finger; he had privately been given a thick tress of her beautiful gold-streaked brown hair; he had privately had made a bronzed silver box to keep it in. Sidelong mentions of these and other relevant matters kept cropping up, but not until 1912 did everything begin to fall into place. Jean Balfour suggests that this may have been because by that time a lively group of automatists had got going, an experienced group of investigators – Eleanor Sidgwick (Balfour's sister), Gerald Balfour (his brother), Oliver Lodge, Alice Johnson, and J. G. Piddington – was well established, and Arthur Balfour himself, for whom the messages seem to have been meant, was relaxing from his political labours, and peacefully engaged in writing his Gifford Lectures. Possibly the very fact that he *was* relaxing, in a time of 'emotion recollected in tranquillity' led to the emergence of a clue; a clue written on the Palm Sunday of 1912. Balfour kept each Palm Sunday as the anniversary of Mary's death, and had spent almost every one of them since 1875 remembering her with his sister Lavinia, now married to Edward Talbot; so that it was a significant day for the production of Mrs Coombe Tennant's script about a dead girl and 'the love that waits beyond death'. The writer, who had never heard of the affair, continued both in scripts and in words spoken in trance and recorded verbatim, to produce allusions of this kind, notably – in the Pre-Raphaelite parlance beloved of the 1870s – to the Palm Maiden, to

---

1. SPR *Proceedings*, Vol 52, 1960.

the May Flower, and to the Faithful Knight (Balfour never married). During the last days of his life – he died well over eighty years old in May 1930 – she went to see him, and as they were listening to music together had a sudden vivid impression of Mary's presence, though she did not know who it was; the figure was only recognized later from her description. Other script writers across the years alluded to the lock of hair, to the silver box, to Rossetti's Blessed Damozel, to the name of Mary by way of the nursery rhyme lines about 'silver bells and cockle shells', to the name of Arthur by way of Arthurian legends and by way of that Duke of Wellington who won the battle of Waterloo. The cumulative effect was impressive, though the impatient reader sometimes gets a feeling that people are searching for the beads of a broken necklace in a dustbin full of Christmas tinsel and cracker mottoes.

The Cross Correspondences continued for many years, throughout the First World War and on, though *diminuendo*, till 1932. Some were claimed to have forecast the war itself; but, as Piddington[1] later observed, this was hardly paranormal, as most educated people at the time were sickeningly conscious that it was coming. One – the Faunus Case – was taken to have predicted the death of Sir Oliver Lodge's son Raymond. Others were assumed to have foreseen the sinking of the *Lusitania* in 1914, the bombing of Fenchurch Street Station in an air raid of 1917, and so on.

The flow of material was not immediately weakened by the death of Mrs Verrall in 1916, at the comparatively early age of fifty-eight. But within a year of this a Miss F. Melian Stawell[2] was arguing that a set of scripts begun in 1910, and dealing with Athenian prisoners kept long ago in a cavern in Syracuse known as the Ear of Dionysius, had emanated unconsciously from the then living Mrs Verrall rather than her dead husband, as had previously been supposed. She also suggested that 'an elaborate association of ideas' was involved, rather than deliberate purpose. This and similar arguments continued in considerable detail for a very long while.

After the War, a few of the 'communicators' were forecasting with the brief euphoria of the time 'the approaching realization of hopes of a Golden Age' and 'the establishment *here on earth* of a universal,

1. SPR *Proceedings*, Vol 33, 1923.
2. SPR *Proceedings*, Vol 29, 1918.

abiding city of Freedom and Clemency, Law and Order'. Alas for the League of Nations! There were also thought to be obscure disquieting hints in another script, about Munich and Berchtesgaden — but hindsight spotlights many details whose total significance is almost impossible to determine, as anyone knows who has tried to work out the *Oracles of Nostradamus*, or the *Prophecies of Malachy*. In all interpretations of this kind Dr Briggs' folk tale of the scholar and the Professor[1] lurks uneasily in the mind. Here is a brief summary. A learned foreign Professor went to Cambridge and decided to examine the students in the language of signs, for a prize. One of them, conspicuous because he had lost an eye, was disconsolate since he knew nothing of this language, and told a friend, an equally conspicuous one-eyed miller, all about it.

The miller, bold as brass, impersonated him and won the prize thus. The Professor said he had held up an apple to signify Adam's fall, and that the 'student' had instantly held up a piece of bread in token of redemption through the Bread of Life. The Professor then held up one finger to show that God is One; the 'student' two, to affirm Christ; the Professor three, as a reminder of the Trinity; and the 'student' clenched his fist to show the Three are One. 'He never faltered or mistook, and richly deserves the prize', said the Professor.

The 'student' miller's version was that 'the quarrelsome old fellow' pulled an apple from his pocket and brandished it as if to say he'd throw it at him; at which he pulled a crust from his own pocket to show he too had something to throw. The Professor then poked one finger at him as if to say he'd poke out his one eye; the miller poked two fingers back to show he would put out two. The Professor held up three fingers, threatening to scratch his face; the miller clenched his fist to show he'd knock him down if he tried; and was then told he'd won the prize.

This example of total misunderstanding is cited as a warning rather than a complete parallel to what happened in interpreting the Cross Correspondence scripts. These were in fact handled with great care. Indeed, W. H. Salter[2] went so far as to carry out an experiment in artificially produced automatic writings of this kind. There were

---

1. Katherine M. Briggs, 'The Professor of Signs', in *British Folk Tales and Legends, A Sampler*, London, 1977.

2. W. H. Salter, 'An Experiment with Pseudo-Scripts', SPR *Proceedings* 36, Salter was President of the Society, 1947–8.

he said, five possible ways of explaining the phenomena found in them. They could have arisen from pure chance – from deliberate collusion – from associations of ideas common to those who took part – from telepathy between the living – and from 'the influence of some discarnate intelligence'. The first two he ruled out; the last he did not discuss. He wanted to test the possibilities that either a common association of ideas or telepathy could account for what had been observed. Twelve highly educated members of the Society, two of them advanced classical scholars, took part. They were asked not to discuss the project with anyone. A list of twelve single phrases or groups of phrases was compiled; one was Greek, one Latin and one French. This list was distributed to the participants, who were asked to make their own choice of items, and to write up to two hundred words in English, French, Greek, Latin or a mixture of languages, on those they had chosen. The replies were all to be sent in by a definite date. Salter himself 'bore certain ideas in mind'. Piddington lodged with the Society a sealed envelope containing his theme. The results were inconclusive. There were no more than possible 'remote allusions' to what Salter and Piddington had had in mind. None of the writers produced 'any allusion outside the range of their normal literary knowledge' as members of the Cross Correspondence groups 'frequently do; and such cross-references as *were* produced were of the simplest kind; there is a momentary contact, after which the streams of association diverge, without the tendency characteristic of the real scripts to come back again and again to a common point of view'.

This has been a necessarily brief survey of an incredibly complex subject. The reader who wants a more detailed study should consult chapters eight to ten of Rosalind Heywood's admirable book *The Sixth Sense*[1] which discusses the matter with warmth, sympathy, learning and the most exemplary patience; and Mr Salter's pamphlet on Trance Mediumship published by the Society for Psychical Research.

---

1. Rosalind Heywood, *The Sixth Sense*, London, 1959.

6

Some Mediums of the Mind

The occurrence of phantasms and of what looked like spontaneous messages from the dead were of course sporadic. To investigate them was sometimes rather like the work of early zoologists, tracking this or that rare species through the jungle, shooting a specimen here or there if they were lucky, and sending skin, bones and a written description to others in a museum at home to classify and record; sometimes with rather odd results, as happened when Stubbs, the 18th century painter, was provided with data of the kind and asked to use it to portray a kangaroo. The result looked like a poor drooping toy that had not had quite enough stuffing.

There were, of course, as has just been seen, admirable records and discussions of spontaneous phenomena in the Society's *Proceedings*; and also in various books, notably Sir William Barrett's collection of *Death Bed Visions* (London, 1926) and Andrew Lang's *Dreams and Ghosts*.[1] The Cross Correspondences, spontaneously begun, and equally spontaneously continued, could be, and were, most carefully observed and evaluated as they unpredictably arose; but they were the product of a small, mostly homogeneous group, and the material was concerned with a loosely linked social circle of characters.

For other types of research it could be useful to deal with a medium. You could make appointments with such a being sure that

---

1. From a collection entitled *Dreamland and Ghostland* originally published in London, 1887 and later issued with shortened title.

you would get some sort of data to work on. It could be like observing a captive kingfisher in an aviary instead of seeing a flash of dazzling blue darting across a mill pond. The trouble was that, as has already been observed, professional mediums could not always be trusted since, as they were paid, they had to deliver the goods.

There was of course — in telepathy sittings — the question of signalling; Gurney wrote an early paper about it, and much later on the use of 'silent' dog whistles was suspected among boys with hearing of canine acuteness. For sittings for communication with the dead, mediums could prepare in other ways. They might of course listen to local gossip in pubs, in shops, at the hairdressers — how useful Figaro might have been — and read local newspapers. In cases like this, moreover, deliberate deception did not have to be suspected, as cryptomnesia, unconscious memory, might well be at work to produce startling results later on. Looking up records of births, deaths, and marriages was of course deliberate; so was consultation with fellow mediums who might have information about such-and-such a family or locality; so were other tricks of the trade described; in detail by Ronald Edwin in *Clock without Hands* (London, 1955). Edwin, who had a remarkable, spontaneous gift for extrasensory perception was persuaded to become a professional medium, but after a while gave it up, outraged by the web of deception in which he had become entangled; a web probably justified by its tireless spinners either because it comforted the bereaved or — as it was by a medium and his semi-philosophical patron in H. G. Wells's *Love and Mr Lewisham* (*Collected Works of H. G. Wells*, London, 1927) — as a means of convincing people of Great Truths that they would not otherwise accept.

Mediums can also consciously or unconsciously use a method called 'fishing'. Here, sitting with an expectant group, he or she produces a common name, or a vague description, functioning rather like a Rorschach blot, a splodge of ink sometimes used by psychiatrists to induce their patients to project their own preoccupations (which can be as diverse as a coat of arms or a teddy bear). The medium then waits for the bereaved to claim the name or the ambivalent image as their own, often giving considerable information as they do so, information later to be fed back to them as proof of the 'communicator's' identity. Here is an illustrative experience of my own. Not very long after the end of

World War II, members of the Society were invited to come along
one Saturday afternoon to test a man who described himself as a
clairvoyant. We were warned not to volunteer information, though
we could of course confirm any unmistakable facts he might
produce. We sat in rows in a large ordinary room. I was at the
back and I do not think it was humanly possible for the
clairvoyant – who was not known to anyone present – to see what
I was inscribing on a piece of paper supported by my bag on my
knee. He began by saying 'I seem to get the name John . . .' and
waited for someone to claim it. No one did, and presently he
continued 'there is a figure in Service uniform behind one of you'
and moved a finger in a wide arc that could have indicated almost
anyone present. Still no claimants; then a figure called Mary, also
in Service uniform, was sighted. Finally he said angrily, pointing
his finger directly at me, 'at any rate, that lady at the back has
something to do with elephants. Maybe she's wearing an elephant
charm, maybe she's been out East, I don't know, but she has
something to do with elephants.' I asked 'Do you mean me?'
'Yes, you' he said. I tend to doodle elephants when bored, and I
had in fact been drawing little elephants on the order paper. I
told him so, and he asked if he could see them. Innocently, I
passed the paper up to him. After a quick look at it, he passed
it back. He must have had a photographic memory for his remarks
thereafter cited the names of several people listed there, including
Lord Charles Hope. This odd little episode usefully demonstrates
the process of 'fishing', the flash of genuine e.s.p. and the
subsequent use of any data obtained.

Two kinds of phenomena can be observed in mediums – mental
and physical. The first deal with information, voices, apparitions,
impressions, imagery, messages. The second involve the inexplicable
movement of various objects, tables, chairs, tambourines, handkerchiefs etc, and sometimes the levitation of the medium himself.
Quite often both sorts of phenomena happen with the same person,
though one seems to predominate. This must be kept in mind
though it is more convenient to discuss them separately. The present
chapter will look mainly at 'mental mediums', 'physical mediums'
will be discussed later.

Professional mediums – as distinct from fortune tellers, oracles,
and those 'possessed' by demigods, who have flourished in most times

and places[1] – seem to have originated in nineteenth century America. They often appear to need a sort of alibi, an extra personality, to act as a master of the ceremonies standing between them and the living on the one hand, and what they believe to be the spirits of the dead on the other. These intermediaries originally took on an archaic form. Popular in the United States were Red Indians (one called Silver Birch still appears in a well-known Spiritualist weekly, whether as a pseudonym or as an inspiration, I am not sure). Red Indians were of course the remotest ancestral spirits indigenous to the New World, part of its primeval landscape in which the new immigrant generations were beginning to put down roots. They belonged to the woods and waters and mountains of an alien scene that was slowly turning into home. It is odd, in a way, that Red Indian 'spirit-guides' should have been so friendly and benevolent, considering the long, bitter wars fought against them. Perhaps the pioneer proverb that the only good Indian was a dead Indian got twisted into an assumption that all dead Indians were good. Perhaps the radiance of Rousseau's Noble Savage had set aglow the Rights of Man. Perhaps the cult of Longfellow's Hiawatha – a New World Orpheus – had something to do with it. Whatever the cause, these 'guides', 'Controls', secondary personalities, alibis, whatever they were, did take on archaic names and associations.

It is impossible to go into detail about all the mediums with whom SPR members have been involved. They were many and widely assorted, and long, long studies of them have been written from a variety of standpoints. I shall however sketch a few of the most famous of those investigated during the great heyday of interest in them, their phenomena, and their psychological processes.

The first of these, reassuringly described by Mrs Sidgwick as a 'stout and matronly figure', was an American lady, a Mrs Piper of Boston, who had been launched on her career in 1884. In pain after a bad accident, she had sittings with a 'psychic healer' named John Cockes. At her second visit to him, she herself went into a trance, and presently began to transmit messages from unknown sources, messages which impressed those who came to hear her by their accurate correspondence with what they knew about dead or distant

---

1. See *Divination and Oracles*, edited by Michael Loewe and Carmen Blacker, London, 1981.

people, or indeed about themselves. In 1885 William James, himself
a qualified physician whose own ill health had once been alleviated
by 'psychic healing', and who opposed a movement to make the
practice illegal – was told about Mrs Piper by his mother-in-law.
Saying nothing about this relationship, he went anonymously to see
her, and was given startlingly accurate information about various
family affairs, including the death, the previous year, of his little son
Herman (though the boy's actual name was given as Herrn). James
wondered if she had found out who he was, but finally came to think
she was in fact tapping some paranormal source of information, and
wondered whether this might be telepathic. As this information had
come through while she was in a state of trance, he asked her one day
when she was her ordinary wide-awake self whether she would allow
him to induce a hypnotic trance. She agreed; he did so, tried some
telepathic experiments and – nothing at all came through, which
was very disappointing.

Heavily loaded with other work, he did not look into her case
again for some five years; but during this time she was under
investigation by Richard Hodgson, an Australian lawyer and philosopher then in charge of the American branch of the SPR (which
later became independent). A careful man, trained to collect, weigh,
and evaluate evidence, he went so far as to have her shadowed by
detectives to see whether she were deliberately trying in any way –
possibly through her husband who worked in a large shop in Boston
– to discover facts about actual or potential sitters which could later
be produced at seances. They could find no trace of such activities,
and he later concluded that she was genuine. So did William James,
when he took up research with her once more, in 1889. A man
without cultural snobbery, he believed that facts should be faced,
however flashy, repellent or idiotic the context in which they were
embedded, and does not seem to have been put off by the
extraordinary phantasmagoria of her Controls. She appears to have
picked up two from John Cockes, who was inspired by Bach, and by
a French doctor called Finney. She retained Bach, and transformed
Finney into Dr Phinuit, who knew little either of medicine or of his
native tongue. (James described him as 'a fictitious being' who talked
'tiresome twaddle'; Walter Leaf, a member of the SPR Council,
noted later that he was deceitful, given to bad language, and
accustomed to 'fish' for information from sitters.) To Phinuit there

were added from time to time Julius Caezar (sic), Walter Scott, who believed there were monkeys in the sun, and a girl improbably named Chlorine. Later on there were many more, as will be seen.

In 1889 James and Hodgson suggested that the SPR should invite Mrs Piper to some seances in England, where she could not have made any conscious investigations about the unknown people she was to see, nor have any unconscious memories of facts connected with them. She was met by Oliver Lodge when she landed at Liverpool on November 19 that year, and taken that evening to see a Mr and Mrs Clark. Mr Clark was, by the way, so ferocious an agnostic that he would not allow his children to play with cousins who were taken to church by their parents. His wife was German by birth. On the evening of her arrival Mrs Piper went into trance in their house, and produced a vivid, unlikely, and accurate piece of information about the family history of her hostess, who was deeply startled and impressed; so much so that her daughter Dora, later a well-known sculptress, still in her old age remembered hearing all about the episode from her and gave me an account of it which tallied almost exactly with that reported in the SPR *Proceedings*.[1] Dora was not and had never been a member of the Society. She produced the story some time in 1978 only because she had been told I was interested in such matters. I had known her for many years through some cousins and often went to see her, especially after she had been disabled by a stroke; she then lived close by.

Next day Frederic Myers[2] escorted Mrs Piper to Cambridge. He thought her 'upright, honest and candid' when she was awake, but noted with caution that 'no one knows about the honesty of trance personalities'. Again, in a series of trances, she produced startlingly accurate information. Lodge, through whose hands all her correspondence passed, put it on record that she had made no enquiries by letter (he would have seen the replies); and that there had been no questioning of children or servants, no study of photograph albums or Family Bibles (in which it was then the custom to inscribe births and deaths) and no consultation of local directories. He believed 'thought transference' to be the 'most commonplace hypothesis' to explain what went on. Myers suggested that this might be amplified

---

1. Cf *Proceedings* VI, 1888–9.
2. Cf *Proceedings* VI, 1888–9.

by the idea of direct clairvoyance, though he recognized that followed
to its limits this led to 'postulating omniscience'.

The trances lasted about an hour. It is interesting, in view of
William Roll's ideas today that there may be some connexion
between psi phenomena and epilepsy, that Mrs Piper seemed to have
slight 'epileptic symptoms' before losing consciousness. Professor
Richet, doctor and physiologist, who worked with her later on, also
noticed 'small epileptiform seizures' just before Phinuit took over.

Mrs Piper stayed in England for several months, supervised by
Myers, Lodge and Leaf who all continued to be impressed. Hodgson
went on working with her when she got back to America, where a
friend of his, George Pelham, died in February 1892, and shortly
afterwards seemed to become a communicator, and later a Control.
Hodgson, who was normally inclined to scepticism, wrote a long
Report[1] on the phenomena, ruling out telepathy as an explanation
and concluding that they had yielded solid evidence for survival and
communication.

Three years afterwards, when the pain of Hodgson's loss had
dulled a little, another and much odder Control began to take over,
that of Stainton Moses, born in 1839, who had in his lifetime been
a clergyman, a schoolmaster, and an amateur medium. He had
joined the SPR in 1882 but resigned in 1886, apparently because of
its current attitude to physical phenomena, which he had himself
experienced during the previous decade. He may also have found the
cool a-septic atmosphere of the Society, and its demand for scientific
detachment and objective proof damping and uncongenial. He was,
he claimed, in touch with no less than eighty-four Principal Spirits,
among them Plato, Seneca, Plotinus, Beethoven, the prophet
Malachi and someone called Rector (perhaps a reminiscence from
some early curacy, though Moses claimed that he was 'St Hippoly-
tus'). These overlapped with a group known as The Imperator Band.
'Rector', who struck sitters as being a wise, benign and rather weary
old man took over as principal Control from 1897 until 1905 (when
Hodgson died suddenly of a heart attack). During this period Mrs
Piper went into trance without much in the way of 'epileptiform
seizures', and produced automatic writing instead of speaking. Her
results remained fascinating, and in 1906 she was invited to England

---

1. SPR *Proceedings* XIII, 1897.

again, in the hope that she might become involved in the Cross Correspondences, as indeed she did. As might have been expected, she sometimes found Hodgson and Myers (who had died in 1901) taking over as communicators and Controls; but, since she had known both for years, evidence of identity apart from her own memories was very hard to prove.

There was indeed a time when 'Hodgson' had his leg successfully pulled. In 1909 a sitter, Dr Hall, asked to be put into touch with an imaginary dead niece called Bessy Beales. His request was granted, and 'Bessy' produced various reminiscences of her uncle. When 'Hodgson' was told the truth 'he' said *his* lady was called Jessie not Bessy, and was related to another sitter. 'The trance consciousness', Rosalind Heywood charitably notes[1] 'is a great myth maker.' Maddeningly for those who like their information clear cut, actual facts remain among the myths, irritating little pearls embedded in the flesh of the oyster (delicious to some, revolting to others).

Whether from Hodgson, or Myers or out of the blue, Mrs Piper did produce a number of classical allusions far outside her own range of knowledge. One of them – made in 1916 long after she had returned to America and was gaining the ability to produce automatic writing without going into trance at all – was interpreted as a warning to Lodge that a terrible blow was about to fall on him, a warning soon followed by the death of his son Raymond on active service in France. This allusion, which was to an Ode of Horace, is known as the Faunus Message, and was succeeded by two others, one from Mrs Piper herself and one from a Dutch medium. The matter is discussed in detail in Volume 19 of *Proceedings*.

Mrs Piper lived to be ninety-one. William James wrote of her, 'If you wish to upset the law that all crows are black, you must not seek to show that no crows are, it is enough if you prove the single crow to be white. My own white crow is Mrs Piper. In the trances of this medium I cannot resist the conviction that knowledge appears which she has never gained by the ordinary waking use of her eyes and ears and wits.' He also declared that he did not know where it came from and had no explanation to offer.

Mrs Gladys Osborne Leonard, some years younger than Mrs Piper,

---

1. *The Sixth Sense*: Revised paperback edition, London, 1959.

was England's first notable specimen of the White Crow genus. A stern Victorian upbringing, modified by childhood experiences of which – once mentioned – she was forbidden ever to speak again, predisposed her later to turn to Spiritualism, which accepted and interpreted what had happened to her. This too was anathema to her parents.

The family became impoverished. Diphtheria ruined the singing voice with which Gladys had hoped to achieve fame, and, more important, fortune. She had to earn a living for some time by playing small parts in repertory theatres; a training in dramatization which may well have helped her unconsciously to impersonate her 'communicators'. It was during this time that she met her husband, who was also on the stage. Marriage seems to have eased financial worries; for after what would now be called a 'crisis-apparition' she was able to spare time to follow up her Spiritualist interests. The experience was very vivid. At two o'clock one morning she woke to see against the darkness her mother looking young and happy in a radiance of light; later in the day a telegram arrived to say, 'Mother passed away at two o'clock this morning'.

Mrs Leonard now began to sit with mediums and to develop her own talents, at first by way of table tilting, which may be regarded as one of the least conscious forms of mind-body interaction, transmitting by way of an agreed code 'messages' of which the person concerned is unaware; messages in which objects from tables to ouija boards are moved most probably through involuntary muscular reactions, but just possibly by some force akin to that at work in metal bending (as observed by Professor Hasted and others over the last few years).

Table tilting introduced Mrs Leonard's only Control (as distinct from communicators), Feda, whom she believed to be the spirit of an Indian girl (brown, not red) who had married one of her ancestors and died in childbed in 1800, at thirteen years old. Feda spoke in a mixture of ordinary English, baby-talk and a sort of Man Friday idiom, always referring to herself in the third person, 'Feda says . . .' 'Feda sees . . .' She tended to order Mrs Leonard about, notably so in the spring of 1914 when she told her 'something big and terrible is going to happen to the world. Feda must help many people through you.' Mrs Leonard obediently took rooms in which to give both private and public sittings, where she produced much accurate information for which no normal sources could be found. Thus, in 1918 she spoke in unmistakable detail of a photograph of Sir Oliver Lodge's son Raymond of which neither she nor her sitter knew anything. It reached him later. A similar flash of information appeared in 1921, when a Mrs Dawson Smith sat with her hoping to get into touch with her son, who had died the previous year, and received information about photographs, papers and 'an old purse with a receipt in it, a counterfoil'. Soon afterwards the Controller, Enemy Debt Clearing Office wrote to this lady asking her to pay a sum of money owed by her son to a Hamburg firm. She knew this debt had been incurred – and paid – in July 1914, wrote to say so and was told her memory was not enough to go on, and the bill must be met. She then recollected the sitting, found the 'old purse' and the counterfoil of a money order payable in Hamburg at that date, and all was settled.

This very practical 'message' (which may of course have sprung from some unconscious memory activated by who knows what in the way of precognition) contrasts agreeably with the reluctance both of Sir Oliver Lodge[1] and of the Editor of *Light* to introduce a medium to a solicitor who wanted to find out, on behalf of a client threatened with bankruptcy by the Inland Revenue, why his previous legal advisers, now dead, had acted in a way that had laid him open to such proceedings.

At the beginning of 1918 the Leonard Committee of the SPR, which already knew and respected Mrs Leonard's activities, arranged with her that for three months, from mid-January to mid-April that year she should give sittings only to people who made appointments through the Society. Sitters were asked to let an independent transcriber take notes (the tape recorder had not yet been invented). This was generally done by one of three Committee members, Mrs Salter, Miss Radclyffe Hall and Lady Troubridge. The last two had already had sittings with her in 1916, when she had produced many details about a dead friend known as 'Lady' or 'A.V.B.'. On this occasion – as happened with Mrs Piper – detectives employed to discover whether she could have acquired her information in any normal way had found nothing.

Some data were produced which alas could have fitted many of the

---

1. See final chapter, dealing with Presidents, for the full story.

dead in the terrible slaughter of the spring of 1918. Some were startlingly accurate, notably detailed descriptions of one young man who died at Neuve Chapelle and of another killed in Bulgaria. But there were startlingly mistaken ones, too. L. P. Jacks was given a message from his 'dead' son, who was in fact very much alive; and conversely a 'missing man' was said to be alive when he was dead. Probably Mrs Leonard was unconsciously echoing back to each sitter what he already believed.

She had very marked telepathic gifts, probably at work when she gave two sitters lively accounts of dear dogs each had owned from time to time; and quite certainly involved when she gave Mr W. Irving (whose report was later printed in *Proceedings* No. 36, 1928) a detailed account of what was actually going on at the house in Tavistock Square to which the Society was just moving (and which she had never visited); the pleasure of the Secretary, Isabel Newton, at being able to see trees and birds outside, the arrival of a new lamp and the present of a red azalea, how some stamps had got lost, the trouble over arranging the furniture so as to make room for steel cupboards . . . and so on. Various attempts were made to rule out telepathy as the explanation of all Mrs Leonard's phenomena. The first, the use of what were called Book Tests, were suggested by 'Feda' some time in 1917.

Book Tests can be fitted into other frames of reference: clairvoyance, for instance; or some sort of feedback from precognition; or the assumption that spirits know everything; or again that everyone knows everything if only the technique can be acquired of drilling down to the source of knowledge and setting it gushing like an oil well. Like many parapsychological exercises it raises more problems than it solves.

Book Tests were later taken up by various other mediums. A fairly recent instance is reported at length in Laura Huxley's *The Timeless Moment* (London, 1969). Part of an attempt to get into touch with the shade of Aldous Huxley, it is typically *odd*, typically unsatisfying, typically hard to explain.

The usual procedure is something like this. A medium (or her Control, or a communicator) indicates that in a room sometimes unknown to her, stands a bookcase whose position is clearly indicated ('just inside the door on the left' for instance, or 'in an embrasure between two windows'). On a certain shelf, say the fourth from the top is a book, three volumes along from the left. On such and such a page, sometimes on such and such lines, is a given sentence or allusion, usually of importance to the sitter. Even if the latter had indeed read the book, he would be most unlikely to remember what was written where (unless he had the very rare kind of photographic memory occasionally found in Orientals).

Of course, as with the *Sortes Virgiliani* or the astrological columns of popular newspapers, many sitters may already be inclined to agree that the 'message' was definitely 'meant' for them. But, accepting this probability, and accepting the possibility that the furniture and arrangements of the room may have been envisaged by some sort of telepathic rapport, there were some very peculiar successes, as when Miss Radclyffe Hall and Lady Troubridge, neither of whom knew Greek, got some Greek books and set them on a shelf in an order known only to themselves; and received an accurate page reference to a sentence in one of them.

Book Tests demanded a great deal of work. So did the subsequent examinations of the results they yielded. In one of those protracted, untiring, statistical papers to which so much labour has been devoted Mrs Sidgwick analysed 532 book tests, and classified some 17% as successful, and 19% as 'nearly successful'. The rest ranged down from the 'dubious' to the failures. A control experiment with sham book tests was then carefully organized in an attempt to gauge whether the results could be attributed to chance coincidence. This, however, yielded under 2% of successes and under 3% of partial successes; so there seems pretty certainly to have been 'something in' the genuine tests; but who knows what? Perhaps because they are so puzzling, so frustrating and so time-consuming, they have gone out of fashion.

Proxy Sittings were another device used to try and eliminate telepathy as an explanation of 'messages' received through mediums. This elaborate procedure was employed by a Miss Nea Walker, herself a medium, whose results impressed the redoubtable rationalist Professor Dodds[1] (who supervised some of them) so much as to make him decide that 'the hypotheses of fraud, rational inference from disclosed facts, telepathy from the actual sitter, and coincidence cannot either singly or in combination account for the results

---

1. President, 1961–3.

obtained' and that 'there seemed to be a clear-cut "either-or"; Mrs
Leonard had supernormal access . . . *either* (a) to some of the thoughts
of a living person or persons who had never held any communication
with her, *or with the sitter*; or *else* (b) to some of the thoughts of a
mind or minds other than that of a living person'. In accordance
with that painful – and admirable – scholarly discipline of fence-
sitting so necessary in psychical research, he declined to commit
himself wholly to either explanation. It is interesting that he does
not seem to have considered the possibility of general clairvoyance
(a theory never so palatable in this country as in France and the
United States) or the relevance of Jung's concept of the collective
unconscious. (Whately Carington's kindred idea of group minds[1]
had not yet been formulated.)

Proxy sittings worked on the following lines. When asked by some
one unknown to get into touch with a dead friend the Proxy Sitter
(at first Miss Walker, though others later followed her example)
would write down the applicant's name, address and relationship to
the dead person, the latter's age, and the date of death. She then
arranged a sitting; and before this – and of course before the medium
came on the scene – would read her notes aloud to a group of invisible
communicators with whom she already believed herself to be in
touch. Then she would sit as proxy for that applicant, still consciously
knowing no more than the facts already set down on paper. A record
of the sitting was afterwards sent to the enquirer for detailed
comment; which could be startling as for instance when what had
seemed like meaningless allusions turned out to be well-known
family jokes, catchwords and pet names.

In examining all these elaborate procedures there are moments
when the boredom threshold interacts with the boggle threshold,
and the exasperated reader begins to ask himself whether the
minuscule facts that might possibly have been elicited were worth all
the interminable hours spent in looking for them; first in sitting
with the mediums themselves, slowly stammering out their often
incoherent impressions; later in going fishing, as it were, in their
streams of consciousness, slow or turbulent; and then in sorting,
weighing, and classifying catches of minnows and tadpoles. It must
be remembered though, that this period marked the heyday of

---

1. Whately Carington, *Telepathy*, London, 1945.

leisured introversion. Where literature was concerned it produced Henry James, and his endless broodings on personal and 'social' interactions, and on emotions cultivated like exotic pot plants, daily to be watered with tears of distilled sensibility. It gave rise to Proust, and his continuous winding exploration of the half-remembered past; and then to Virginia Woolf, her prose iridescent with reflections of the unsaid. In another sphere it burgeoned into Freudian analyses that could last for years of complicated self-torture. These forms of research, then, accorded with the preoccupations of the time.

It was during this extremely analytical and introverted epoch that interest in the *dramatis personae* of mediumship – as distinct from their messages – developed in detail. The identities of the Controls and the communicators came to fascinate those investigators who could not accept the idea that every single one of them was just what he said he was, an idea made peculiarly unacceptable by the more exotic members of both groups, such as the prophet Malachi among the former, and Androcles' Lion among the latter.

From the late 1880s onwards it was surmised that these apparently independent beings were what came to be called 'secondary personalities', prevalent moods repressed beyond recognition, solidified, sealed off from the general flow of consciousness to emerge at times of stress – or relaxation – and take over for themselves. This process cannot accurately be described in a few non-technical words. One can only suggest it by analogies. There is for instance the fit of coughing at a concert which can be held back for a time, and then, just as one is beginning to forget about it and think it conquered, explodes with irresistible – and shattering – violence. There is the anger too long controlled which suddenly bursts the dam and produces an overwhelming torrent of rage.

These are of course much over-simplified images of what can be an extremely complicated process. These secondary beings, though possibly generated by moods or complexes were capable of taking on recognizable traits of their own, and of acting characteristically over long periods of time. It is worth noting moreover, that they can be used either as scapegoats or as inspirations, and that those in whom they emerge need not feel personally responsible for their activities, whatever form they take.

Much research work consists of course in fitting new concepts to old observations. Frederic Myers was one of the earliest people to apply the notion of the secondary personality to parapsychological ideas when, as early as 1889, he identified Socrates' Daimon – which was on occasion associated with twenty-four-hour-long trances – with 'a wiser self' that could 'use the products of unconscious thought'.

Fascinating pioneer work on such personalities began to become known in the 1890s; it was carried out by an American physician, T. Morton Prince. Myers discussed one of his early investigations in a lecture to the Society, and wrote a paper about it in *Proceedings* XIV (1898–9), later reprinted in the specialist periodical *Brain*. Two years later *Proceedings* XV contained, together with a fuller account of T. Morton Prince's best known work, several articles applying its ideas to various psychical phenomena. Mrs Sidgwick for instance used them to interpret Mrs Piper's Controls and communicators[1] in general, suggesting in addition that some of them might possibly be modelled on material drawn from memories telepathically received from living people who had known those whose names were used. Andrew Lang put on record his conviction that Phinuit was definitely a secondary personality, and that the 'GP' in whom Richard Hodgson had thought to recognize his dead friend George Pelham might well be another.

T. Morton Prince's study set out *The Development and Genealogy of the Misses Beauchamp* and was subtitled *A Case of Multiple Personality*. The original 'Miss Beauchamp (B1)' was reserved, and morbidly conscientious (she sounds as if she had been modelled by some very fusspot kind of governess). Under hypnosis two more personalities emerged, B2, 'serious, weary and sad', and B3, a complete contrast to the others. Spontaneous, childish and mischievous, she was aware of the rival personalities (and of an irritable shadowy fourth who turned up later) though they were not conscious of her existence. She despised B2 as 'asleep', and heartily detested the 'stupid' B1, whose memory she shared, and on whom she played all manner of tricks, unravelling her knitting, putting a boxful of spiders among her

---

1. It is interesting that on October 29, 1901 an American paper, the *Sunday Sentinel* of Milwaukee, published a full page interview with Mrs Piper, reporting her as saying she believed in a 'telepathic explanation' of much of her work, and remained for the rest 'an open minded student'. This interview was with a fully conscious Mrs Piper. In her trance states she seems to have accepted her Controls and communicators as wholeheartedly as ever.

possessions, and so on (it seems just possible that certain poltergeist manifestations may be explainable in the same sort of way). She also wrote scurrilous letters and 'poems' about her and left them about for her to read on her return to the physical organism they shared; and obviously for other people to read too.

Some years later Professor William MacDougall, FRS, reviewing the case in *Proceedings* XIX (1905–7) pointed out that it yielded evidence that the spirit was not wholly dependent on the physical brain and that the personalities might be 'discarnate'. The affair could in fact be used to support 'the spiritistic explanation of such cases as Mrs Piper's' and to justify belief in survival after the death of the body (and also, though he did not say so, a belief in 'possession'). He seems, however, to have modified his ideas by 1920, when he wrote in his Presidential Address that he regarded his own (conscious) self as 'a general in command of many subordinates' who might 'take over' when he was 'asleep or relaxed'. Plainly these subordinates were linked with his own being, not alien ghosts.

Interest in multiple personalities – psychological and para-psychological – has fluctuated down the years. In 1904 a Dr Wilson had described (*Proceedings* XVIII) a twelve-year-old boy in whom an attack of meningitis had precipitated the appearance of no less than ten separate personalities, one after another: (did he, one wonders, grow up to be an actor?) and Alice Johnson had painstakingly noted their resemblance to Controls. The discussion was continued in later *Proceedings*. There was comment on the 'play-acting' of a child Control, Nelly, the *alter ego* of a Mrs Thomson, who had been employed by the widow of Archbishop Benson to try to get into touch with her husband and her brother. (Mrs Benson thought telepathy alone had been at work.)

In 1931 Dr Mitchell discussed (*Proceedings* XXXI) an additional case of the kind discovered (confusingly) by another American physician, also named Morton Prince. (This one's initials were W. F. and he later became a President of the Society.) It was that of a girl, Doris Fischer, whom he and his wife finally adopted and who had had a terrifying childhood with a violent drunken father. From her there emanated alternatively 'Margaret', 'Sleeping Margaret' and, after her mother's death 'Sick Doris'. On the theme of dissociation in general and of such personalities in particular he suggested that they sometimes represented characters whom their originators would have liked to be; as if for instance, Walter Mitty had taken to *acting* his fantasies instead of projecting them on to his interior cinema screen. Dr Mitchell also put forward the idea that 'child guides' were popular because so many people longed to be children again. But do they? Childhood can as often be boring and frustrating as joyful and irresponsible. On the other hand, of course, it is pre-eminently the time for invisible playmates (my own family has produced three, Mrs Deddy, Mrs Jumbly Jobbly and Doggie Blacksands, all of whom evaporated when their owners went to school); and, perhaps equally significant, the ability to 'be' someone else. 'Come on, I'm Robin Hood, and you can be Maid Marian!' 'No, I'm going to be Little John' and so on with the utmost conviction till teatime.

Much research, of course, consists in fitting new concepts to old observations. During the next two decades C. Whately Carington, a shy, dedicated retiring man, whose services to psychical research have never been fully recognized, began to work out – and presently to use – objective methods of trying to establish whether Controls were indeed budded-off parts of the medium through whom they operated. One of these methods was to employ a word-association test akin to those described by Jung in volume XXIV of the Society's *Proceedings*. In such tests – I quote Rosalind Heywood's admirable description.[1] 'The sitter is asked to respond with the first word that comes into his head to a series of words read aloud to him. The more a word affects him emotionally, the longer he takes to reply. Hence, to a string of words each individual will have an individual reaction pattern' which can of course be recorded in the manner of a temperature chart.

Applied to the case of Mrs Leonard and 'Feda', this test showed that where the medium's conscious reactions were slow, the Control's were fast, and *vice-versa*, and that the patterns they yielded fitted into one another like two pieces of a jigsaw puzzle; or, in Carington's own words in a discussion[2] of Controls in general, 'like the outside and inside of a *repoussé* plaque'.

He also suggested that the word-association test might be supplemented by the use of a 'psycho-galvanic reflex' (or electrical

---

1. *The Sixth Sense*, London, 1959.
2. *Proceedings* 52, 1935.

skin resistance test), of the kind used in the 'lie-detectors' once popular with the American police. 'Any evocation of emotion', he explained, 'is accompanied by a change in the electrical properties of the skin, which can be accurately measured by the use of electrical apparatus. This change can be used with confidence as a measure of the intensity of the emotion'; but not, of course, to show its nature – fear, joy, grief, guilt, illumination – or its source.

Carington applied both tests to the celebrated medium Eileen Garrett, who had aroused much interest by her vivid subsequent awareness of the personal and (even more surprising) the technical, details of what seemed to have happened during the fatal crash of the world's largest airship, the R101, at Beauvais in 1931. Like Mrs Piper and Mrs Leonard, Mrs Garrett was always ready and willing to be investigated. More, she had a lively intellectual curiosity about the processes through which her information came. In the end, in fact, she ceased to work as a trance-medium, and succeeded in establishing in New York in 1952, the Parapsychology Foundation which was and is devoted to various methods of encouraging the study of extra sensory perception. Meanwhile, she co-operated gladly with Carington's attempts to discover the nature of her two Controls. He concluded that they too were indeed secondary personalities.

Though her work aroused a good deal of controversy – and a heated correspondence – no such feelings seem to have been stimulated by a much more recent attempt to investigate Controls (now alternatively known as 'guides') by physical means; perhaps because it was described in terms so technical as to remind the reader of Gibbon's attempts to 'veil in the decent obscurity of a learned language' the more startling practices of the Roman Empire in decline. This attempt was recorded in a paper by G. L. Heseltine and J. H. Kirk presented at the Society's Third International Conference at Edinburgh in 1979. It set out a series of experiments undertaken to find out whether the patterns of electrical brain activity in a trance medium differed when his two 'guides' 'Hotep' and 'Shoalin' were present. It was discovered that they were indeed different; though the writers regretfully had to own that the experiment could not give much information about the 'guides' themselves.

It looks as if, though the Society has no collective opinions, there could be a very common assumption that such entities are indeed secondary personalities, while the communicators may sometimes be given the benefit of the doubt. (Carington had concluded that the latter were either what they claimed to be, or 'histrionic poses'.)

Thus, one may be pretty certain that whatever the source of Mrs Rosemary Brown's music, so confidently ascribed to various composers in the Beyond, the fact that she knows as 'Liszt' the Control who leads her round the local supermarket,[1] points out the best bananas and adds up her bill for her at the check out does not mean that Liszt himself is recalled from celestial harmonies to carry out these useful functions; though 'Chopin' may possibly be who he says he is, even though he has forgotten how to speak French as he did to George Sand — Mrs Brown understands French — and talks Polish, which needs to be translated by 'an interpreter' in the spirit world.

Now that the theory of reincarnation has become popular, and with it the practice of hypnotizing volunteers and 'regressing' them, in their dissociated state, to remember their 'earlier lives' (the belief that they had them is of course strongly implicit in the suggestion that these can indeed be remembered!) it has been suggested that tests for multiple personality[2] might usefully be applied to the beings who emerge; the old lady of mediaeval times who was so poor that she had nothing to eat but potatoes (not in fact known here until the late 16th century), the girl about to be tried as a witch who gave the name of the Assizes but cited again and again the date given (as a printer's error) on the cover of a pamphlet on the subject, the 'member of the early Celtic Church' who believed it had priestesses, and lacked any complex ritual and any preoccupation with morals.

The investigation of mediums has of course continued over the years, though not perhaps with the same sustained enthusiasm, the same assessment and reassessment of recorded data that had been involved with Mrs Piper and Mrs Leonard, not to mention the amateur sensitives involved in the Cross Correspondences. This may have been due in part to a dearth of such mediums, a dearth which has been attributed to various different causes; among them a change in the general intellectual climate; the unexamined assumption that

---

1. Cf Rosemary Brown: *Unfinished Symphonies*, London, 1971.
2. For a full and carefully documented discussion see Ian Wilson *Mind out of Time*, London, 1981.

anyone who 'sees' visions or 'hears' voices is necessarily 'as nutty as a fruit cake'; and the enormously increased use of electrical apparatus for industrial, medical and household purposes, as well as for radio and television. It has been suggested that this may affect the electrical activities of the brain (only discovered in 1929), which is thought to receive – or to become aware of – paranormally transmitted information most efficiently when it is involved in producing alpha waves. One might also suggest that the distractions instantly on tap from radio and television could dispel (much faster than those of the written word) the atmosphere of relaxation, of inner solitude, and sometimes of near-boredom in which spontaneous extrasensory perception tends to come through.

The use of tape recorders has helped to dispel some, though not all, of the debatable doubts of what had in fact been said at a seance, or in a hypnotic trance, at a time when it was necessary for notes to be written by hand, often in darkness, however swift and efficient the note-taker. Even now, however, something depends on the personality and interests of the person who transcribes the tapes. I have myself received a transcript of a perfectly mundane tape-recorded literary lecture, and have been amazed at the number of irrelevant allusions to King Arthur and the Round Table which kept cropping up. References to my own notes, and to one or two members of the audience, confirmed my own impression that I had never once mentioned them. They must have been of paramount interest to the transcriber.

Moreover, tape recordings replayed as they stand may produce curious impressions. The grunts, the groans, the heavy breathing of the 'regressed' may well devalue the episode, irresistibly reminding the listener of the story of the scared girl at the cinema who began to move away from her panting neighbour only to be reassured by the remark, 'Don't be so silly, it isn't passion, it's asthma.'

Notable mediums there were however, pre-eminent among them such figures as that of Miss Geraldine Cummins, a wiry athletic little Irishwoman who died in 1968. She had been an international hockey champion in her youth (a refreshing challenge to the popular image of a medium as a fleshy sedentary lady uttering cryptic messages in a darkness heavy with the disagreeable, ammoniac odour of joss sticks). Her integrity was undoubted, her own interpretation of her work was open to discussion. She had flashes of precognition; she made occasional accurate paranormal medical diagnoses (her father was a Professor of Medicine); and she produced a great deal of automatic writing, set down at the rate of 1500 words or so an hour. Some of this appeared in book form. Two of these works purported to have come from Frederic Myers and one, *Swan on a Black Sea*, from Mrs Willett (Coombe Tennant) of the Cross Correspondences.

The most famous, *The Scripts of Cleophas*, written in the 1930s, ran to some eight volumes and described events experienced during the development of first century Christianity; these impressed various Biblical scholars by their accuracy in small details usually known to experts alone. Incidentally, though Miss Cummins believed the work to have been dictated by a group who called themselves 'The Messengers', she disclaimed the idea of having any Control. She preferred, she said 'Socrates' own name for his subliminal caretaker, which was Daimon'.

She herself interpreted her automatic writings as communications from the dead. However, they yielded evidence of telepathy with the living – as when she produced a story recognized by W. B. Yeats, who was present at the time, as the plot of a new play on which he was at work – and of unconscious memory – as when she recorded as a message from a Colonel Fawcett (who had disappeared in the jungles of Brazil) much of an article written and published before his departure. The case remains open to discussion; and, maddening though this is to most of us who like Either/Or decisions, it looks as if the diagnosis of what is medically known as multiple aetiology, the interaction of several different causes, was probably the most accurate in this and many other cases.

It is impossible to survey all the investigations of mediums, amateur or professional, carried out by members of the Society. Some reports of such work remain in its confidential archives. Others, though available for consultation, have never been published. Some cases, like the very interesting one of Edgar Vandy[1] (thought to have communicated at various sittings the facts of his mysterious and fatal fall into a swimming pool) have involved more than one sensitive.

It should be said moreover that – contrary to a general opinion shown by several calls a day, the Society does not have a large team

---

1. Cf 'The Case of Edgar Vandy', edited by Kathleen Gay, SPR *Journal*, March 1957, and Andrew MacKenzie, *The Unexplained*, London, 1966.

of 'approved mediums' on its books; nor does it recommend favoured individuals.

An aspect of psychical research which has cropped up sporadically over many years is the appearance of 'drop-in' communicators, who seem to be more often involved with an amateur 'home circle' of experimenters than with a single medium. The visitor 'drops in' and gives – often by way of the ouija board, or of coded raps, and sometimes through automatic writing – details of his or her name, where he lived, what he did and when and how he died; rather as a lonely person walking in the countryside at night might make for a warm lighted pub for a little company, explain himself, and maybe leave a message for someone he had known thereabouts. Dr Alan Gauld published in the Society's *Proceedings* (Vol. 55, July 1971) a careful study of a number of such cases recorded from 1937 onwards by one particular home circle, with which he himself sat on occasion towards the end of the period.

There were about 240 'alleged communicators', one of whom was said to be alive but in a coma. This proved impossible to check – maddeningly, since telepathic incidents do seem to occur during this state. (The best example I know is that of a woman who slept for several nights in a room in a clergy house normally occupied by a priest on duty, who was wakened early every morning by the sexton. The sexton was at the time unconscious in a hospital ward. *She* was awoken regularly every morning – at the hour of the sexton's usual call, of which she knew nothing – by loud knockings at the door. Directly the patient recovered consciousness and entered convalescence the knockings ceased.)[1]

Of the 240 communicators studied by Dr Gauld, well over half were friends or relatives of the sitters, and were excluded from consideration, since memory might well be at work; from the remainder he excluded eminent or historical communicators about whom plenty was known to the public. He also ruled out communicators whose statements could not be verified at Somerset House, in public directories, service records, street maps, and so on, Ten were left whose statements were to some extent accurate. There followed careful examinations of births, deaths and marriages columns in national and local papers; and a hunt for possible obituaries which

---

1. Personal communication.

members of the home circle might have seen without realizing the fact, printed say next a crossword puzzle. Dr Gauld pointed out that deliberate fraud was not only unlikely, but would have demanded the most unlikely and elaborate investigations; and that 'Super ESP' would also have involved an extraordinarily complex series of operations in picking out relevant details all over the country, and in wartime activities abroad. He concluded that several cases 'can be given a perfectly natural though perhaps entirely specious explanation in terms of the survival hypothesis'.

This kind of research means of course that a vast deal of time, energy and detective ingenuity has to be spent in tracing and verifying details large and small; a fact vividly exemplified in the case of 'Grace Roads' set out by Brian C. Nisbet in two *Journal* articles in July and September 1975. The first event was startling. It occurred in a non-Spiritualist group who had been doing table tilting experiments together for some years. To them 'Grace Roads' correctly gave her name, the date and place of her death (slightly overelaborated) and an address at which her son could be — and was — found and interviewed. Later communications were interwoven with fantasy, and produced the — apparently fictitious — figure of a Mr Jones, whom she feared because he was anti-Semitic and she was Jewish. An enormous amount of painstaking research finally unearthed an obituary of this lady in the local paper, the *Hackney Gazette*. It looked as though the whole affair might well be explained by unconscious memory.

The most recent piece of work on this theme, 'An Analysis of Some Suspect Communicators' by John Beloff and Ian Stevenson appeared in the *Journal* for September 1980. It discussed a number of cases written down — in response to what was felt as an urgent impulse — by Mrs Margo Williams, in the Isle of Wight. John Beloff had at first been impressed, but later — in conjunction with Ian Stevenson — thought that much of the information could have been derived, possibly by way of cryptomnesia, from natural sources; that some of it seemed to be incorrect; and that the 'communicators' were all oddly alike in possessing an extraordinary sense of guilt, and in sharing the same kind of personality. 'The effect', he wrote, 'was like that which might be produced if the same copy editor had undertaken to "correct" the styles of such distinctive writers as Dr Johnson, Sir Walter Scott, James Joyce and William James.'

7

Wildfire

Before going on to discuss the Society's long, tangled, painstaking investigations of 'physical mediums' (who seem to affect objects in the outside world) we must return to that main theme of interaction between mind and body which re-echoes throughout the history of psychical research, often to the discomfort of those who disdain all that is 'material'. This theme is continually cropping up and continually posing new questions, the new and tantalizing answers to which spawn fresh enquiries.

What is involved is the possibility that one individual psyche – possibly reinforced by a group – can influence its own body, the bodies of other people and, maybe, inanimate objects – stones, saucepans, crockery, metal.

It is not difficult to believe to some extent in the first of these possibilities – tears of grief or rage, the blush of embarrassment, the sweat of fear, form part of all human experience from earliest childhood. The rise of psychosomatic medicine has moreover shown – for instance – how worry can bring about the development of gastric ulcers (which have even been hailed as the badge of the successful tycoon). But when it comes to such possibilities as fire-walking and levitation, however authentic the evidence put forward may seem to be, the boggle-threshold is low, and the impulse to reject such ideas comes into play.

That the mind can influence other people's minds, and *through* them their bodies by way of suggestion is also becoming easy to accept. The theories of Christian Science in the last century, the practice of Coué-ism in the 1920s, the use of hypnotic suggestion by orthodox medicine have all helped to bring this about. The dermatology departments of some hospitals have produced a new version of the traditional practice of 'wart-charming'; here a ritually white-coated doctor will successfully 'buy' the warts of unsophisticated children. Individual doctors[1] have moreover managed by a very carefully controlled piece of work to clear up by direct suggestion under hypnosis a case of congenital ichthyosis (a disfiguring and disgusting lifelong condition known as fish skin disease) previously considered incurable; and an instance of congenital birthmark.

Perhaps this kind of influence has been most easily recognized, though, in the work of unofficial 'healers', from the 17th century Valentine Greatrakes with his 'warm and balsamic touch' to Harry Edwards in our own time. It has been argued that the effect of powerful suggestion is to make the patient mobilize, at an unconscious level, his own physiological resources towards the disabled part of his body; in fact to speed up the process of natural defence and healing. It also seems possible that some electro-magnetic activity as yet unknown is at work. Obviously, both may be involved (to a degree varying from healer to healer) and can reinforce one another. It may be significant that wounds exposed to a magnetic field heal faster than others, just as do wounds over which the hands of certain healers are held; though so far no magnetic field[2] has been detected in the latter. That a strong sense of heat is often experienced in such healings is neither here nor there, as it could be induced either by some external stimulus or by an inner, psychosomatic process. In this connexion it is interesting to remember a medical observation that 'people can be taught to *think* their hands warm': the tradition that certain Tibetan lamas used to be trained deliberately to produce very high temperatures in themselves, and were tested by observing how soon they could dry out a cold wet sheet wrapped round their naked bodies; and the curious fact that spontaneous very high temperatures have been recorded in one or two European contemplatives[3] – notably Catherine of Genoa and

---

1. See Stephen Black, MD *Mind and Body*, London, 1969.

2. Professor Hasted, however, contributed a paper to the Fourth International Conference of the SPR (1981) on *electrical* signals recorded around the bodies of psychic subjects.

3. Cf Herbert Thurston, *The Physical Phenomena of Mysticism*, London, 1953.

Philip Neri – apparently as a by-product of concentration on prayer. (This was considered as odd rather than holy.)

It looks as if levitation of the human body may occur in the same kinds of way. There is, again, the tradition that lamas could be taught the technique of doing this. There is good evidence that it has occurred, as an involuntary by-product of prayer, among contemplatives, notably Philip Neri once more, Teresa of Avila – who found it extremely embarrassing, and clung on one occasion to the iron bars of a window in a vain attempt to prevent herself rising – and Joseph of Copertino. He, too, was ashamed of what he called 'these frivolities'. (Like the heat phenomena, levitation was not thought to be evidence for sanctity.)

Various spontaneous instances are reported among shamans, fakirs, and of course in the famous 19th century medium D. D. Home, who was never caught faking, and whose various flights convinced a number of contemporary eye witnesses, both at the time when they occurred and throughout their lives. E. A. Smythies, CIE, then Forest Adviser to the Government of Nepal made instant careful notes[1] of a case observed by himself and several other European observers in Katmandu in 1941. A young orderly, sitting cross-legged and with his hands clasped, on the brick floor of a small room brightly lit by an unshaded electric ceiling lamp was seen to rise in the same position, some two feet from the ground, and after about a second to be bumped hard and painfully down. This happened three times. The Hindus among his fellow servants said he was being punished by the Bhagwan, the spirit of his home village to whom he had omitted to sacrifice during his last leave.

The idea that the psyche may directly affect inanimate objects is even harder to face than its two predecessors, since these objects are not amenable to suggestion. It was long possible to explain that those who believed they had spontaneously seen such objects moving about had been deceived, either by incredibly elaborate trickery, or by hallucinations deliberately suggested. This interpretation of events has been made much harder to maintain – at any rate where experimental work is concerned – by such inventions as infra-red photography, and by the use of modern laboratory equipment.

It is interesting to see how much opinion on this subject has

---

1. SPR *Journal*.

changed over the years. Where what is called psychokinesis used to be doubted – partly on the *a priori* ground that it was impossible, partly because of the fear of superstition, partly because it was fairly easy to fake by mediums whose powers were on the wane, partly because a number of sitters were known to be marvel-gluttons – the wheel has come full circle, and it seems to attract more scientific attention than any other theme. It is a far cry from the time when the redoubtable W. H. Salter[1] could praise Mrs Piper on the grounds that 'through her, communications were given which could be considered seriously on their own merits, without the support of *dubious physical phenomena*' (my italics). It is a far cry from the time when various SPR members seemed to feel either that such matters should not be taken seriously, or (with an almost prudish delicacy) that they were 'not quite nice'. (Of course, some of their manifestations could be indelicate.) Perhaps I should add that this is a purely personal impression of my own, received when I first joined the Society and tried to discuss several poltergeist hauntings personally known to me.

Poltergeist outbreaks were however among the phenomena earliest investigated by the Society. Such events have been recorded at very many times and in very many places; in China, in India, in Russia, in the South Seas, and all over Europe. Robert Boyle suggested in the early 18th century that the Royal Society should investigate one in the home of a Protestant minister in France; whence another very interesting case was reported in the late summer of 1980. England has provided many well-documented instances. There were those of the Just Devil of Woodstock which plagued some Roundheads during the Civil Wars; of the outbreak at Tedworth, attributed to the curse of a wandering drummer who had been imprisoned by Mr Mompesson, magistrate owner of the haunted house; the Cock Lane Ghost and the Wesley case in the eighteenth century; several others in Victorian days; and yet more in our own, even without the controversial reports of events at Borley and at Enfield. Whatever may be thought to cause them, these events engender high emotional temperatures rising to fury point among investigators.

Poltergeist outbreaks often begin with mysterious noises; inexplicable 'footsteps' are heard, or the 'shifting' of furniture (later found in

---

1. *Trance Mediums*, W. H. Salter, SPR.

its usual place) in another room, or the 'bumping about' of some invisible creature 'about the size of a calf', or rappings on walls or bedheads, or even, in old houses, the ringing of domestic bells.[1] All these alarm not only humans but family dogs (though cats seem less timorous). There may also be gruff voices, and the movements of small objects – beads on a mantelpiece, fruit in a bowl – not to mention large ones. In the case of little Virginia Campbell[2] in Scotland in 1963, detached observers, a doctor, a minister, a schoolmistress, saw a school desk and a heavy chest full of blankets repeatedly raised from the floor and set down again by some invisible means. More frightening still are movements – sometimes flights – of saucepans, ornaments or crockery indoors and of stones out-of-doors. These are not seen till they are in motion, and they follow a curious curved trajectory unlike the course of anything thrown in the normal way. Sometimes the stones are hot. Sometimes there are apparently causeless fires.

Not all these phenomena occur in every outbreak. In modern ones, there can also – or alternatively – be interference with electricity installations and with automatic equipment such as that used to record telephone calls. In a house of my acquaintance which produced other apparently poltergeist events – the noises, the sudden opening of doors, the twisting of doorhandles, the turning over of a nightgown left on a bathroom chair while its owner was in the bath alongside – the lights would occasionally come on in the middle of the night; and in the famous Rosenheim case electrical engineers, telephone experts and the local authority were summoned – in vain – to trace and put right the cause of all the trouble (which ceased after the departure of an unfortunate typist whose ordinary quiet progress down a corridor was once observed to set all the ceiling lamps swinging).

In earlier times the favourite explanation was that evil or mischievous spirits were at work (poltergeist is the German for 'noisy spirit'). In parts of Ireland the Little People were blamed; and Shakespeare's Puck, like the Yorkshire Lubber Fiend seems to have

---

1. Professor Hasted suggests in his fascinating book *The Metal Benders* (London, 1981) that in the case of Victorian bells hung on wires, this may arise from the presence of an (unconscious) metal bender.

2. See A. R. G. Owen, *Can we explain the Poltergeist*, New York, 1964, and, in general, A. Cornell and A. Gauld, *Poltergeists*, London, 1980.

had tricks up his green sleeve. Witches – who were also thought to raise whirlwinds and thunderstorms – could be held responsible too; they were thought to use their magic powers either for gruesome fun, or, more often, to avenge some slight. Even in the comparatively rationalist times of the Wesley outbreak the villagers were saying darkly that the Rector of Epworth (father of Samuel, Charles, and many others) had offended the local 'cunning men' by his preaching, and that they were getting back at him. (He himself seems to have attributed the phenomena sometimes to rats and sometimes to his daughters' suitors, presumably playing practical jokes – though how they could make a wooden breadboard 'dance' of its own accord in full view by daylight was never explained.) With hindsight some of the trouble may be attributed to acute family tensions, personal and political. The unhappy Mrs Wesley did not only have to teach each one of her eleven children to 'cry quietly' from its first year onward so as not to disturb her husband while he was writing sermons; she also had to stand up against his pressure to make her join in prayers for the Hanoverian King, whom as a passionate supporter of the Stuarts, she believed to be a base usurper. It is possible that all this frustration, anger and misery may have exploded into poltergeist phenomena, possibly through unconscious interaction between Mrs Wesley herself and her daughter Hetty, just entering adolescence, the age at which psychokinesis is most commonly discharged.

Early in the Society's history the chief divergence seems to have been between the followers of Podmore and of Lang respectively. Podmore[1] considered almost all poltergeist outbreaks fraudulent (though he did reluctantly ascribe to 'supernatural agency' an incident in 1895 associated with one Annie, a foster child of thirteen years old, at Durweston). For the rest he dismissed such first hand evidence as 'untrustworthy' because the witnesses were 'uneducated' and (therefore) 'bad observers'. (But unsophisticated observers can on occasion be more accurate than sophisticated ones who *know* they cannot believe their eyes. It was children who could dare to admit to themselves and to say to other people that 'the Emperor had no clothes on'.)

Of the cases Podmore examines in detail, that of Emma Davies, a 'nursegirl' is particularly interesting. Her presence set various

---

1. Cf his paper on Poltergeist Cases in *Proceedings* XIII, 1896–7.

objects into movement; saucepans, bricks, clothes hung out to dry. She was, not surprisingly, dismissed; (hardly an ideal person to look after children!). The phenomena followed her when she left. He took this to mean first that the *place* where she originally worked had not been haunted (fair enough), and second that she was a fraud and had faked everything wherever she was. He noted too that 'she afterwards had fits'. This was an additional bad mark at a time when epilepsy was still associated both with insanity and with 'moral degeneration'. It has quite different implications in our own era, when William Roll[1] has pointed out that this illness may well be associated with psychokinesis.

Summing up, Podmore laid it down that in eleven of the cases he had investigated, those observed by 'educated persons' were adequately explained by 'trickery', that 'the appearance of objects moving slowly or flying' was 'a sensory illusion due to the excited condition of the percipients' and that 'genuine hallucinations may apparently be associated with fraudulent physical phenomena'. Q.E.D.

These conclusions were reprinted in his *Modern Spiritualism*;[2] and Andrew Lang took issue with him in a later *Proceedings*,[3] citing Lord Chesterfield's remark that 'if a man indubitably rose from the dead, within three days the Archbishop of Canterbury would disbelieve it' and noting more mildly on his own account that 'among the educated, memory is often inclined to minimize extraordinary occurrences'. He asserted the evidential value of history, cited contemporary, 17th, 18th and early 19th century documents – including those of an instance at Willington Mill in the 1840s and 50s – and stressed the 'uniformity of phenomena', the extraordinary likeness between such cases, wherever and whenever they were recorded – among the Eskimos, in the Red Indians of the New World, in 8th century Europe or in Victorian England. He also stressed the fact that many of those who reported them believed them to be unique and had no idea that anything of the kind had ever occurred elsewhere. In the next issue of *Proceedings* (XVIII, 1903–4) he discussed a case at Cideville in France in 1852, when a

---

1. W. R. Roll, 'Towards a Theory of The Poltergeist', *European Journal of Parapsychology*, Vol 2, No 2, Utrecht, 1978.

2. London, 1902.

3. 'The Poltergeist Historically Considered', SPR *Proceedings*, XVII, 1901–1903.

shepherd named Thurel brought a libel action against the local *curé*, who had accused him of practising 'sorcery' upon two pupils staying in the presbytery, boys of twelve and fourteen; a quilt had 'darted' from the surface of their bed, a stocking from beside it, 'raps beat out the rhythms of tunes, and also answered questions'. The case was dismissed, because Thurel himself had been heard by witnesses to claim responsibility for what had happened. (Maybe the boys had been chasing his sheep, and he had made threats of terrible consequences, and the suggestion had worked itself out, subconsciously, in this mode; maybe, like the English witches cited by Keith Thomas,[1] he had thought to get his own way – and protect his flocks – in the future, by claiming responsibility for any misfortune that overtook those who had offended him.)

As early as 1897, a third interpretation of poltergeist hauntings began to emerge in a correspondence in *The Times* about the haunting of Ballechin Castle, a haunting which had been reported in what can only be called full technicolour by an enthusiastic lady, a Miss Ada Goodrich Freer. One of the correspondents, Professor Milne, a well-known seismologist, suggested that they might be explained by 'seismic disturbances' such as earth tremors along some geological fault in a rocky formation. To these were later added the pressure of underground water along ancient sewers or culverts after a period of heavy rain; or during exceptionally high tides if the places affected were near the sea; or subsidences in disused mine-workings. All such events might well produce strange noises of various kinds, bangs, tappings, sounds like the shifting of heavy furniture, and sounds like footsteps. They might even shake objects off shelves indoors and set frost-loosened stones falling off walls outside.

This useful hypothesis – ultimately known as the 'geophysical theory' of poltergeists – might have been expected to appeal to researchers who could not believe all the phenomena to be caused *either* by trickery *or* by the activity of spirits. Whether it was discussed in private does not appear, but not for over fifty years does it seem to have been examined in detail and set forth in print. This process was begun by G. W. Lambert (President of the Society 1956–8) with all his usual indefatigable scholarly research in the

---

1. Keith Thomas, *The Decline of Religion and Magic in 17th century England*, London, 1973.

Journal for June 1955. He noted that many incidents occurred within
three miles of tidal water; examined relevant geological patterns in
England, Ireland, Scotland, Wales and France; listed cases and
'primary effects' both here and in a far wider field – America, Europe,
Russia; and gave map references. Further equally well researched
articles followed. It was argued that such happenings might well
frighten people into full-blown hallucinations of sight, hearing,
smell or temperature; or into misinterpreting normal events in
accordance with their fears, 'seeing' white figures for instance where
they would normally have noticed no more than drifts of mist.
Luminous appearances were said to be formed of phosphorescent
gases given off by the decaying matter in cracked and worn out
drains. Such figures were thought to have become rarer as drainage
systems were rebuilt.

This theory may well serve to explain many poltergeist hauntings,
especially those traditionally observed at certain times of year;
coinciding for instance with spring tides. As such hauntings are very
often associated with ancient 'stately homes', however, it is not
possible to check them by these cracks in the walls usually produced
by underground disturbances, since such cracks could well be due to
old age alone.

Once formulated, a good working hypothesis – the heart's desire
of psychical researchers – tends to be stretched to cover a much wider
field than the one in which it arose. This was no exception. Although
E. J. Dingwall and Trevor Hall reiterated as early as 1958[1] the
useful distinction between 'person-centred' and 'place-centred'
hauntings, the geophysical theory was advanced to explain a larger
number of instances than it could conveniently fit. The idea of
multiple causation was ignored.

It was all to the good that the *Journal* should carry in September
1959 the first of G. W. Lambert's two admirably researched papers
on 'Scottish Haunts and Poltergeists' complete with tide tables, maps
and a comparison of the incidence of poltergeist cases in dry years
and wet; and also all to the good that Alan Gauld and Anthony
Cornell should report a year later on 'A Fenland Poltergeist', also
citing tide tables and rainfall statistics, which showed that this
outbreak would not fit into the given pattern. It was all to the good

---

1. *Four Modern Ghosts*, E. J. Dingwall and Trevor Hall, London, 1958.

that the December 1960 number should carry a fascinating survey, again by G. W. Lambert, of 'The Geography of London Ghosts', pointing out how many haunted houses in the area were built above underground watercourses like that of the little river Tyburn – bourne, like the Scottish burn, is an old name for a stream – which runs down past the site of Tyburn Tree, the ancient gallows near Marble Arch, into the Serpentine and onwards to the Thames; and that of the Westbourne, whose waters flow through a large pipe still to be seen at a London Underground railway station. This carefully documented and closely reasoned paper certainly reinforced the argument that some of the hauntings reported over that area might well be explained in terms of the geophysical theory; some, but not all, not for instance the curious voices singing eighteenth century music[1] 'heard' by Maurice Baring and Philip Kershaw in a house in Barton Street, Westminster, some 80 years ago.

The same sense of partial but not total explanation is generated by a most interesting and ingenious study of 'Family Death Warnings' in the *Journal* for December 1963. It suggests, for instance, that the 'knockings' heard on several occasions in the 17th century before the deaths of members of the Woodd family were caused by a rise in the height of underground water, which in turn caused a migration of rats, which in their turn carried the plague. It suggests too that sick members of families with a tradition of such warnings will be scared into letting go their hold on life if any sounds are heard that could be interpreted in this way. These very sensible arguments, useful in their special contexts, do not however cover all the traditions concerned (not for instance that of the unseen 'Drummer of Airlie' whose taps outraged the Sabbatarian controllers of a South African prison camp during the Boer War, and presaged a family death in action next day). The best brief summary of the situation is still perhaps the very careful critique of the geophysical theory contributed to the *Journal* for September 1961 by Gauld and Cornell, thanking Lambert for formulating and applying it, acknowledging its usefulness in some instances, and pointing out that it could not possibly be stretched to cover the whole field.

Meanwhile yet another interpretation had been gaining ground. *Proceedings* (Vol. 47, 1942–5) contained (together with a report on

---

1. See Renée Haynes, *The Seeing Eye, The Seeing I*, London, 1976.

psychokinetic experiments of various kinds including work with dice,) a paper by John Layard, an anthropologist who had carried out field studies in the South Seas, and had become an ardent follower of Jung. Layard suggested – in the Jungian tradition – that both the noises and the mysterious movements of objects in poltergeist outbreaks might themselves be psychokinetic in origin, brought about by some form of energy, released by certain individuals at times of frustration or fury, that could not be expressed in any other way. (It was later suggested[1] that there could be some likeness between such people and those who reacted to emotional stress by producing allergies; asthma, hay fever, migraine, rashes and so on which can be set going either by physical or by emotional stimuli.)

Predictably, the paper provoked a fiery correspondence from researchers of various different points of view. The Society is not monolithic and disclaims collective opinions; which means that individual ones are sometimes formulated with considerable punch, and that struggles for the *general* acceptance of this or that interpretation of events, this or that methodology, this or that set of standards can be very lively indeed. To re-read this particular correspondence is a little like going out on a fine, dark Guy Fawkes night among burning bonfires with rockets rising, fizzing and bursting into a shower of many coloured stars.

K. M. Goldney rejected the paper's hypothesis out of hand. So, rather surprisingly, did Whately Carington, perhaps too closely schooled in mathematical modes of thought, careful measurement, statistical methods, to unlock his mind's door to such an alien argument. Dr Wiesner was mildly in favour of the theory. That learned and judicious educationalist and thinker, Dr Robert Thouless (President 1942–4), welcomed as 'valuable and useful' the idea that 'poltergeist phenomena are telekinetic expressions of an unconscious conflict in the mind of the agent'. (Telekinetic – and telekinesis – were long used instead of psychokinetic and psychokinesis.) Rosalind Heywood thanked Layard for formulating the concept. E. J. Dingwall discounted the presentation as 'confused' and some of its points as 'dubious', but said the theory had been discussed verbally, though not in print, for the last fifteen years.

It caught on, however; and G. N. M. Tyrrell (President 1945–6)

---

1. Owen, op cit.

in his study, *The Personality of Man*,[1] envisaged poltergeist phenomena as 'the expression of a subconscious level of personality *via*
physical force'. What that physical force could be, and how it works
was not then and is not yet established, though experimental
investigations – like those, soon to be considered, of Professor Hasted
and others with metal-bending children – may one day yield useful
results. Perhaps it should be said that this curious talent seems to
have been released in such children by watching Uri Geller's feats on
television; which is why they are known to Italian researchers by the
charming name of *gellerinos*.

That spontaneous poltergeist outbreaks could and did occur, and
had been observed by so many people independent of one another in
so many times and places served to validate some of the despised
'spiritualistic phenomena' of mediums; who had in fact often begun
their careers as what would now be called poltergeist foci. It would
be fascinating to know how they managed to retain their powers of
setting off psychokinetic explosions after the original stimulus had
faded. After all, one can move away from some house whose
associations, consciously known or unconsciously felt, can act like
dynamite upon the brooding psyche; and the turmoils of adolescence,
family tensions and frustrations, violent anger that cannot be
expressed in words, all these usually conform in the end to the old
saying *tout lasse, tout casse, tout passe*. Perhaps a habit of psychokinetic
reaction was set up in those mediums so that it became 'second
nature' to produce in the exterior physical world the equivalent of a
temper tantrum in a naughty child, kicking, screaming, hitting
everyone and everything within reach, throwing things about,
holding its breath with rage. Perhaps, having once discovered
consciously how to release an energy that set objects flying around it
was fun to exercise that secret skill; particularly if one believed that
in doing so one was the important instrument of spirits. It is well
established that physiological techniques can be – and are – used to
bring about conditions in which general psi-phenomena may emerge.
Stillness, deep breathing, special diets, the kind of meditation
concentrated not on an idea but on an imagined sound, may
sometimes (but not always) yield experiences of telepathy, precognition, clairvoyance. It looks as if other physiological techniques may

---

1. London, 1946.

induce conditions favourable to psychokinesis; witness, for instance, the fact that Rudi Schneider, a physical medium of genuine powers who will presently be discussed, used to pant like a dog during seances. William Roll's suggestions that psychokinesis is particularly prone to occur among epileptics — almost as the equivalent of a *grand-mal* fit — has already been noticed.

It is interesting that the Greeks should have called this malady 'the sacred disease' whether they believed the sufferer to have been temporarily taken over by a spirit or because his utterances in or out of a fit seemed to have some paranormal content. Adrian Boshier, the South African anthropologist who was initiated as a tribal witch doctor or shaman, certainly suffered from *petit-mal*. I saw him succumb to it on several occasions at an American conference on Parasychology and Anthropology to which I had been invited. Sitting at the long conference table, he would go into what the Scots call a 'dwam', a dissociated state, grind his teeth, shudder, mutter a few groaning words and, after being given a drink of water by a neighbour, recover, and join in the proceedings again. In view of this it was particularly interesting to hear him say that the witch doctors had recognized him at once as one of themselves. (Was it for this reason?) I asked him later in general terms whether he had ever discussed epilepsy with them. He said 'No, but they can tell you how to use it'.

William Roll has also suggested that psychokinesis is especially likely to occur in women at times of pre-menstrual tension; an idea which, if true, may well contribute to the widespread primitive beliefs that women are mysterious unaccountable creatures who can be extremely sinister. The association of psychokinetic effects with menstruation may account for the rural superstition that women should not work in dairies during a period, since they are liable at such times to turn the milk and cream sour, as thundery weather is supposed to do. Probably this would not hold good of modern dairies, where there is efficient refrigeration and butter and cheese are machine made; but it would be interesting to test the theory in an old building kept cool only by thick walls and a northerly aspect.

In connexion with traditional beliefs, that in the Evil Eye — still extant in the Mediterranean countries — may be relevant to psychokinesis. I do not mean any deliberate willed conscious attempt to suggest doom, to curse someone with sickness or with the kind of accident-proneness that may bring disaster. I have in mind what looks like an unconscious explosion of ill-feeling into pk; as when in A's presence B's luggage slides off a quay into the water, or a pot plant hanging from the ceiling falls on C's head at a party. These two instances were given me by someone who had seen both happen. The person concerned was in fact an erudite literary critic who had among his fellow countrymen the reputation of causing such incidents. I have lately been given an account of a similar occurrence by an American friend who had been much shaken when something of the kind, inexplicable in ordinary terms, had happened when he himself was internally angry with a colleague by his side.

It seems justifiable to conclude that the continued careful observation of 'wild' psychokinesis, occurring in its natural ecological context, the jungle of human actions and reactions and interactions, has reinforced the convictions of those who studied it so long, so patiently and so carefully in professional mediums, under the artificial conditions as it were of a Zoo; or even a circus, where trained animals go through the hoops punctually at given times.

Those students seem to have been justified in their conclusion that despite ingenious trickery on occasion the unexplained movements of objects, strange and unaccountable noises, vivid lights, streams of cold air, did indeed occur quite genuinely from time to time, and could not invariably be dismissed as deliberate fraud on the part of the mediums involved; or as conscious or unconscious suggestion producing hallucinations among the sitters – as Sir William Barrett once hazarded; or even as plain lunacy on the part of all concerned.

A curious secondary result of poltergeist incidents is worth reiterating; the extraordinary violent feelings, for and against paranormality that they engender among observers. This was particularly vivid in a recent outbreak in a small house at Enfield, in North London in September 1977. The house was inhabited by a mother, two daughters aged 11 and 14, and two younger sons. The trouble began with the usual inexplicable knockings and furniture movements. Two members of the SPR, Maurice Grosse and Guy Lyon Playfair were asked to investigate, and recorded these, and many more phenomena, including levitations of the girls and, in December, a loud lewd male voice coming from one of the girls which when tested seemed to be produced by the false vocal chords sometimes used by ventriloquists. Grosse and Playfair were joined by the Press and by television operators, an amateur photographer and others, to whom they gave every chance to check what went on.

The Rev. Stewart Lamont,[1] who acted as reporter on this case for BBC Scottish Television observes that doubts about the voice were raised at the Second International SPR Conference at Cambridge in 1978, where video cassettes of the case were shown; and that these doubts were reflected back, so to speak, on earlier events, even though these had been tape recorded and photographed at the time when they happened, and were so typical of poltergeist hauntings. His view — with which I should be inclined to agree — is that the original occurrences were genuinely paranormal, but that possibly as time went on and the power faded one of them at any rate may have done some faking, particularly where the voice was concerned (and possibly in the levitation line; she was an athletic girl). I viewed one of the later video tapes, and I have never seen a child's face show more mischievous conspiratorial joy at teasing the grown-ups than hers when she smiled at her sister.

Oddly enough the later, more official observers do not seem to have given much weight to such an explanation as has just been put forward. The whole episode has met with a scepticism infuriating to those involved from the beginning — a scepticism itself inflamed to anger by the publication of a popularly written book on the subject,[2] whose photographs in particular arouse unending controversy.

1. *Is There Anybody There?* Edinburgh, 1980.
2. *This House is Haunted*, Guy Lyon Playfair, London, 1980.

8

(i) Physical Mediums in Full Swing

It is as well to have from 'wild PK' evidence that paranormal physical phenomena can and do happen, explode spontaneously from out of the blue. Otherwise there could have been justifiable doubt whether this form of mind-body interaction did in fact exist, at any rate until the careful investigation of metal bending children began four years ago.

Statistically based experiments with dice throwing did not yield any very striking results; it looks as if the subjects needed a particularly high emotional charge and a rather high boggle threshold to set the process going in this context. Investigations with physical mediums have all too often shown up the use of conscious or unconscious fraud at times when their odd, fluctuating powers were weak. And a knowledge of all the commercial gadgets at their disposal could produce still further doubt, not permanently dispelled by the reflection that unless nature were there first art could not copy it. Thus, *Gambols with the Ghosts*, that splendid catalogue of 'effects used by nearly all prominent mediums, entertainers and others of the entire world' issued in America at the turn of the century produced (as well as the items cited in Chapter I) mechanisms for causing 'Raps here there and every where, standing or sitting, in light or in dark in any room or circle as often as you like'; a gadget for 'Vest (*anglicé* waistcoat) turning, or, Matter through Matter'; a Telescopic Reaching Rod for use in the dark, 'which will pick up any small object'; a self-playing Guitar; and a kit for 'a complete Spiritualist seance', including a Spirit Telephone and 'The Medium's

Fire Test which enables you to handle heated [paraffin] lamp chimneys with bare hands'.

It would be interesting to see them all. The Society for Psychical Research possesses no more than D. D. Home's elegant accordion – which yields no clue to the way in which it played without being touched; a piece of 'ectoplasm' from the Scottish medium Mrs Duncan, consisting in this case (she furnished several different varieties) of a piece of scruffy though much washed cream coloured 'sateen'; and some wax casts of 'spirit hands' over whose origins there seems to be some uncertainty. They are curiously small.

It would be impossible to discuss in detail all the physical mediums investigated by SPR members, alone or with others, over the last century. Two of the most famous – D. D. Home and Florence Cook – were no longer in very lively eruption when the Society was founded; but their activities continued to be examined, re-examined, discussed and still found mysterious by SPR members for many years and so need to be noticed.

D. D. Home was never in fact discovered to be cheating, though many elaborate suggestions have been put forward as to how he *might* have done so. Some of his phenomena are more credible now than they were at the time; though even then the fact that they were often so inconvenient to him personally might have been taken to show that they were genuine. There were, for instance the explosions of rapping that made the aunt with whom he lived as a young man in America turn him out of her home; explosions that recurred later on when, back in Britain, he stayed in the house, and under the medical care, of Dr Gully of Malvern (who wrapped his patients in sheets soaked in cold water, a kind of shock treatment that often seemed to work). Home was also observed by careful and trustworthy witnesses to handle glowing coals without hurting himself; to grow suddenly and temporarily taller; to materialize 'human hands, arms and forms'; to play an accordion without touching it; and to levitate various objects and sometimes himself (on one much discussed occasion out of one window and into another).

It is possible that all these peculiar occurrences might have been accepted more readily if he – and many others – had not attributed them to 'spirits'. Certainly Professor Richet, that hard boiled materialist expert in physiology accepted such phenomena as explicable in normal terms once they were properly understood;

equally certainly, it would seem, does the redoubtable Dutch researcher Mr George Zorab who has suggested that 'a special phantom forming predisposition' was one of Home's own paranormal powers, and that the production of 'spirit hands' and 'spirit forms' arose from these rather than from 'supernatural agencies'.[1] He seems perfectly well satisfied that they were indeed produced.

On the other hand, to relegate such happenings to the realm of intricate mechanism to be explored and explained after the manner of James Clerk Maxwell could well have confined interest in them to no more than a handful of specialists driven by an intellectual passion to 'see wheels go round'; to discover *how* they worked, rather than why. Mr Rupert Sheldrake[2] has observed that there are two ways of explaining psi phenomena. 'One is to start from the assumption that they depend on laws of physics as yet unknown; the other is to suppose that they depend on non-physical causal factors or connecting principles'. The first will appeal primarily to the physical scientist, the second to the kind of mind – a good deal commoner – more interested in meaning than in measurement. In such minds if no significance can be found for a strange event, if there is no framework, however ricketty, into which to fit it, it may simply fade from attention. This seems to have happened, as the years went by, to Lord Adare a first hand observer of many of Home's phenomena. Admiral Strutt,[3] a connexion of the Rayleigh family, and a great pillar of the SPR in his time, once told me that sailing one summer in the nineteen-twenties, he put into harbour and found the boat moored next to him belonged to this witness who had by now inherited the Earldom of Dunraven. They talked together for a while. The gist of his remarks was that yes, he *had* seen the man levitate; yes, he had been fascinated at the time; yes, he had felt that something extraordinarily significant was going on; but that now, looking back, he could see no particular meaning in the incident. It seemed pointless. This 'so what' reaction probably happens quite often; if something doesn't seem to make sense, why bother with it?

Making sense of curious happenings is, however, a long, tedious, chancy business, as Sir William Crookes was to discover. President

---

1. SPR *Journal*, Vol 48, 763, 1975.

2. Sheldrake, Rupert, *A New Science of Life, the hypothesis of formative causation*, London, 1981.

3. Personal communication.

of the Society from 1896 to 1899, and of the British Association for the Advancement of Science in 1898, he had some twenty years earlier approached D. D. Home's phenomena from a purely scientific angle, using careful observation and experiment; but had never quite succeeded in fitting his findings into a satisfactory general setting. In fact, because he recognized and reported the occurrence of strange, inexplicable events which had previously found a popular interpretation in terms of Spiritualism, he was accused by the *Quarterly Review* (still as 'savage and tartarly' as it had been in Keats's time) of being a convert to that faith. It was rather as if a man studying the appearance and behaviour and constituents of marsh gas should be assumed to believe in a mischievous entity called Will o' the Wisp. He replied that this was not so, and that all he wanted to do was to find out the facts. He posited 'the discovery of a new force connected in some way with the human organism'. Incidentally, that objective body the Dialectical Society, after no less than forty meetings for 'trial and test' agreed with him, affirming, in the words of the distinguished lawyer, E. W. Cox that 'there is a force proceeding from the nerve system capable of imparting motion and weight to solid bodies' ('weight' could have indicated among other things the pressure on the keys of the accordion that made it play tunes). Crookes noted the fluctuations of this 'force' from time to time in D. D. Home, labelled it 'psychic', observed that it drew on 'nervous energy' and recorded that he had seen the medium 'lying almost fainting on the floor, pale and speechless' after producing phenomena. The same physical exhaustion occurred in 'Stella C' in the 1920s and has been noticed in the Russian Kulagina in our own time.

Crookes' first studies of Home appeared during the early eighteen seventies in the quarterly *Journal of Modern Science*, of which he was editor. They included descriptions of the use of a spring balance to test the medium's ability to affect weights, and of a cage to enclose the famous accordion so that it could not be touched. The last of these papers, 'Notes on Phenomena called Spiritual' appeared in 1874; Crookes is said to have been surprised when this was not accepted as easily as his papers on physics had been; and still surprised when his 'Notes on Seances with D. D. Home' in the SPR *Proceedings* for 1887 also met a rather mixed reaction. Personally grounded in what he called 'the *vital* knowledge of my own ignorance', he had not realized the general tendency to resist at all costs what William James called 'the greatest pain in the world, the pain of a new idea'.

'Notes on Phenomena called Spiritual' produced a number of such pains; they reported that their author had himself seen Home (whose seances were held in full light) levitate on three occasions, once sitting on a chair, once kneeling on a chair, and once standing on the ground; and that no less than a hundred people had seen such movements at other times. Crookes also vouched for the fact that when the medium came to his own house (where no gadgets for fraud could be suspected), objects moved about inexplicably, 'clouds of light' were sometimes seen, and there were also 'luminous appearances' of sparks, and of 'something like a turkey's egg'.

The paper suggested various ways of explaining such events. (1) Trickery; (2) The delusions of those present at a seance (delusions produced by hypnotic suggestion?); (3) Conscious or unconscious cerebral action – foreshadowing perhaps as his Presidential Address of 1896 did more specifically) the discovery of 'brain waves', not actually confirmed until 1929, and even then – alas for parapsychological theory – found to work on so small a scale that they could not even account for telepathy at a distance; (4) The activities of the spirit of the medium and of those present (an idea which looks ahead to the phenomenon of 'Philip the imaginary Ghost' produced in Canada in our own time by Professor George Owen, a member of the Society); (5) The action of evil spirits; (6) The action of fairies, gnomes and similar entities; (7) The action of the dead and (8) Psychic Force, 'known to Spiritualists as Magnetism', which can be used in connexion with theories 4, 5, 6 and 7. (Why not, one wonders, with theory 3?).

Still odder were Crookes' experiences with Florence Cook, who had been expelled at fifteen from a London school where she was working as a pupil teacher, expelled because in her presence tables and chairs, books and pencils kept moving about without being touched; very distracting for her class, and extremely awkward for her head mistress, who complained that she was 'accused of Spiritualism'.

Crookes reported in seances with her the levitation of people, as well as of objects of various sizes; also 'luminous appearances'; 'percussive sounds', and 'materialized hands' all paralleled by D. D. Home's phenomena. What she is also said to have produced are 'materializations' of her Control, Katie King. This female psycho-pomp, reputedly daughter of the famous 19th century buccaneer Sir Harry Morgan (said to have retired into private life as Henry King) was rather popular among mediums at the time. 'Katie King' resembled Florence Cook, but not in detail; one was taller than the other, one had and the other had not ears pierced for earrings, their pulse rates differed, their hands were differently shaped. Both, however, were solid and warm to the touch. Katie King appeared, clad in white, while her originator, dressed in black, remained tied to a chair in a curtained cabinet. Crookes reported that he had walked arm in arm with Katie; his wife said she had seen her about the house when Florence Cook was staying with them . . .

The promenade surmounts my own boggle threshold; though Richet in 1899 and George Zorab today – both staunch materialists – have accepted it as factual. The latter cites the curious case of a young Swiss schoolmistress seen simultaneously by one set of her pupils in the class room and by another set in the garden, and refers to the widespread folklore tradition of the döppelganger, the double, and the 'fetch'. But all these are surely more closely connected with phantasms of the living than with any solid creature; none of the schoolgirls walked arm in arm with their teacher. I know of no tradition in which anyone dared to handle the 'fetch', and massive hallucinations of the sense of touch are rare. Uncomfortably, one has to suspend judgment.

Crookes has since been accused – on the testimony of one Anderson, who claimed that Florence Cook herself told him so after she had married, become Mrs Corner and lost most of her powers – of having been seduced by this lady, of having continued the seances as a means of keeping the liaison going, and of having subsequently covered up her frauds. 'What the soldier said isn't evidence'; and this story seems inherently unlikely, given Crookes' scientific conscience, his lifelong devotion to his wife (who was fond of the medium) and the fact that there would have been many much easier ways of carrying on an illicit love affair.

Although Crookes finally abandoned parapsychological work in favour of his brilliant scientific studies, he served on the SPR Committee dealing with Physical Phenomena from 1888 to 1890 and invariably maintained that he had 'nothing to retract' even in his Presidential Address to the British Association for the Advancement of Science.

It is interesting that Professor Richet, later President of the SPR, could not accept Crookes' statements until after he had himself observed some events that seemed to correspond with them in the case of Eusapia Paladino, an almost illiterate Italian peasant woman whom he first tested in Milan. She could elongate and levitate herself, set furniture rising and moving about, and produce isolated notes – not tunes – from musical instruments without touching them; all this most frequently in the light of day. (It must have been in dusk or darkness that 'luminosities' could be seen proceeding from her.) She also appeared to grow long protuberances (later, presumably, retracted) which moved about and touched sitters. They sound like the 'arms' of an octopus – and very creepy, too. These were dubbed pseudo-pods. Even after he had seen such things for himself, Richet records that he twice swung back from certainty that they had really happened to an incredulous inability to accept them. (He finally concluded[1] that certainty is a matter of habit as much as scientific proof, and that as 'it flies away with time, we must continue our experiments' as a safeguard against 'neophobia'.)

Experiments were carried on in Milan, in Warsaw, in Rome. Occasionally Eusapia – who functioned in a trance condition – was observed to cheat with a childlike clumsiness (later she was always angry with the experimenters for having allowed it to happen!). More strictly controlled, she produced results that seemed to be entirely paranormal. These were best when she was in a good humour. In the summer of 1894 Richet had a house party at his villa on the tiny Mediterranean island of Rouband, where she could have no confederates, and no apparatus could be rigged up. Myers, Lodge and the Polish researcher Ochorowitz were among the guests invited to study her phenomena; which occurred in full bloom, helped perhaps by the fact that everything was genial and relaxed. Conversation went on in English, French, German and Italian, people were at ease with one another, and Richet was an admirable host, if a little inclined to talk so much that his wife had to remind him to get on with the carving. Later, the Sidgwicks attended tests of her in Paris, and were impressed. In 1895 the very sceptical Richard Hodgson suggested

---

1. 'On Conditions of Certainty', SPR *Proceedings* XIV, 1898–9.

that various esoteric gadgets had been used, and that the 'pseudopods' might be faked by some 'folded umbrella-like object or steel rod attached to the knee'; Ochorowitz, who had been involved in the Warsaw experiment, pointed out that she had been searched, and given special clothes to wear during seances.

That summer the Society asked her to come for seances in Cambridge, where she stayed with Myers and his wife; the latter on one occasion when sitting on the floor holding the medium's feet saw 'projections, like the necks of swans' apparently issuing from her body and nudging people. (The French investigator Jules Bois later compared her to an amoeba, capable of projecting outside itself 'more or less material bodily structures'.) All went well at first; then the Sidgwicks came, accompanied by Richard Hodgson, ever suspicious, ever determined that no one should fool *him*, ever convinced that mediums were all, and at all times, guilty of fraud until they could be proved innocent. To keep Eusapia happy and relaxed, games of croquet were organized (at which she cheated abominably) and when this did not seem to work, Professor Sidgwick was seconded to conduct a decorous Cambridge flirtation with her, as she had been observed to enjoy masculine attentions![1] alas, despite these kind arrangements, the presence of a hostile experimenter had its usual effect, and Eusapia's results were unimpressive.

The experimenters had already been informed that if precautions were relaxed while she was in trance the medium would cheat. They did so; she did so; and instead of tightening up the procedures again – as had previously been done, with interesting results, they decided that 'as systematic fraud had been used' there was no point in continuing the work. The creature they were examining *must* be black or white throughout; no one drew any analogy with the striped zebra or the changing ermine, dark in summer, snowy in winter, and as for the relevance of chameleons . . . Four years later the Society refused to publish the interesting results of some very strictly controlled experiments in France. She had been condemned and that was that. The same held good of some more experiments in Italy during the early 1900s.

However, when Richet was the Society's President in 1905 he

---

1. I was told this by old Mr Salter in November 1962, and wrote it down at the time.

began to work on yet another series of French experiments with Eusapia Paladino. They went on till 1908, were held at the Sorbonne, very carefully controlled, and carried out in full light. With Richet were Henri Bergson (who was also, in 1913, to serve as President), and Pierre and Marie Curie. The results were most interesting. After this the Society sent three men, an expert conjurer named Baggally, Hereward Carrington, an authority on fraud in physical phenomena, and Everard Feilding, who had a reputation for general scepticism, to test her in Naples.

All three seem to have been convinced that on this occasion at any rate the phenomena were genuine. Feilding put it on record that he had seen 'movements of objects such as a table and a letter-balance without any physical contact'; noted 'the tendency of the mind to reject bizarre fact'; and said he was convinced of 'the existence of some force not generally recognized which was able to impress itself on, or create the appearance of matter'.

Whatever their psychosomatic make-up, tall or short, fat or lean, in whatever ways it is affected by heredity, social class, national culture pattern, health, sickness, circumstance and luck, major physical mediums seem to be very rare birds; birds whose powers often decline as time goes by. After a while Paladino became a stout old lady who no longer attracted much attention.

Not until three years after her death in 1920 was any comparable figure discussed – a woman of a quite different, and very English temperament known as 'Stella C'. Quiet, detached and sensible, she was interested by the fact that 'cold breezes' sometimes emanated from her. Discovered by Harry Price as the result of a chance meeting in a train, she agreed to have a series of seances with him in 1923. Among the sitters were Everard Feilding, Lord Charles Hope, W. J. Woolley, then Research Officer of the SPR, and E. J. Dingwall who was to succeed him. She lapsed quickly and quietly into a trance state in which her hands became very cold, her breathing weak. Raps and 'blue flashes' took place, and a table was moved paranormally. A thermometer registered a drop in temperature, and the sitters became aware for themselves of her 'cold breezes'.

The SPR organized sittings with her that autumn. Raps, creakings and blue flashes occurred once more, and a rubber dog was inexplicably thrown across the room. However 'Stella C' found herself so much exhausted by what happened that she refused to be tested again till March 1926, when at a seance attended by Professor Driesch (President that year) more blue flashes were seen, and a sealed-off mouth organ produced musical notes.

Two years later, there was another series of tests observed by Lord Charles Hope, Julian and Juliette Huxley, and Dr E. B. Strauss of St Bartholomew's Hospital. On March 21st Julian Huxley heard raps, and he and Dr Strauss experienced 'a strange feeling up their arms'. A week later Dr Strauss and Lord Charles felt 'cold breezes'. In April Julian Huxley had a cold draught 'blowing up his sleeve'. In June a table was observed to move.

In the end 'Stella C' gave up seances because of their effect on her health. Soon afterwards she married. This may well have diminished her powers. She was intellectually interested in these odd gifts rather than emotionally committed to them or to any overriding interpretation of them. Juliette Huxley, who sat with her husband at seances with many other mediums (some quite certainly bogus) recollects her as eminently cool and sensible; moreover she did not speak of 'controls' or use the idiom of the professional mediums. Incidentally, as there seems to be a general tendency to believe that all observations made in the past are untrustworthy, since one cannot talk to those who made them, may I say that I personally discussed with Professor Huxley and Dr Strauss — both now dead — their experiences with 'Stella C', and checked them, and her own with Lady Huxley in the summer of 1981.

She also told me of two fruitless sittings later on with the famous Rudi Schneider, whose hand she held on one occasion. She remembered particularly vividly the way he panted, like a dog in a car in a traffic jam. He began directly they sat down, and continued throughout the proceedings in an attempt, she thought, to 'wind himself up' into a state in which phenomena would occur. But none took place when she was there.

This 'overbreathing', once well known to naughty schoolgirls who wanted to enliven the morning assembly by fainting, probably did bring him into the trance state in which his powers were often released. Interestingly enough, it did not stop there; he could and did sometimes go on panting for two or three hours without getting exhausted. Moreover it was sometimes synchronized with the working of the oddest gift of all, that of obscuring a beam of infra-red light (which could be used in a dark seance room) to guard some object against being touched in any normal way, so that if it did move psychokinesis seemed to be the only possible explanation. The beam *was* repeatedly obstructed, as if something were trying to reach the object (though it was not often moved); and later a quick galvanometer was used to record what happened during the process itself. It was found that the obscuration of the beam was somehow synchronized with Rudi's panting. To breathe in and to breathe out 'each involved a muscular effort, and the number of obscurations of the infra-red corresponded with the number of muscular efforts', wrote Lord Rayleigh[1] of the experiments recorded by Messrs Osty in *Les Pouvoirs Inconnus de L'Esprit sur la Matiére*, (Paris, 1932.) Later a highly technical doubt as to 'resonance' was put forward. Rudi himself is said to have made remarks 'as to the movements, position and quality of what he called "the force" ' which were often justified.[2] Was 'the force' what had been described – and sometimes visualized – by earlier experimenters in terms of 'invisible cantilevers' and of 'pseudopods'?

Rudi Schneider was the youngest of six Austrian brothers, survivors of a family of twelve. They came from Braunau am Inn, a valley in the mountains next to the one where Adolf Hitler was born and reared. Rudi's elder brother Willy was the first to show psychic phenomena, and as early as 1922 Dr Dingwall sat with him in Munich; but he did not come to England till 1924, by which time, this distinguished researcher remarked,[3] his powers had weakened. (They faded out completely after his marriage in 1926.) Willy – or his rather bossy Control 'Olga', who also claimed to have been Lola Montez – found noise and music helpful in getting him going. It is worth remembering that many Spiritualist seances in Victorian times were begun in this way, and that similar means were found useful in the experimental work of Batcheldor, Brookes Smith and Owen, to be discussed later. Like Rudi, Willy employed rapid breathing. Like 'Stella C' he produced 'cool breezes' (though oddly enough these were not considered important). A tinkling tambourine was seen to move about, as were handkerchiefs and strips of luminous

---

1. In his Presidential address 1937, SPR *Proceedings* 152, 1938.

2. M. Osty's Myers Memorial Lecture, rather incomprehensibly translated from the French. SPR, 1933.

3. E. J. Dingwall: 'Twelve sittings with Willy Schneider', SPR *Proceedings* 36, 1928.

cardboard; but the oddest thing observed was the repeated levitation of a luminous ring, which 'hovered in the air like a snowflake'. One of those who saw it was an experienced conjuror, a member of the Magic Circle (an equivalent among his profession say of the Royal Society among scientists) who could not suggest any normal way in which this could have been done, given the careful precautions observed. (He did suggest ordinary explanations of some of the other happenings, as that someone could have made the tambourine tinkle by blowing at it.)

It was shortly after the sixteen-year-old Willy's gifts had been discovered that 'Olga' decreed that his brother Rudi, then eleven, shared them and must participate in seances: and the boy is said to have come sleepwalking down from his bed to join the home sitting seance. In the end of course he attracted more attention than his elder. Though American and British researchers, including W. F. Prince and Everard Feilding (who distrusted the father of the family) worked with him abroad, he did not visit England till 1929, when Harry Price invited him to come over for tests at the National Laboratory for Psychical Research, which he had founded three years before. Here Rudi, panting away, produced sounds from untouched bells, the movements of various objects, the billowing of curtains and again 'cold breezes', observed by Lord Charles Hope and the philosopher C. E. M. Joad.

Price later made a contract with Rudi for a further series of sittings from February to May 1929; but was very angry when he found out that Lord Charles had arranged to have an independent series of his own (carried out with the physicist Rayleigh) after that contract had run out. He went on working with Rudi, but privately informed two people (previously, and most unfairly, sworn to silence about what he was going to say) that he had caught him cheating. For many months he warned no one else, least of all Hope and Rayleigh, and allowed it to be thought publicly that he had no doubt of the medium's integrity. A year after the new series had begun, however, he took his revenge – and did himself no good – by publishing an article in the *Sunday Despatch* stating that he had found Rudi to be fraudulent, and that he could prove this by 'incriminating photographs'. Anita Gregory, who had investigated the case during her time as a Perrott Warrick Student, published in *Annals of Science* (34, 1977) a paper entitled 'The Anatomy of a Fraud' – the part of her thesis which dealt with this episode. She believed Price had deliberately faked the photographs. Alan Gauld, who discussed in the SPR *Journal* (June 1978) that issue of the Annals did not agree, but thought that in any case the photographs did not necessarily support Price's allegations, but could be interpreted in other ways. Whichever hypothesis is true, the latter plainly had no conception of the responsibilty a research worker owes his colleagues.

Rudi continued to collaborate with other investigators, and his reputation remained so high that the detached and critical Dr Donald West (then Research Officer to the Society – he served as President 1963–5) was able to maintain in the *Journal* for January 1948 that 'the mediums with the best claim to produce PK phenomena had been able to withstand all kinds of tests, notably Rudi Schneider'.

This was after the failure of any medium to win the prize of £250 offered by the Society between May and the end of December 1947 for someone able and willing to demonstrate supernormal physical phenomena under test conditions. This well advertised offer gained little response. Mrs Duncan, who will be discussed later, said she would not sit with the SPR 'for a million'. Some of those who seemed attracted withdrew. Those who stayed the course did not produce anything significant.

(ii) From Guru to Guinea-pig

A later offer of £1,000 was withdrawn; and after this, investigations took on a much more technological flavour, neatly symbolized by a change of label. Those formerly known as 'physical mediums' came to be called 'PK subjects'. PK of course stands for psychokinesis (and RSPK for recurrent spontaneous psychokinesis – which should serve to refrigerate poltergeist outbreaks if anything can).

Words – and even more, acronyms – are often used as forceps to pick up facts without touching them, feeling them, or attempting to fit them into any general framework of meaning. The question asked about them will be not why they happen but how; not what they imply as to the nature of things but what is the chain of physical causation that brings them about; not their significance but their mechanism.

This modification of the assumptions of psychical research workers – many members of the Society among them – was perhaps most marked after the publication of Dr Rhine's fascinating large scale card experiments in the 1930s. It probably sprang in part from the need to prove to minds conditioned by a training exclusively in scientific method that the subject being investigated did indeed exist, and was not simply a by-product of that belief in spirits which had so long been put forward to explain it.

The new approach may well have been necessary (though most of its supporters did not realize that those they sought to convince would spring to defend their threatened boggle thresholds by accusations of gullibility, negligence and fraud). But it gives only half the picture. One might just as well try to account for Blake's paintings by studying the mechanisms of sight and the compositions of the pigments he used. It is however powerful and all-pervading; it carries the odour of disinfectant respectability, a reassuring whiff of Lysol. Though the Behaviourists' refusal even to consider the existence of consciousness has faded a little, the study of the moods in which people become aware of psi in any of its forms has become largely physiological, concerned primarily to record the variations in brain electricity which accompany this awareness, rather than with what emerges, or why or whence it comes. The electro-encephalographic patterns of persons engaged in meditation are considered infinitely more important than the subjects they are meditating about and the flashes of insight that may come through. Indeed meditation itself is sometimes equated with no more than a successful attempt to clear the mind of thought, logical or associative; an attempt which brings about some psychophysical state rather like hibernation in hedgehogs. This state, which is said to ease tension and lower blood pressure, may well conduce to bodily well-being and mental efficiency, but is totally irrelevant to human concerns with meaning, ethics, choice and behaviour. One remembers here

Arthur Koestler's[1] study of the Nazi officer who found his exercises in Zen meditation gave him greater lucidity and energy with which to organize and carry out the extermination of Jews in horror, squalor, torment and despair.

This kind of meditation is in fact a means which can be used to yield power for any end. Despite the odour of incense – or joss sticks – still associated with the word, it retains no more religious connotation than the Ganzfeld technique[2] now often and so fruitfully used in experiments with paranormal cognition. Here the human guinea pig lies completely relaxed at a comfortable temperature. Each eye is protected against light by half a ping-pong ball and a gentle incessant waterfall of 'white noise' occupies his hearing. In this well organized isolation from every stimulus of the outer world he should be more liable to perceive what goes on within him, whether it be the shrill arpeggios of his own indigestion, the flux of his own thoughts, or, possibly, incoming ideas, images, messages transmitted by way of psi, whatever it is, however it works, or wherever it comes from. It is worth mentioning that conditions like these may make it easier to yield to hypnotic suggestion and that hypnotic suggestion by way of telepathy may well be possible, judging by some of the late 19th century experiments which so much interested Myers, and by the more recent work of L. L. Vasilieff[3] and others in the USSR.

In a way this technique of instant protection against the impact of messages brought in by the senses is a carpentered version of the attempts made by contemplatives in all religions to detach themselves from the world so that, no longer distracted by such interruptions they may become more and more fully aware of the Presence of God. Theirs is a very much more difficult process, demanding a continual exercise both of the active will and of passive receptivity. Morover, of course, where the Ganzfeld guinea pig is on the look out for extra-sensory perceptions of all sorts the contemplative rejects those which have no connexion with his main purpose. It could be that by the time he is given some flash of its fruition he will have become a person more capable of co-operating with that sudden glory; just as

---

1. Arthur Koestler, *Drinkers of Infinity*, London, 1968.
2. Carl Sargent, *Exploring Psi in the Ganzfeld*, New York, 1980.
3. Cf L. L. Vasilieff, *Mental Suggestion*, Galley Hill Press, Hants, 1963.

the Mexican *curandera* who went through long rituals of dedication before taking mescalin was not knocked out by the numinous current of phantasmagoria that swept away so many consumers of 'five drops of instant Zen on a sugar-lump'.

Of course it must be recognized that though there are people who cannot stand Ganzfeld conditions for very long (finding them alarming, perhaps, as families evacuated from noisy cities during the war found the silence of the countryside) it is plainly not so risky as the chemical means sometimes used on perfectly sane volunteers in the 1950s in an attempt to discover the cause of schizophrenia (and just possibly, as a byproduct, to shed light on extra sensory perception, which does sometimes seem to occur spontaneously in this connexion,[1] even though Zener card experiments with sufferers have yielded no result). Some of these volunteers were members of the SPR; Rosalind Heywood gave a fascinating account of her own experience in *The Infinite Hive*.[2]

Neither meditation, nor psychedelic drugs, nor sensory shielding – except for variations of light – was used by those who took part in a series of PK experiments recorded by K. J. Batcheldor in the SPR *Journal* for September 1966. His article, 'Report on a case of Table Levitation and Associated Phenomena', was concerned less with scientific proof that psychokinesis existed than with showing its results, and how they were obtained. He acknowledged that the experiments he was describing would not convince any careful sceptic on the look-out for fraud, and only asked readers to suspend disbelief enough to try something of the sort for themselves.

His group consisted primarily of three old friends interested in the subject, who knew and trusted one another. He was himself a Principal Clinical Psychologist, the other two were a Miss Coghlan, a nurse, and a Mr Chick, proprietor of a guest house. None was a Spiritualist, none went into a trance, none claimed to be 'mediumistic'; though Mr Chick was present at 70 out of the 80 fruitful experiments (out of 200), he had no success when sitting alone. They sat together at regular intervals between April 1964 and September 1965, their hands resting on the top of a succession of tables whose corners were touched with luminous paint and whose

---

1. Cf Laurence Bendit, *Paranormal Cognition*, London, 1934.
2. London, 1964.

weights ranged between two pounds and forty pounds. They had
expected to produce and to study the well known occurrence of
movements resulting from unconscious muscular action, described
by Faraday over a century before.

The first events at a sitting tended to be raps, scraping noises or
soft thuds. Then the table could begin to slide about, to tilt and to
rock; all occurrences that might have arisen from that cause. At the
eleventh sitting though, the table rose from the floor – an effect that
could hardly have been produced by hands pressing on the top of it.
After that, a table was used which had been equipped with electrical
apparatus that would signal whenever all four legs left the floor at
once; and at the next, the twelfth sitting, there were livelier
movements than ever. The table shook, tilted, danced, levitated
chest high, remaining there for eight seconds, and then floated across
the room. There were many other incidents of this kind.

It should be noted that no music, and no religious or scientific
silence was used to bring about a suitable atmosphere, and that
people were free to talk and comment throughout; and did.

In the *Journal* for June 1970 Colin Brookes Smith and D. W.
Hunt followed up this report – and referred to some unpublished
papers by Mr Batcheldor – in an article describing two lots of
experiments they had made in 1968 and 1969, founded on his
published and unpublished work. (It must have been in the latter
that he suggested 'a wide range of paranormal phenomena may be
produced experimentally without any "physical medium" '; in his
published paper Mr Chick was plainly the chief generator – and/or
releaser – of power.) The main argument was however that PK was
'a psychological skill that could be acquired by most people', given
aptitude, experience, expectancy of success, and absence of scepticism
(and probably of detachment too; they had to be committed to the
dance rather than lookers on).

The four people concerned were an electronics engineer, a
secretary, a photographer and a dentist. They functioned in full light,
under remote photographic control, used extremely sophisticated
apparatus, and, having 'by-passed the inhibition barrier' they too
obtained – and were mechanically recorded as obtaining – knockings,
rappings and movements and ultimately levitations of their ingeniously and elaborately fraud-proofed table.

The general principles underlying their work were extended in the fascinating experiment mentioned earlier, which was carried out in Toronto, with members of the local psychical research society, by Dr A. R. G. Owen, a geneticist Fellow of Trinity College, Cambridge, and a very distinguished SPR member, who had been interested in psychical research by his senior colleague Professor Broad, and who had later studied the case of little Virginia Campbell at Sauchie.[1] They invented in 1972 an imaginary 17th century Cavalier called Philip, worked out his biography in considerable detail, and once a week for a year sat round a large ordinary table, meditating about him, with little result. In 1973 they adopted the British tactics, talked, laughed, relaxed; and when raps began to sound obtained 'messages' from 'Philip' through them, 'messages' clear and definite so long as they fitted in with the myth they had made. Something or somebody jibbed, however, when a questioner described Rupert of the Rhine as the brother of Elizabeth of Bohemia. Which of those jolly Canadian housewives who were finally filmed at work – or play – had long ago read that he was Elizabeth's son, and had managed telepathically to inject some doubt into the signals conveyed by the communal force?

Once that force has been shown to exist, research is back again with the main questions. How does it work, and in what setting? What does it convey, and whence? Above all, what does it imply?

To the first, there is so far no overall answer. There have been, and there are many attempts to record, under laboratory conditions, its manifestations in different fields, and to interpret them in relation to various scientific disciplines; the search continues – with a certain amount of acrimony among those who pursue it – but the end is not yet, though fascinating sidelights continue to come in, like the observation that the bangs tape-recorded in poltergeist outbreaks seem to differ from normal bangs recorded for comparison. The normal ones begin sharply and fade out in a series of diminishing vibrations. The paranormal ones build up, with increasing vibrations in a crescendo leading to an especially loud noise and only then fade out. It seems quite certainly to have some connexion with electro-magnetic activity; but what sets this going remains as mysterious as the stimulus recorded by the plethysmograph[2] – a device for recording

---

1. Cf Chapter Seven.
2. Cf *Journal* Vol 44, 731, March, 1967.

small changes in blood pressure. In these experiments a plastic 'finger cup', connected to a self-recording cardiac dynamometer was fitted to the left finger tip of each volunteer, to whom an agent at a distance tried to transmit names which might evoke some emotional reaction. The timing was recorded at both places, and it was found that the plethysmograph did indeed show significantly often that emotionally charged names coincided with blood pressure changes, though the volunteers themselves were unconscious of the fact.

It seems most unlikely that what happened could have come about through purely physical causes; to my mind at any rate it looks as if the stimulus had been to the psyche and had led straight to a psychosomatic reaction without ever rising into the conscious mind (as the smell of a rose associated with some deep shock can set off a bout of asthma. It is the shock, not the rose, that is at work.)

The setting of psychokinesis remains more mysterious still. Just possibly it can only be formulated in terms of quantum theory and of the new physics, terms that can hardly be translated from the language of mathematics into the language of words, if one can judge from suggestions such as that time runs backward from effect to cause; which does not happen in life as humans experience it, however true it may be of the infinitesimal units of energy studied by physicists. Perhaps to make the comparison at all is to miss the point, as with the in-joke of mediaeval philosophers who asked how many angels could dance on the point of a needle. (Angels were conceived to be incorporeal and intangible; they occupied no more space than the square root of minus one.)

To the question of what do PK phenomena convey there are many possible answers. It could be a profound relief of tension, in that its raw manifestations may demonstrate the conflicts, frustrations, agonies of the psyche just as infant tantrums do, and just as did the heels of hysterical ladies drumming on the floor in Victorian days when the word hysteria carried no moral stigma, and these activities were thought interesting rather than reprehensible. At a slightly more sophisticated level it looks as if it could be directed into other channels. Matthew Manning (of whom more later) found out how to divert much of the force that first exploded as poltergeist activity into automatic writing and drawing.[1] And in communal experiments

---

1. Matthew Manning, *The Link*, London, 1974.

it may emerge in some symbolic way, so that tappings and creakings sometimes arrange themselves into codified messages; or the movements of objects, and the appearance of unexplained lights may seem somehow to be integrated, like the ritual gestures of ballet. Earlier phenomena may relate to later ones as a child's first scribblings with a pencil do to graffiti on a wall, or later still to writing poetry.

Where do the codified messages or the significant gestures – where indeed does the whole storm – come from? Pretty certainly from the unconscious mind of one, or more, or all of those present at an experiment or at a spontaneous explosion. But what is the stimulus that sets the unconscious mind going? There is a wide choice of answers, none of them official, or likely to be. Thus the veteran George Zorab, a Dutch member of the Society ascribes *all* psychokinetic disturbances to unknown physiological powers released by the unconscious mind of someone intolerably irked by frustration in general, and the sexual frustrations of adolescence in particular. (He also tends to interpret hauntings of all kinds in accordance with this reductionist formula.) Others suggest that certain places contain something analogous to tape recordings of some unbearable emotion, which, picked up by sensitives, can spark off poltergeist phenomena from them. Yet others think it possible that such sensitives, telepathically aware of stress in others can discharge it as it were by proxy, as seems to have happened with the Curé d'Ars, in whose presbytery some quite terrifying outbreaks used to occur – and were witnessed by many of his neighbours – the night *before* some particularly agonized penitent came to his confessional. Perhaps it should be said that these penitents came from all parts of France, so he had no normal local knowledge about them; the enterprising French railways of the time ran excursion trains for them. What looks like a small-scale modern instance of proxy PK is the case investigated by Professor Archie Roy[1] in which a boy sensitive seems to have discharged the tensions of a neighbouring family in this way.

The advent of Uri Geller in the early 1970s opened up a new approach to psychokinesis. This handsome Israeli displayed both in private and to large audiences in the flesh and still larger ones on television, apparently extraordinary powers of affecting metal

---

1. Described in a lecture delivered to the Society in March 1980.

objects. Spoons, forks, keys, were seen to be bent or twisted either without touch or by gentle stroking. This sometimes happened in the capricious way characteristic of poltergeist outbreaks; so that, for instance, objects presented to him on stage might not be affected, but keys on a ring in the owner's pocket were later found to be distorted; in fact *trying* to carry out some feat did not always work, whereas he sometimes produced unintentional effects. Another odd thing that happened was that some watches belonging to his hearers seemed to stop; and others that had already stopped, began going.

Geller was much distrusted because he was a showman, and many attempts were made to explain what he did as ingenious conjuring tricks. His compatriot, H. C. Berendt, a member of the SPR and Chairman of the Israeli Parapsychology Society contributed to the *Journal* for December 1974 a fascinating assessment of his character and achievements, giving the impression that like many others before him he may well have used trickery when his psychokinetic powers were under par. On the other hand, carefully studied evidence did for a time convince Dr John Taylor that something paranormal was involved (though later he turned away from the whole field of psychical research).

Geller was, unfortunately for himself, further devalued in many people's minds by the attempts of an American physicist to involve him in the wilder fantasies of 'ufology' (a word invented from UFO, an acronym for unidentified flying object). It may have been good for publicity to suggest that he had been taken for trips in flying saucers by benevolent celestial beings anxious to murmur moral platitudes in his ear for the benefit of humanity at large; but it was not the kind of thing to prove an encouragement to serious research.

But if the first impact of Geller's performances diminished after a while, its secondary effects expanded to attract ever increasing attention; and still do.

To begin with the effect on his audiences; to see him on television apparently doing inexplicable things seemed to release among some of the spectators powers akin to his own. Reports kept coming in that in the homes of some viewers clocks and watches that had not gone for years began merrily ticking, and continued to do so. (The possibility that time-pieces can react to human sensations is suggested by the widespread tradition expressed in the works of the old song –

> And the clock stopped, never to go again
> When the old man died

maybe because the shock of his death set some PK process going among the bereaved – especially in English-speaking cultures where the cult of the stiff upper lip forbids tears, fainting or the discharge of emotion in ritual mourning.)

Equally surprising, and much easier to test were tales of children who, uninhibited by any preconceived ideas of what was or was not possible, had experimented on their own with the family cutlery, sometimes with shattering success.

Several people in this country have carefully investigated such children in their own laboratories, notably Professor Arthur Ellison (President of the SPR 1976–9 and 1981–2), Head of the Department of Electricity and Electronics at the City University, and Professor John Hasted, Head of the Physics Department at Birkbeck College, London University, another distinguished member of the Society. After discussing various aspects of his work in the *Journal* and at more than one SPR Conference Professor Hasted produced in 1981 the first full length study of the subject in his book *The Metal Benders*. This general survey details much of his own work over the years. He enumerates his precautions against cheating and fraud (a few of which have been attacked by critics as insufficient); and sets out clearly some of the technical methods involved in his researches, including the use of videotape recordings, the electron microscope, and sensors of various kinds. He discusses the problem of what actually happens to the distorted, softened or broken metal objects: the fact that psychokinetic 'quasi-forces' can play a part in deflecting compass needles as well as in metal bending; and the difficulty of using the concept of electro-magnetism to explain telepathy. A fascinating chapter deals with some startling events experienced in the author's own house when Geller was his guest; and another examines the idea that certain inexplicable movements of objects, and their sudden disappearance and re-appearance, may be interpreted as the result of 'many universes' impinging on one another. These are 'material' in as much as they can be envisaged by physicists; and minds, seen as 'transtemporal – and transspatial' can move about in them, and presumably perceive simultaneously what goes on in more than one. Difficult, but perhaps rewarding to brood over. It looks as if we may indeed, quite literally be moving about in worlds not realized – worlds brimming with meaning.

Professor Hasted, who has himself observed metal benders from France and Japan, is well aware of another secondary effect of Geller's performances – which has been to make the study of psychokinesis scientifically *fashionable* for the first time since the Industrial Revolution. (Crookes' important work swam against the whole stream of thought in his time.) By the beginning of the 1980s the subject was under investigation not only in Britain and the United States but also in Australia – whence D. C. Scutt, of the Caulfield Institute of Technology contributed an account of his work to the *Journal* of February 1981 – Belgium, Canada, China, Denmark, France, Germany, Israel, Italy and probably the USSR. Psychokinesis might, of course, have military implications, but there would be enormous difficulties in putting it to large-scale practical use, notably because the power to produce PK is fairly rare, because it tends to flare and fade from time to time in the individuals who do possess it, because its manifestations are gusty, capricious, and inexact, and because the law of reversed effort seems to apply to attempts to produce it to order – in fact the more you *try* to do it the less happens, at any rate in the desired direction.

Nevertheless, mixed feelings may be aroused by the suggestion made a year or two ago by Julian Isaacs, one of the liveliest of the younger SPR parapsychologists, that people should be tested for this faculty and that those in whom it is found should be deliberately trained to develop it further. All very well in the interests of science perhaps; but traditional legends of witchcraft and black magic sound very much as if some form of psychokinesis may already have been developed and used. Like any other human faculty it could be employed for good or evil purposes. And what about the legend of the Sorcerer's Apprentice, who let it loose but could not control it?

It is reassuring that Matthew Manning, one of the most remarkable physical mediums of our own day, has said firmly that he will never exercise his power in any way even remotely connected with military interests or with espionage. This young man was early investigated by Dr A. R. G. Owen, who has already been mentioned.

Poltergeist activity began to erupt around Matthew in February 1967 when he was a boy of 11 worrying about his Common Entrance examination; there were the usual strange noises, and the usual inexplicable movements of objects – a tankard, a vase, chairs – frightening and exhausting to live with. Dr Owen reassured the family that the house was not 'haunted' in the usual sense, and predicted that the phenomena would fade out after a while; as they did indeed soon after Easter. But they recurred (after a few minor manifestations) very vividly indeed four years later, during the April holidays when the boy was growing anxious about his O-level examinations. They continued after he got back to school and produced alarming upheavals until the end of May when they began to decline.

Dr Owen was by then in Toronto as Professor of Genetics and as Director of the New Horizons Research Association, but remained in touch with the Mannings, and wrote to the Headmaster of the school discussing the trouble and stressing the point that poltergeist events were not necessarily 'supernatural' but 'due to unusual physical forces sometimes developed by people unaware of them'.

Three years later he invited Matthew, by now 18 years old, to Toronto to be studied at a seminar on psychokinesis attended by 21 scientists from various parts of the world, among them Professor Brian Josephson, FRS, Britain's young Nobel Prize winner in physics, who proved particularly open-minded to new, unexplained facts. Uri Geller's feats had by then aroused interest in metal bending, and Matthew was asked to try it; he found he could do so, but was bored by what seemed to be a pointless exercise. However, during experiments with this, a curious new variation was found in the pattern of brain waves recorded in him by an electroencephalograph. Just *before* the metal object – key, spoon, fork, whatever it might be – was distorted the machine traced a movement towards the theta and delta frequencies. The slope outlined looked exactly like a ramp, so the phenomenon was called the ramp effect. One may connect this with Professor Grey Walter's remark[1] that 'there is objective evidence that spontaneous impulses' (of thought) 'to explore are *preceded* (my italics) and accompanied by electric events'. It was later discovered that Matthew was able to produce a similar ramp effect in the e.e.g.

---

1. W. Grey Walter: *Twenty-third Eddington Memorial Lecture*, Cambridge, 1969.

of a person holding his hand; one such person was the President of Toronto University. This may perhaps be compared to the process[1] by which a dowser, touching with two fingers the wrist of an experimenter may cause the latter's muscles unconsciously to twitch the rod when passing over a hidden underground stream a minute or two later.

Since the Toronto seminar, Matthew Manning has been subjected to all sorts of further investigation, and has appeared on television channels as far afield as Japan, but has experienced considerable disappointment because, though his strange abilities have so often been demonstrated, checked, repeated and verified, so few of the investigators have publicly discussed their data or put forward theories to interpret them. He has in fact come up against the boggle threshold that defends so many careful people against the shattering impact of the incomprehensible.

It must be extremely galling to feel one is regarded as a guinea pig, passive for scientists or actively performing for the television screen; and to conclude that a great deal of hard work has had very little result. Neither feeling is well founded, however. Reports are slowly crystallizing. Thus, the Society's *Journal* for December 1979 published two accounts of American experiments with Manning. One, by Charles T. Tart and John Palmer gave details of tests with coin-spinning, with aura detection and with a machine; the last of these was found extremely frustrating. The other paper, by William Braud, Gary Davis and Robert Wood, dealt with 'psychokinetic influences upon biological systems', i.e. living creatures, among them gerbils and a species of fish that emits electrical signals. This series was a good deal more fruitful, and may well have played some part in forming Manning's decision to devote his powers to healing.

Moreover, the impact of much of his work – and that of others – has been indirect, like that of heavy rain seeping through various channels to form a flood and psychokinesis has become over the last few years one of the most popular of all subjects for psychical research – partly perhaps because it does not necessarily involve so many metaphysical problems (as to the nature of human consciousness, for instance, or the concept of time) as other forms

---

1. Personal experience.

of psi. The primary questions asked are: does this power exist, can it be *proved* – as well as observed – to exist, and if so, how does it work?

The answers vary widely. Some depend on the belief that the pure milk of research ought to be not just pasteurized but sterilized so as to be uncontaminated by any nasty living germs that might generate new ideas. Others are bolder and risk both development from within and attack from without; their work will be discussed in a later chapter.

9

Fact, Fraud and
Furor Scholasticus

In every branch of learning there are both rivalries and perfectly legitimate different interpretations of fact, often advocated with passionate conviction. Hence suspicions germinate and grow; that Mr Smith or Mr Jones must be at least very stupid not to agree with Mr Jones or Mr Smith; that his methods of research are probably slipshod, inaccurate, inefficient and misleading; that he cannot have checked his references or his mathematics; that he *must* have invented his sources or fudged his experiments; and, at last, that deliberate fraud must have been used.

Sometimes of course such suspicions are amply justified, as when the 18th century Thomas Chatterton's pseudo-mediaeval poems were found to have been written by a living boy, who thought no one would notice them if they were signed by his own name (nowadays he might well claim that he had remembered them from a previous incarnation). Sometimes they can be disproved and forgotten. More often a maddening tangle of truth, falsehood, misapprehension and ill-feeling is involved. This tangle is usually very hard to unravel.

For obvious reasons, psychical research is a particularly good breeding ground for such suspicions. Its subject matter tends to raise the hackles – and lower the boggle thresholds – of minds conditioned to assume that nothing is real which cannot instantly be weighed, measured and computed. Fraud has definitely been shown to play some part in producing this or that 'psychic' manifestation; and of course we all know what the 'will to believe' can do.

The 'will to disbelieve', less widely recognized, is equally important; and the interplay between the two tends to be violent, especially when complicated by different codes of honour, different standards of professional behaviour, different points of view, almost different patterns of culture among those involved. (As an instance of this last, in a very different context, contrast the man agonized with grief who knows he *must* not cry with Stanley Holloway's sorrowful funeral-goer shocked to the core because the chief mourner is wearing Brown Boots.)

In this chapter I shall set out a few large-scale examples of such violent interplay, in which the Society has been involved from time to time. In one or two it is plain that the will to disbelieve was largely justified, in others that it was not; in all the clash of viewpoints echoes loudly.

I shall not deal in detail with cases that took place before the Society was founded. There is no room to do so. One ought perhaps to mention D. D. Home again. He was never discovered cheating, despite all the virulent feelings he aroused, despite Robert Browning's ferocious poem about him as *Mr Sludge the Medium*, and despite all the ingenious attempts made down the decades to explain some of his phenomena; attempts that ranged from a suggestion that he faked levitation by placing boots on his hands and putting them in a dim light on the seance table while arranging for his voice to be relayed somehow from the ceiling, to Guy Lambert's argument that, before coming to London, he managed to discover which houses were built over underground rivers or sewers, and carefully arranged to hold seances in them, presumably after periods of heavy rainfall or during spring tides.

The first highly controversial case recorded after the Society had been founded was the investigation of some early claims made by the Theosophical movement in the 1880s. This movement had been founded by the Russian Madame Blavatsky and the American Colonel Olcott in 1875. Their headquarters had been moved to Bombay in 1878, and they had settled at Adhyar in Madras in 1882. Here a Shrine had been set up.

Their teachings echoed those of the mysterious East; the first English book concerned with them was A. P. Sinnett's *The Occult World*, the second a study of *Esoteric Buddhism*. In the summer of 1884 Madame Blavatsky, Colonel Olcott and a Brahmin adherent, a Mr M. M. Chatterji, came to England and met Henry Sidgwick, who was sufficiently impressed by them to set up a Committee to look into the phenomena they claimed to have observed and produced. The Committee included – as well as his wife and himself – Gurney, Richard Hodgson, Myers and Podmore.

Theosophists took the Hindu tenet of reincarnation for granted. They also held at that time that there existed in Tibet a Great White Brotherhood with various paranormal powers. They were called Adepts or Mahatmas, and Madame Blavatsky was a *chela* (disciple) of theirs. One of them particularly interested in the new movement was called Koot Humi, another was named Morya.

These Mahatmas had learned – and could teach their disciples – a number of strange skills. One was that of producing phantasms of themselves, so-called 'astral forms' which could not only visit distant places but talk to people there. The Committee noted the likeness between this phenomenon, and the instances of 'phantasms of the living' and of 'alleged voluntary apparitions' already reported to the SPR in this country. There was also a resemblance between the ability claimed on behalf of the Mahatmas 'to evoke sound without physical means' and the occasional veridical hallucinations of voices also known here; sometimes in connexion with crises, more rarely as the result of deliberate experiment.[1]

Other powers ascribed to the Mahatmas and their pupils were that of 'the transportation, even through solid matter, of ponderable objects, including letters' . . . and the 'precipitation' of handwriting and drawings on to previously blank paper. To these activities no parallel had been found.

A preliminary report was compiled and issued confidentially to all members and associates of the SPR; and Council decided the matter warranted sending Richard Hodgson to India for three months to investigate. He sailed in November 1884 – the voyage took some weeks – and returned the following May. Part of his task in the end was to try to establish the facts about some letters allegedly sent by Madame Blavatsky and 'Koot Humi' to a Monsieur and Madame Coulomb who ran the Shrine at Adhyar, letters which implied a conspiracy to deceive the public. In the summer of 1884 (while the leaders were in England) this couple had been expelled from the Theosophist Society in India, for 'speaking ill of' it. Some of the letters were printed in the September/October number of the Madras

---

1. See chapter 3 for a first-hand instance.

Christian College magazine, and Madame Coulomb personally produced a pamphlet on the subject, describing apertures in the ceilings of the building through which mysterious messages would flutter down, and a panel that opened at the back of the Shrine itself and could be used for the same purpose. Madame Blavatsky hotly, volubly and repeatedly denied any fraud. The couple were said to be lying.

Hodgson had set out for India with what he called 'a prejudice in favour of Theosophy'; but this disappeared, possibly because his Anglo-Saxon culture pattern was outraged by a display of 'temperament' normal among Slavs at that time, as in prima donnas at all periods. His investigations, however, were careful and objective; and he concluded after much discussion of the likeness in style, spelling and handwriting (as to which experts were consulted) that Madame Blavatsky, not Koot Humi, had written the letters attributed to this great Mahatma.

Although Hodgson finally decided that he could not himself find enough evidence to substantiate that 'occult phenomena' had occurred in connexion with the Theosophical Society, his Report[1] duly quoted the more moderate remarks of a distinguished Civil Servant, A. O. Hume, once an ardent Theosophist, who concluded that though there had been frauds, there had also been some genuinely paranormal events, and that Koot Humi was 'a real entity but by no means the powerful and godlike being he has been painted, and that he has had some share directly in the letters'. (It is possible to speculate, at this distance of time, as to whether he was a secondary personality of Madame Blavatsky's, an over life-size version of Imperator or Phinuit; this would explain a great deal.)

Perhaps the most illuminating episode of the whole affair is concerned with a Mr Massey, who had wanted to have definite proof of the existence of Adepts in general. In connexion with this he was shown a missive from Madame Blavatsky to a (non-professional) medium of his acquaintance, whose name is only given as Mr X. Mr X had a 'control' equally anonymously called Z. This missive asked Mr X to get Z 'to take the enclosed letter and put it in M's pocket or in some still more mysterious place. But he must not know that it was Z' [who did it] as 'he distrusts Z'. Taxed with this, Madame

---

1. *Proceedings* Vol III, 1885.

Blavatsky said she had 'not intended to deceive or impose upon Mr Massey (!)' and added, 'That I saw nothing in it then . . . as now, of so dreadful, is only a proof . . . that our notions of the honourable and the dishonourable differ'. She never spoke a truer word as to this situation (and hundreds more. The trouble about pious fraud is that it sows general distrust).

The Society has several times been pressed to withdraw this Report, but has throughout replied that it has no collective opinions, and can neither endorse nor deny those presented. They rest as evidence from which the reader may form his own judgment.

The second tangled case, that of Mrs Duncan, is on a very much smaller scale (psychologically, not physically; she is described as a large ungainly woman). She wanted to make a living, and to be admired, rather than raise the standard of a new cult. Born in Scotland in 1898, she married a cabinet-maker (who later served as her impresario) by whom she had a large family. Her phenomena included the production of 'ectoplasm', which sometimes formed materializations of the dead (duly recognized by her sitters). Her method was to enter a small cabinet, go into trance, and get taken over by her Control, Albert Smith. The London Spiritualist Alliance had fifty sittings with her between October 1930 and June 1931; for these sittings she was stripped, searched and dressed in 'seance garments'. Two interim reports in *Light* were favourable, a third found indications of fraud.

Pieces of 'ectoplasm' found from time to time differed in composition. Two early specimens consisted of paper or cloth mixed with something like white of egg. Two others were pads of surgical gauze soaked in 'a resinous fluid'; yet another consisted of layers of lavatory paper stuck together. The most usual material for 'ectoplasm' however, seemed to be butter muslin or cheesecloth, probably swallowed and regurgitated. Distressing choking noises were sometimes heard from within the cabinet; and it was interesting that when she was persuaded to swallow a tablet of methylene blue before one of the seances at the London Spiritualist Alliance, no ectoplasm whatsoever appeared.

An investigation by Harry Price and other members of the Society for Psychical Research, to which he belonged at the time, showed that she certainly did use cheesecloth on occasion; flashlight photographs of her 'ectoplasm' clearly showed the weave, the selvedge marks, and even one or two tears (had it been thriftily used again and again?). After this exposure she was still backed by passionate admirers; among them, probably, those who had 'recognized' their dead relations among the crumpled folds. It has to be realized that a light-coloured mass of stuff, can, like the dark-coloured Rorschach blot used in psychiatry, reflect the preoccupations of those who look at it. It is interesting that Theodore Besterman, then Research Officer to the Society, organized in 1931 a fake seance to test sitters' powers of accurate observation; and found that, although they knew they were being tested no less than thirteen of them reported hallucinations or illusions.

In 1933, at a seance in Scotland, 'a little girl called Peggy' emerged from the cabinet. Someone grabbed her, the light was switched on, and there stood Mrs Duncan. She was prosecuted and fined £10. That does not seem to have deterred her. Eleven years later two naval lieutenants who had already been given false information at an earlier seance attended another and watched two 'white forms' glide by. As a third came along one of them seized it, the other turned on his torch – and there, once more, stood the medium. This time she – and four travelling companions – were prosecuted at the Old Bailey for 'conspiracy to pretend that she was in touch with spirits'. All were convicted, and she was sent to prison for nine months. It has been suggested – in general discussion – that oddly enough a flash of genuine extra sensory perception had led up to the prosecution in that Mrs Duncan had revealed to a sitter before the news had been released, and before she could have got hold of it in any ordinary way the fact that a certain British battleship had been sunk. She was then suspected of being an enemy agent. I cannot vouch for the truth of this; but a comparison might well be made with the curious case of the crossword puzzle published in a most respectable newspaper just before the Allied invasion of Europe in World War II. It contained a number of highly secret code words for the various operations involved; and this naturally excited the suspicions of Military Intelligence. The compiler, a man of the utmost integrity who had been contributing such puzzles for many years could only say that, as happened with his other work, the words simply came into his head as he was fitting the pattern together.

Much as individual members of the Society were interested in the

Duncan episode there was not quite such a general polarization of
feeling as resulted from the case of Borley Rectory, best remembered
perhaps as Harry Price's theme in *The Most Haunted House in
England.*[1]

Here the acrid flavour of what were known for centuries at Oxford
as 'town and gown rows', riots between city and university people,
begins to smell strong. The trouble was due in part to the
development of the SPR from a small group of people linked by
family and university ties, and sharing similar intellectual backgrounds and assumptions, to a much larger association whose
members had widely differing points of view.

Harry Price, one of the most fascinating and storm-provoking
figures in psychical research has already been mentioned in connexion
both with Rudi Schneider and with Mrs Duncan herself. He was a
man of great ability, great energy and great kindness. (I have never
ceased to be grateful for all the trouble he took to reply with careful
source references and useful comments when I wrote to him out of
the blue some years ago enquiring about the 17th century story of
the Just Devil of Woodstock.) He was also very ambitious, and
suffered acutely from an ingrowing chip on his shoulder about his
lack of a university degree – for which his engineering training did
not seem to him to compensate – and, I rather suspect, about his
social origins; he was born in 1881, when such things mattered. As
a result, he was inclined to be prickly with people he regarded as his
superiors in the class hierarchy, and to attribute to patronizing
contempt their occasional reluctance to work with him. This
reluctance had in fact very different origins. Like Madame Blavatsky,
Price was uninhibited by a sense of honour, general or scholarly; and
he combined an infinite capacity for drama with a great talent for,
and addiction to, publicity, sometimes of a ridiculous kind, as when
he associated himself with the story of a talking mongoose called
Jeff, said to appear from time to time on the Isle of Man, and to
speak – and sing hymns – in six European languages (thus
distinguishing himself from the animal 'familiars' of folklore witches,
who had an aversion to all things ecclesiastical).

Sadly, but not unnaturally these characteristics led to distrust of
his work (some of which was very valuable) and to a distaste for being

---

1. London, 1940.

associated with him. He joined the Society for Psychical Research in 1920 and remained a member until his death in 1948; but his efforts to amalgamate with it the National Laboratory for Psychical Research, which he founded in 1926 and directed were singularly unsuccessful. Mrs Sidgwick has often been reproached for snobbery in saying she did not want him on the Society's Council 'because he is not a gentleman'; but it is forgotten that at that period the word had an ethical connotation. The questions raised persist. Should an investigator for instance attempt to trick his colleagues – as seems to have happened in the Schneider case – or more generally to cite their unpublished work without their consent – or to claim sole credit for a collective achievement, or tell lies – however interesting the results might be – to the subjects he is testing? In fact, can he be trusted, or must an attitude of eternal vigilance be maintained when working with him?[1]

What happened at Borley looks like an inextricable tangle of fact, fantasy and possible fraud; and the whole affair typifies not only the perennial difficulties of research, and their exacerbation by reporters in quest of thrills, but also the fury that can be generated among investigators. This is why I have included it.

The 19th century Rector of Borley, H. D. E. Bull, had built the Rectory in 1863 (a fictitious later legend said over the site of a monastery) and lived and brought up 14 children there. As early as 1886 stories of its being haunted were current. I am grateful to Mr David Jenkins for telling me that a very old lady from the village, a Mrs Saulez, confirmed this tradition in conversation with him some years ago. When H. D. E. Bull died, his son, the Rev. H. E. (Harry) Bull, succeeded him, and continued to live there with some of his siblings. He 'saw' an apparition of his mother in the garden, and in 1900 four of his sisters 'saw' a nun; but they do not seem to have been unduly alarmed, as the sisters stayed on in the Rectory after their brother had married and moved for a time to a house across the road. He died in 1927 and his successor in the benefice, G. Eric Smith moved in to the Rectory with his wife; the building

---

1. For a general discussion of this problem, which still exists, cf Anita Gregory, 'Ethics and Psychical Research' SPR *Journal*, March 1974, Vol 47, 759, which distinguishes very clearly between, for instance, the standards of business men and of academics.

was in very poor condition by that time. Mr Smith, worried both by
the village rumours of ghosts and by certain experiences of his own
(which he did not confide to his wife for fear of alarming her) wrote
to the editor of the *Daily Mirror* for help. The editor got into touch
with Harry Price, who was by that time well known. He visited the
place in June 1929. Various poltergeist phenomena broke out – stone
throwing and the appearance of 'apports' – and a maid reported
seeing a ghostly figure.

The Smiths did not stay long – which was hardly surprising – and
in 1930 an elderly Mr Lionel Foyster (a cousin of the Bulls) moved
in with his very much younger wife, Marianne, whose second
husband he was. Soon afterwards Mr Foyster too began to report odd
phenomena, later confirmed by some neighbours, Sir George and
Lady Whitehouse and their nephew Edwin, a young Benedictine
monk. There were mysterious noises, bell-ringings, footsteps, and
knockings; and 'spirit writings' presently appeared on the walls. In
1931 Harry Price went again, but though, as he later wrote to
Everard Feilding, in early 1930 'the place was alive with *something*',
this time he suspected Mrs Foyster of fraud. She found this out,
resented it bitterly, and he was refused permission to make a further
visit in 1932.

The Foysters moved out in 1935 – he had become an arthritic
invalid – and the new Rector went to live at Liston. By this time a
fine legend had developed in connexion with the supposed 'convent'
on which the Rectory had been said to be built, and the phantom
nun said to have been sometimes sighted.

In May 1937 Price took the empty building for a year, advertised
in *The Times* for investigators, 'responsible persons of leisure and
intelligence, with cars' (but not necessarily with any knowledge of
psychical research). He issued them with an account of events so far,
and with careful instructions as to how to deal with any experiences
that might come their way. It has been argued that all these could
have acted as powerful suggestions of what to expect. The phenomena
reported by these investigators were augmented by various planchette
scripts, involving the 'nun' (now supposed to have eloped with a
monk from a not too distant monastery, to have been caught and to
have died in prison – the story grew like a Busy Lizzy plant) and by
a threat from a 'spirit' to burn the place down. Price broadcast about
this after his tenancy had ended, and was heard by the new tenant,

Captain Gregson. In February 1939 the place was indeed burned down.

Price, by that time writing *The Most Haunted House in England*, had become so far reconciled with the Foysters that the former Rector, who had made written records of those events which he had known at first hand, allowed him to use them in this book. There were three sets. One described the hauntings in detail, one was called 'Fifteen Months in a Haunted House', and one was a 'Summary of Experiences'. The book, published in 1940, was an immense success.

Fifteen years later a well documented survey was published by E. J. Dingwall, K.M. Goldney and Trevor Hall, as Volume 51, 186 of the SPR *Proceedings*. It presented with the cold, controlled, unremitting fury of a road drill what could be called the case for the prosecution against Harry Price, who had died in 1948. Every incident recorded in the book was interpreted to put him in the worst possible light, to demonstrate that he had exploited for his own personal advantage every available occurrence, legend or putative hallucination, and that he had probably faked evidence. Many damaging conclusions were put forward preceded by such phrases as 'may have been', 'appears to have been' and 'it is not unreasonable to postulate'. Only one rather grudging attempt to mitigate the many offences ascribed to the figure in the dock was the remark, 'he may have thought there was some genuine basis' (for the phenomena reported) 'and that by supplying what he thought to be a proper psychological *milieu* the genuine elements might more easily emerge'. Apart from this, the production seemed to be based on the French system of criminal procedure, in which the accused is presumed to be guilty until he can prove himself innocent. This raised the hackles of the average reader, particularly as the accused was dead and past self-defence. (It is only fair to add that efforts to establish the truth were no longer hampered by the laws of libel).

Slowly the pressure of opinion increased. In 1965 the Society's Research Advisory Committee authorized an investigator, Robert J. Hastings, to re-examine all the evidence; and in March 1969 he produced a further issue of *Proceedings* (Number 55, 201). He surveyed the earlier issue in careful detail, pointing out errors that had been made and showing that various incidents used as evidence of fraud could bear different interpretations. He noted for instance in connexion with the appearance out of nowhere (as an 'apport') of an ecclesiastical medal, that there was no available evidence for the statement that Price collected such objects; and pointed out that as the latter suffered from angina pectoris he could not possibly – as alleged – have done the heavy digging necessary to 'plant' some human bones found buried at Borley. Hastings also put forward an alternative explanation for the impression reported by a journalist named Sutton that he had 'seen' Price throw a brick and heard him ascribe it to poltergeist activity; and pointed out that at the time when the earlier *Proceedings* had appeared Price had been unable to defend himself against this and other accusations because of his heart condition, though his secretaries had indeed protested.

The 1969 *Proceedings* also included some comments from Peter Underwood of the Ghost Club, who had been at Borley on many occasions. He pointed out that the three previous writers had assumed that at the time when Richard Whitehouse was involved in the phenomena he was suffering from the effects of a nervous breakdown; but that this had occurred no less than six years previously and he had long completely recovered. Underwood also noted that he himself had been an eye-witness of the apparently paranormal movements of a stiletto and some bottles, ascribed to 'stories' told by Marianne Foyster.

Summing up, Hastings put it on record that though *The Most Haunted House in England* was indeed popularly written, Price's own contemporary files dealing with the case had been lodged in the Library of the University of London and were available for consultation; and that though some of his opinions seemed to have altered over the years this was evidence not of dishonesty but of development. He suggested that Price had wanted to find out whether the phenomena that had recurred at Borley over different periods had in fact been sparked off by different people; this could have been most useful evidence that such outbreaks could depend *both* on places and on persons.

Considerable feeling was inflamed by the Hastings Report, but it died down again and not until 1979 did the subject come up once more in a *Journal* article by Iris Owen and Paulene Mitchell based on interviews with Marianne, now a sprightly eighty-year-old, who had married yet again and had gone back to Canada. She said that three years after her marriage to Lionel Foyster he had had a heart attack and begun to develop arthritis; that he had gone to Borley for health reasons; and that during the Smiths' incumbency there had been poltergeist phenomena connected with their fifteen-year-old servant, Mary.

Some little time after Marianne and her husband had moved in, the account continued, he had realized his health was getting worse and that he would die a bedridden invalid. Anxious to leave his wife enough to live on, he planned to make money by writing a book on the Borley ghosts (about which he had already heard from his cousins, the Bulls). He was inspired to do this by the great success of a contemporary volume on the American Amherst Mystery. The three pieces he wrote were intended to form part of his book. He faked phenomena on occasion. Richard Whitehouse was either his accomplice or a poltergeist focus. And so on.

Peter Underwood protested in the *Journal* (June 1980) that Lionel Foyster, a conscientious Anglican priest, was most unlikely to have behaved in this way, and to have asserted that his three carefully compiled records were true if they were not. He characterized the new allegations as 'unreliable and unimpressive'. There the case rests; an admirable example of the difficulties of psychical research in ascertaining what actually happened, in dealing with the persons concerned, and in deciding between all the interpretations put forward, entangled as they often are with assumptions, suspicions, emotions and sometimes deliberate deceit.

The camera cannot lie. The machine cannot be mistaken. Properly worked out mathematical calculations must be true. Such axioms are very welcome to researchers tired of conflicting human evidence, exhausting human emotions, tangled ethical issues. Generations of scientific members of the Society have hoped to establish fact, to approach truth, and to convince their sceptical colleagues by employing strictly controlled scientific methods to investigate parapsychology.

But here too this elusive subject tends to run into the sand. Those who advocated such an approach did not, in their innocence, realize what its effect might be. What happened, of course (though not with those rare birds the genuinely open-minded) was that those whose deepest-rooted and most comfortably settled convictions were threatened, quite simply declared that the scientific methods in question had not been properly used, shifted the argument to a technological ground, and began to develop that disease which Brian Inglis has delightfully called *protocolitis*. The patient rather enjoys his condition. His attention becomes deflected from the subject to be investigated to the modes of investigation employed. The itch to pick holes in them is irresistible; its satisfaction is an all-absorbing occupation.

Quantitative experimental work had been envisaged very early on in the development of the Society; the use of playing cards, coloured discs and so on had been suggested and tried. But work on the large scale that permitted statistical evaluation developed most speedily in the 1930s, when Dr Rhine's fascinating experiments with American university students began to become widely known. The advantages were obvious (particularly after the invention of Zener cards had narrowed down to five instead of fifty-two the number of images that could be guessed). One of them – not always recognized – was that the investigator could feel secure, in full control of his material. Fear of the mysterious, of the uncomprehended, could be abolished if he were properly protected by mathematical formulæ to which he could cling like the child at the Zoo whom Belloc told 'always keep a-hold of Nurse, for fear of finding something Worse'. If things came to a final crunch the computer could keep the Numinous at bay. If any cold breath of air from the unknown should seem to blow in, then the mechanism had not been properly used, to say the least of it, and fraud was highly probable.

The strangest and one of the saddest examples of what can happen in such circumstances can be seen in the case of Dr S.G. Soal, D.Sc., a distinguished mathematician, and a fanatically conscientious psychical research worker whose scruples could make him discontinue any experiment in whose course what looked like even the most harmless interruption had occurred.

As a very young man mourning the loss of his brother Frank in World War I he went regularly for a while to weekly Spiritualist demonstrations of clairvoyance, without much concrete result; (he found them very vague). Later he sat with various mediums, one or two of whom repeated to him several words and phrases – family slang, as it were – that he and his brother had shared. He realized that this might be the result of telepathy, but continued to go to seances. At one of these, with a Mrs Blanche Cooper, in 1922, he was told that a 'spirit communicator' Gordon Davies, with whom he had been at school, was present. He, like Frank, had been killed in the war, and he gave convincing proofs of his identity. Later she described in vivid detail the house in Southend in which he had lived. Dr Soal afterwards found out that Gordon Davies had *not* been killed, but was in fact living in Southend at a house which corresponded inside and out, furnishings, pictures and all, with the description given by Mrs Cooper. But at the time when she had given it, Gordon Davis had been living in London, had had no idea of moving to Southend, and had not even bought some of the items she had described. This case, which interested the Society's accurate down-to-earth Hon Secretary, Mr Salter very much, was published in *Proceedings* in December 1925.

Dr Soal continued to explore various lines of psychical research, always with the most rigorous precautions. Between 1936 and 1939 he carried out a series of card guessing experiments of the kind used by Dr Rhine to test telepathy, examined 160 people, recorded 128,350 guesses – and achieved no results that could not have been forecast by probability theory.

When war broke out the college in the University of London at which he was a lecturer – Queen Mary College – was evacuated to Cambridge, where he met Whately Carington and was 'received somewhat coldly since . . . my reputation for scepticism had become a byword among members of the SPR'. However, they became friends. Carington remembered that 'time displacement' had occurred in some of his own smaller scale experimental work ('viewers' guessing at a distance what objects were being displayed night by night in his study had significantly often described those on show the night either *before* or *after* the one with which they were concerned). He then persuaded Soal to undertake, with the help of independent workers (among them Mrs Goldney and Carington himself) the enormous task of re-examining all those records on the chance that they might contain evidence for precognition. At first Soal was most unwilling to do so, protesting – rather oddly, one might think, after the Gordon Davis experience – 'how *can* anyone know about something that hasn't happened yet'. He yielded in the end however; the work was carried out and in the cases of two of the people concerned, Mrs Stewart and Mr Basil Shackleton, the examiners did indeed find 'positive deviations from chance expectation both on the card before and the card after that shown'. *Nature* published in 1940 a letter on the subject signed by both Carington and Soal (Professor Broad exclaimed in some amazement, 'Is Soal also among the prophets!'). No attack has ever been made upon these experiments – which had in fact been set aside as records of a massive failure to demonstrate telepathy – or on the findings later drawn from them. It is interesting, and may be significant, that precognition was involved both in the qualitative data obtained with Mrs Cooper and in the long and apparently fruitless quantitative work with card guessing; was 'experimenter effect' involved?

Dr Soal then began to work in the main with his two talented subjects. This was not easy in wartime conditions with continual slow blacked-out train journeys between London and Cambridge, and the long exhaustion of sleepless air raid nights. One or two record sheets were lost, but he managed in 1943 to publish a paper in *Proceedings* on his work with Shackleton. His Presidential Address of 1950 made clear his conviction that paranormal cognition did indeed occur; for he urged that people should stop experimenting over and over again to prove to sceptics the existence of telepathy, but should instead deal with specific problems as to its workings. He published in 1954 a book based on his own researches, *Modern Experiments in Telepathy*. Six years later, a psychologist, Dr C. E. M. Hansel attacked him in a paper published in another *Proceedings* (May 1960) based on the *a priori* reasoning that 'as the probability of precognition is infinitesimally small . . . all possible evidence for trickery or error is overwhelming'. He then pointed out in elaborate detail what *might* have happened, accidentally or deliberately, to affect the results of the experiments; ' "voice clues", taps, coughs, whispers, memorized signals, and every possible form of dishonest collusion.' Soal replied with aplomb.

In the September *Journal* that same year Dr Soal and Mrs Goldney published a letter rebutting the suggestion made by a foreign lady with a curious obsession about 'drugged cigarettes', that she had seen him altering figures on the score sheets. Another observer, duly on the *qui vive* had seen nothing; later the lady acknowledged that she could have been mistaken. A member wrote asking whether the Society ought not to abandon concern with all these accusations and rebuttals and get on with further investigations; but was told very properly that 'we cannot cover up any serious criticism of members' research'. Maybe his letter did have some effect, for it was not until 1971 that the affair began to take off into the sphere of the higher mathematics with Dr R. G. Medhurst's article in the March *Journal*, 'On the Origin of the Prepared Random Numbers used in the Shackleton Experiments' which showed, he argued, that the statement of the method of constructing quasi-random series used during the Shackleton experiments was incorrect. A note in the September *Journal* listed some minor errors in the paper, whose proofs the author had not been able to correct before his death; and a letter from Christopher Scott came out in December observing that those cited could not have affected Dr Medhurst's conclusions, and indicated two similar ones, plus a third which might have made him modify a statement.

In 1974 a further attack developed in force when Scott, with Philip Haskell and others published yet another hostile discussion of the Shackleton experiment. This was followed by papers defending Dr Soal, written by Professors Mundle, Pratt, Smythies and Stevenson, Dr Beloff, Miss M. R. Barrington and Mrs Goldney, who had worked closely with Dr Soal for some forty years. It is to be hoped that they comforted him, for he died in 1975. He could do nothing to defend himself when three years afterwards Miss Betty Markwick produced a long, complex, highly technical paper in which this lifelong investigator was tried by computer and found guilty of fraud.

Three explanations of the verdict have been put forward. One was that the culprit – who had in the past produced some remarkable automatic writing – was prone to dissociation, and that a secondary personality might have emerged and falsified his results; another that he had deliberately and consciously cheated in order to gain 'scientific recognition for parapsychology'. Both Mrs Goldney and the late Professor Pratt modified their previous defence of him, though the former found it almost impossible to believe in conscious deception on the part of someone so much absorbed in research and so extraordinarily conscientious in conducting experiments according to protocol. The latter suggested that 'when preparing the lists of random numbers on the record sheets before the sittings were held (Soal) used precognition when inserting digits into the columns of numbers he was copying down, unconsciously choosing numbers that would score hits on the calls the subject would make later'. A third and rather ingenious suggestion was put forward by John Randall (*Journal*, December 1978). He pointed out that many investigators working with psychokinetic subjects report that electronic equipment is likely to malfunction in their presence, that the human brain is 'a highly sophisticated piece of electrical equipment', and that in the presence of psi activity the brains of experimenters may malfunction.

No one seems to have queried the verdict itself. Evidence for character cannot be considered by a computer – and the computer's Sacred Cow status is still widely respected in many quarters despite the very odd results it has yielded from time to time in other fields than those of psychical research: banking for instance.

However, in the middle of 1981, an American correspondent asked the Society if he might have copies of the score sheets for re-examination. Who knows what the results may be? *Quis computet ipsos computatores?*

There have been many such imbroglios in the history of the Society for Psychical Research – that aroused by the recent Enfield case is yet another – and there will probably be many more. There is not space to examine them all in a book devoted to its work rather than to chronicling the lively personal and academic hostilities sometimes involved; but the four chosen here seem to me to illustrate the main themes that recur. A large number of variations can be played upon them: and are.

10

Achievements. What Next?

Though the swings of intellectual fashion in psychical research are strongly marked in the Society, a certain essential continuity remains, partly perhaps because it disclaims corporate views, and those of its members remain individual.

As has been noted, the pendulum has jolted from an overwhelming interest in mediums and their psychology to an overwhelming interest in the use of mass experiments evaluated by statistical methods; from a profound concern with the geological and/or emotional causes of poltergeist outbreaks towards a passionate preoccupation with the electroencephalographic charts of meditators and of psychokinetically-gifted people. What is more, the trend towards what might be called the technology of psi continues. Julian Isaacs, for instance, has as a result of his laboratory work distinguished first between the willed and the involuntary production of psycho-kinetic events; and then between those which take place slowly, and those which, like paranormal metal bending, happen fast. He suggests that though people may not ever be able consciously to control other forms of psychokinesis, this last may possibly be learned, or at any rate improved by practice; but that – as happens with piano playing at concert level – the skill wears off if practising is discontinued. Isaacs has also had some fun in developing and working with a largely automated device originally designed in America, the Cox Minilab (is it unkind to suggest that the seventeenth century doctrine of the Divine Right of Kings has reappeared today as a belief in the Infallibility of Automata?). The Cox Minilab is a sealed, locked, transparent box within which are a layer of sand – to show traces of movement – and a number of small objects which, it is claimed, can be shifted about by some psychokinetic process exerted by people concentrating on it from another room; these movements trigger off a ciné-camera which records them![1]

The assumption that psychokinesis 'is the measure of all things' has been developing for some time. It was even put forward, years ago by Admiral Tanagras, a distinguished Greek member of the Society, as an explanation of precognition (which does indeed happen, however uncomfortable the fact makes one feel). It occurred, he suggested, because one person was consciously or unconsciously 'ill wishing' another. This looks like a scientific reformulation of traditional belief in the power of the Evil Eye. It does not however explain happy or neutral precognitions, say of an unknown landscape or of such odd incidents as have been recorded by those who followed J. W. Dunne's admonition to write down their dreams on waking, and who were able to check back from time to time and find them fulfilled.

There has also been an attempt to explain in psychokinetic terms the events known as 'the Electronic Voice Phenomena' or more colloquially as the Raudive Voices, which aroused considerable interest (and controversy) in the nineteen sixties and seventies. These originated in Sweden, with the work of a Dr Jurgenson and were further developed, studied and reported in detail by Dr Konstantin Raudive, a Latvian philosopher who moved from Sweden to Germany.

Dr Jurgenson had noticed that some tape recordings he had made contained 'extra' voices, which would speak a few words at a time, on occasion in more than one language. He published a book about this in 1964; Raudive read it, began experimenting for himself – he ultimately managed to hear no less than 70,000 phrases – and wrote his own book in 1968. The voices spoke in Swedish, German, Russian, Latvian, French and English; all were languages known to Raudive. If any other tongues were used, presumably they would not have been recognized.

A translation entitled *Breakthrough* appeared in England in 1971 and the thing caught on here as rapidly as it had in Sweden,

---

1. The SPR *Journal* for October 1981 contains an animated correspondence on this subject.

Germany and Austria. Perhaps the technology involved in this new way of transmitting what were assumed to be the voices of the dead was so ingenious, complicated and up-to-date that what they actually *said* was thought unimportant. Otherwise the mind might well have boggled at the idea that Winston Churchill had managed to produce a few words each in a separate language; Churchill, whose linguistic attainments never seem to have gone beyond schoolboy French on the level of that famous fabled statement '*Quand je regarde ma derrière je vois que c'est diviseé en deux parties*' (When I look at what lies behind me I see that it is divided into two parts).

These tapes, then, had for a while a great vogue (and there are indeed those who still believe they are what they purport to be). So of course had that Talking Dog broadcast on radio some years ago whose owner, offering him a biscuit, interpreted as 'I *want* one' what sounded to some of his hearers like no more than a well barked 'Bow *wow* wow'. Dr Raudive believed that most listeners to the electronic voices had to spend some time in learning to pick them out from background noise, and to decipher their meaning.

The Trustees of the Perrott-Warrick Studentship enabled a young SPR member, David Ellis, to study the phenomena at first hand. He began to work with a distinct readiness to accept the voices as paranormal, and to go along with Dr Raudive's argument. In a fascinating study[1] he set out the reasons for changing his mind. Some of these were highly technical; he noted in this connexion that Dr Raudive's knowledge of electronics was 'minimal'. He also pointed out that some of the later voices tallied with an announcement in English from Radio Luxembourg; that others could have come from different radio signals; and that many of the sounds interpreted as words could have arisen from indistinct transmissions, mechanical noises and the imagination. 'The listener', he wrote 'does seem to develop with practice . . . a faculty for producing interpretations by a process of guess work'.

Even if one accepts Mr Ellis's conclusions – as I do – psychokinesis can still be cited, as Professors Bersani, Peduto and Trevisan, SPR members from the University of Bologna (where Lambertini wrote his survey of extra sensory perception two hundred years ago) showed, in papers read at the conferences of 1980 and 1981 on the 'psycho-

---

1. *The Mediumship of the Tape Recorder*, D. J. Ellis, 1978.

linguistic' effect of the voices. Though the authors doubted whether the original sounds were intrinsically paranormal, they suggested that an 'emotionally motivated' listener, reading his own meaning into them, and unconsciously anxious to transmit it to other people, might affect the actual recording in some psychokinetic way. Various ingenious technical modes of testing the idea were worked out.

If parapsychologists, like football supporters, were given to writing their sentiments on walls, a popular current inscription might well run PK RULES, OK.

Other subjects are still studied, however, and other forms of research continue among members of the Society. There remains a powerful undercurrent of interest, for instance, in anthropology, folklore, biology, history, hypnosis – witness the volumes edited by the indefatigable Dr Dingwall[1] – medicine, healing, psychiatry and philosophy.

In this last can be traced developments running from Gerald and Arthur Balfour to C. D. Broad, H. H. Price, Shivesh Thakur and that staunch and lucid dualist John Beloff; from Henri Bergson to the vitalist Hans Driesch and on to Whately Carington's ideas about telepathy and the group mind as developed by the distinguished marine biologist Alister Hardy in his paper 'Biology and Psychical Research'.[2] This suggested in animal species 'a group mind holding the whole plan of structural form, and particularly development' which can become 'a unit of life . . . building itself up from the unconsciously shared experience of all the members of the race': which seems to link up with the botanist, Rupert Sheldrake's argument[3] that 'a plant develops the form typical of its species because previous members of the species took up that form', and that 'an animal acts instinctively in a particular manner because similar animals behaved in that way in the past'. He extends the process to include on the one hand the given patterns into which crystalline solutions harden, and on the other the development of new skills in groups of laboratory rats at a distance from one another (easier to

---

1. E. J. Dingwall (ed): *Abnormal Hypnotic Phenomena*, London 1967 and 1968. Research Officer to the Society 1927–28.

2. SPR *Proceedings*, 1953, later developed in his Gifford Lectures, Vol I, *The Living Stream*, 1964.

3. Rupert Sheldrake: *A New Science of Life, the Hypothesis of Formative Causation*, London 1981.

observe at close quarters than the extraordinary way in which blue tits all over the country learnt, almost simultaneously how to open the cardboard tops of milk bottles and get at the cream; a fact cited by Hardy). Neither Hardy nor Sheldrake commits himself to much speculation about the *first* impulse to such processes in general, though the former has gone so far as to write of 'a morph', 'a form and behaviour design outside space and time'.

Philosophers and other members of the Society retain a passionate interest in the nature of time, uncomfortable as it is to try to consider something in which we are all immersed as naturally as fish in the depths of the sea. True, the discussion contrasting time as experienced with time as mechanically recorded, so popular in earlier years, has been swallowed up in wider speculations as to the ages of space travellers as compared with those of terrestrians born on the same dates; (was Rip Van Winkle carried off in a flying saucer perhaps; were the fairies who kidnapped little Bridget of the song little green men from another galaxy?). We are left with even more ground than St Augustine for reflecting that we know quite well what time is until we begin to think about it.

Among so many giddying speculations, though, it is good to know that biological studies may have cleared up one temporal problem. Early psychical researchers were long and deeply puzzled as to how post-hypnotic suggestions were so punctually fulfilled; why it was for instance, that a man who had been told in a trance state that precisely two hours after coming round he would go and open a certain window, would indeed feel impelled to do so at the exact moment indicated, telling himself and his neighbours that the room was intolerably stuffy, or much too hot, or full of cigarette smoke, since he did not remember the real cause of his action. The discovery that a biological clock exists in many animal species suggests pretty conclusively that something of the kind is inherent in our own. (The unpunctual probably withdraw their attention from it; to ignore a stimulus is a human talent.)

Nevertheless an enormous stumbling block remains – the fact of precognition. Its spontaneous occurrence has been recorded over thousands of years in many great civilizations, Greece, Rome, China, Japan; though attempts to organize it on a regular rationalized basis, as with the Roman College of Augurs, were not in the long term successful. It has been studied experimentally by the Rhines in

America and was found to be involved in a number of British tests
conducted to study telepathy, long laid aside as non-significant and
re-examined, at the suggestion of Whately Carington, for 'time
displacement' (see Chapter Nine).

Precognition has been confirmed again and again by numerous
studies carried out by other members of the SPR during its century-
long existence. Instances have been collected, checked, recorded and
published in Dame Edith Lyttelton's *Some Cases of Prediction* (London,
1937), in Andrew MacKenzie's admirably researched *Riddle of the
Future* (London, 1974) and in Dr J. C. Barker's *Scared to Death*
(London, 1968).

This last made two very important points. The first established
the remarkable effects of suggestion – long term or short term,
intentional or accidental – in bringing about illness, in making the
sick yield to death, or in stimulating them to live; as when a very
authoritative Sister in a military hospital threatened to put a sinking
patient on 'Colonel's Orders' if he did not survive the night (he did!
and recovered). The second point was that accurate precognitions of
death could and did occur without any evidence that suggestion had
been at work. Dr Barker cited several instances, the most startling
of them concerned with the Aberfan disaster of 21 October 1966,
when a mountain of rubble fell upon a Welsh village school and
buried many of its pupils alive. Some of these precognitions came
from the children themselves, some from other parts of the country
where Aberfan was hardly known, even as a name. One woman in
Plymouth for instance, had a vision of it the previous night, at once
told six witnesses – who subsequently confirmed this in writing –
what she had seen, and spoke of it next morning to a neighbour.
Later, she saw it again on television, and recognized not only the
scene but 'a little boy with a long fringe, looking absolutely terrified'
and the man with 'an unusual peaked cap' who rescued him.

Professor Mundle contributed a commentary, 'Experimental Evidence for PK and Precognition' to *Proceedings* in 1949–52[1] and H.
A. C. Dobbs followed this up with another, 'Time and ESP' some
years later.[2] He remarked that 'precognition represents a glimpse of
one of a number of possibilities the future may hold', opposed the

---

1. *Proceedings* 49.
2. *Proceedings* 55, 1963.

theory that psychokinesis is involved, and differentiated between forecasts – for example that a kettle will boil under certain conditions – from actual predictions; but then proceeded to arguments very hard for a reader not versed in modern physics to understand. Like J. W. Dunne, explaining his findings about dream fulfilment in *An Experiment with Time* and later works, Dobbs postulated another Time Dimension; he also used concepts such as those of the Block Universe, and of the interaction of photons and positrons, which demand more elucidation than they get. The facts stand out, but to follow the interpretations calls for a strenuous, almost acrobatic intellectual exercise, like say 'turning cartwheels' along a steep and twisting road.

Interest continues in trustworthy historical records of what looks like precognition. This is exemplified in the attention still paid to the strange prophecies of the French Doctor, Michel de Nostre Dame (Nostradamus) born in 1503 who, during the course of a successful medical career – he was given a pension by the city of Aix for his services during the plague of 1546 – found himself in middle life impelled to record (by a process that sounds like automatic writing) first in prose and then in verse quatrains a series of prophecies. At first they dealt with the immediate future, so accurately that they were published in almanac form and convinced various European monarchs that he was inspired. In 1555 and 1558 he published his *Ten Centuries of Prophecies* whose scope extended to the fourth millennium AD. Full of anagrams, symbols and allegories – partly perhaps because the unconscious mind tends to work in that way anyhow, partly perhaps because the writer justifiably feared ecclesiastical censure if he made himself too plain – they yet contained a clear statement of the date when Henri II of France would die, and what look like other predictions, notably of the outbreak and ravages of the Thirty Years War, of the beheading of Charles I of England, and of the flight and capture of Louis XVI and Marie Antoinette during the French Revolution. Professor Archie Roy, the Scottish astronomer who contributed a paper on 'Time and Consciousness' to the Society's International Conference in 1980, reviewed two recent studies of the quatrains in the *Journal* for June 1981 and concluded that some of them might well be genuinely precognitive; a more cautious assessment than that of Dr J. E. Orme[1] who had argued earlier that 265 of them *might* be accurate, that 42 of these were particularly striking, and that most of them differed from the usual run of predictions in that they dealt mainly with events Nostradamus did not live to see, many in a future very far distant from him, and that they tended to be as much political as personal.

Primitive communities, ancient and modern, take matters of this kind in their stride, as has been shown in Ronald Rose's *Living Magic*,[2] a study of psi among Australian aborigines, which covers space as well as time, telepathy as well as precognition. Anthropological studies of out of the body experiences published in the *Journal* over recent years include a long, carefully organized paper by Dean Shiels, 'A Cross Cultural Study of the Out Of The Body Experience'[3] (long investigated in this country by R. Crookall and others, notably Celia Green).[4] His data, culled from 'non-Western cultures' have, he maintains 'a remarkable uniformity'; from which he deduces that Out of the Body Beliefs exist because out of the body experiences do in fact happen, even though they are not always interpreted in the same way. Thus, in only one of the groups investigated did he find any such ideas about a 'silver cord' linking the separated self with the body as have been popular in England; and as are still popular, in the form of 'a magic thread of cotton' among the Rigo people of Papua-New Guinea as reported in Alistair McIntosh's fascinating individual survey of 'Beliefs about Out of the Body Experiences'[5] among the tribal groups of this area where he worked as a volunteer teacher for two years, later being helped by an SPR grant for a further period of research there.

These experiences are rationalized in terms of folk lore. Sometimes it is assumed that everyone has them during sleep; more often that they occur during fright, and at death; occasionally that they are self-induced by witches and sorcerers, sometimes by incantations, sometimes by the use of certain herbs. Like Celia Green's carefully

---

1. *Journal*, September 1979 (Vol 50, No 781).
2. London, 1957.
3. *Journal*, March 1978 (Vol 49, No 775).
4. *Out of the Body Experiences* by Celia Green, with a Preface by H. H. Price (a former President of the Society) Oxford, 1968.
5. *Journal*, Sept. 1980.

researched volume[1] dealing with such experiences among ordinary English people, it is especially interesting because it comes from individual sources, in his case persons he knew in an everyday context of living and working. The information has not been processed into large generalizations which valuable though they can be, tend to be used in abstract frames of reference, as with a paper published in the same issue[2] on the investigation of OOBEs among students in an Australian university, an investigation intended to examine the 'separationist' and the 'psychological' theories of what went on. The first is self explanatory, assuming that the self is separated from the body; the latter suggests that out of the body experiences are hallucinatory, though psi may introduce a veridical element into what is apparently 'seen'. The author examines the idea that those who have them are 'adroit in their mental imagery skills'. The paper is full of acronyms for the processes used in assessing the students (WOT is the Ways of Thinking questionnaire, DPQ The Differential Personality questionnaire, VVI the Vividness of Visual Imagery questionnaire). It is debatable how much solid fact can be discovered in this way, and what happens if any of those questioned have a taste and talent for leg-pulling. There is of course much mathematical evaluation of 'mean scores'. The processes involved seem to resemble those of plucking, cleaning, and boiling a chicken down for stock. The end product may be wholesome and nourishing; but nothing characteristic of the original remains, life, colour, shape are gone, regarded as irrelevant.

How fascinating, nevertheless, that Dr Irwin should have found his subjects actually lacked vividness in their visual imagery; and held that the evidence obtained did not support the theory that 'the OOBE is a visual hallucination conjured up by individuals with pronounced imaginal skills'. Another explanation is to be sought, in terms of 'neuroticism' and other carefully tabulated psychological characteristics; it would be good to have a definition of 'neuroticism'.

It is interesting to note how strong here – as in Dr Susan Blackmore's work on this subject – is the influence of an unexamined assumption, that of monism. The interpretation of out of the body experiences usually made by those who have them is dualist; that the

---

1. Op. cit.
2. 'Out of the Body Down Under', by Harvey J. Irwin.

body and the essential self are separable, and have temporarily been separated. (That this sometimes leads to secondary speculations about 'astral bodies' and the like does not necessarily disprove the original impression.) Neither the monist or the dualist assumption need be excluded, but neither should be taken for granted as axiomatic. To clarify argument, the existence of both needs to be recognized and acknowledged.

All this is closely linked, of course, with the increasingly popular theory of reincarnation, as to which opinions in the Society differ as vividly as they do out of it. The latest piece of research published by a member is Ian Wilson's 'Mind out of Time',[1] which interprets in a new way the supposed evidence for it.

Research then, is continuous. What has it in fact achieved so far? What solid results can the Society present after a century of varied and intensive work? One surely is the formation of many other serious psychical research societies in various parts of the world. The earliest were perhaps in the United States, where a branch of the English one became autonomous, and more sprang up. Members of the London Society were often members of one of the others, and in any case close contact was maintained with them; as it was with the European societies, of which the *Institut Métapsychique* in Paris was one of the first. The SPR has had several distinguished foreign Presidents, American, French and German. Later-established Psychical Research societies now exist in China, India, Japan, Latin America and South Africa.

What of 'those faculties of man, real or supposed, which appear to be inexplicable in terms of any recognized hypotheses'?

The first thing to be observed is how much those 'recognized hypotheses' have changed over the years. Studies of animal behaviour have been very useful in this connexion. Thus the apparently intuitive flight of bats which so puzzled Gilbert Murray[2] has now been interpreted as a natural form of radar and the longer term direction-finding of migrant birds looks as if it were due in part to some inbuilt sensitivity to the earth's magnetic field. A small quantity of a substance called magnetite has been found in the brain of the homing pigeon, and the probability is that it exists in other species

1. London, 1981.
2. Presidential Address.

– even perhaps in those humans gifted with an outstanding 'sense of direction'. It should be noted, though, that this yields no explanation for what has been called 'psi-trailing' in which a pet cat or dog given to kind neighbours when its owners have moved perhaps hundreds of miles away to a place where it has never been, will successfully cut across country to join them. It also does not explain why grown members of different species of stork, even when they have hatched and developed together from eggs deliberately mixed in the same nest, will separate and fly each by their ancestral migration routes.

Among the subjects originally put forward for investigation by members of the Society were Dowsing, 'physical' or 'Spiritualistic phenomena', 'Reichenbach effects' (concerned largely with human abilities to perceive unfamiliar forms of light), Mesmerism, Apparitions and 'Thought Transference' now more familiar as telepathy.

An explanation of dowsing in terms of sensitivity to changes in electro-magnetic fields generated by underground water or minerals has been put forward. The subject has long been the sphere of inconclusive experiments by various members of the SPR (scientists and others), and of practical use by architects, builders, surveyors and soldiers (in arid unfamiliar countries). These were concerned more with the fact that it worked than with how or why it did so. Like many primitive abilities, that of the dowser tends to dry up if he is made self-conscious, or put on the defensive. It would be interesting to know whether magnetite is involved in the physiological make-up of such people. If, as the American work already discussed seems to indicate, dowsers do not get any result when the areas over the pineal and adrenal glands are protected from electro-magnetic radiation, these would plainly be the parts of the body to search for magnetite. But neither this substance, nor any other means of increasing sensitivity to electro-magnetic fields can account for 'map dowsing', in which a dowser with a pendulum – sometimes no more than a ring on a piece of string – works as successfully from a printed map of the region to be searched as he would in the field.

Here at any rate are recognizable hypotheses to account for two apparently paranormal faculties, now shown to be real rather than supposed. It needs to be repeated loud and clear that these hypotheses do not account for *all* the ways in which these faculties work; the form of direction-finding known as psi-trailing and the form of dowsing carried out with a map differ from the others as the perception of a veridical hallucination differs from the perception of a person physically present.

'Reichenbach effects' seem to have received little attention for some time. They were largely concerned with the ability – rare in people, but probably commonplace in some animals and insects – to perceive certain forms of light in association with magnets, and to see 'auras' (or haloes) of various different and fluctuating colours and intensities around the human body.

'Physical and Spiritualistic phenomena' once attributed either to 'spirits' or to 'nerve force' are now considered in terms of psychokinesis; but the attempt to explain them solely by some form of electromagnetic activity as yet unknown comes up against difficulties inherent in all modes of studying mind-body interaction. Here the complex interplay of psyche and *soma*, concentration and relaxation, the emotions, miseries and glories of the unconscious, the activities of the will and of the self-observing intellect have to be considered. For myself – I can speak for no others – the occurrence of psychokinesis has been established, both by the careful observation and recording of spontaneous cases when they erupt, and by experimental work. The low boggle threshold created at first by its 'sheer impossibility' (like the 'influence at distance' implied by the theory of gravitation, the existence of globe lightning and the invention of the telephone, and maintained by the ingenious frauds of so many mediums, has been heightened; and these phenomena have been shown to occur, whatever the explanation – or explanations – may prove to be. As Rupert Sheldrake has written[1] 'There are two ways of explaining ESP or PK. One is to start from the assumption that they depend on laws of physics as yet unknown; the second is to suppose that they depend on non-physical causal factors or connecting principles'. The third way is of course to accept the possibility of multiple causation, the maddening possibility that different instances may be attributed *either* to one, *or* to the other, *or* to the interaction of both.

As to Mesmerism (known today as hypnosis) the Society's clear-eyed work, alone and with other bodies, from the time of Myers and Charcot onwards has cleared up the first, mistaken interpretations of

1. Op. cit.

what went on, the esoteric vocabulary that developed around it, and the phosphorescent miasma of occultism so long associated with the whole subject. As early as 1893 a sub-committee of the BMA recognized its value in relieving pain and in treating functional disorders. Today it is employed by surgeons and by dentists for anaesthetic purposes and used by psychiatrists and dermatologists as a means of therapy. Legal measures – supported by members of the Society – have been passed to prevent its misuse by music hall performers; and sociologists and historians have begun to recognize the ways in which it was exploited for political purposes by such virtuosi as Hitler and Mussolini (to name only the dead). To face, to examine, to evaluate mysterious phenomena is of the greatest value in discovering what they are, and in working out a defence against their misuse.

The often renewed study of Apparitions has shown that these are seen from time to time by some persons who are in good health; and that though they are by definition hallucinations – since they are not physically present to the senses – they can be veridical, representing some incident taking place at a distance which could not be known in any normal way.

Sometimes such an incident may involve precognition. Sometimes, as in the case of Haunted Houses, it may have happened long ago as well as far away. A possible explanation of this last, once very popular, is that something analogous to videotape is involved, which is replayed to any 'sensitive' who relaxes in the house. Professor Hasted[1] has suggested that where bell ringing is concerned, a 'metal bender' all unconscious of this curious talent, may be around. It has at any rate been established that, whatever the explanation may be, the existence of haunted houses cannot be discounted as superstition, imagination or the desire to tell and believe good stories.

The occurrence of veridical hallucinations in which one person is vividly and unaccountably aware of what is happening to another far away is now of course attributed to telepathy, originally studied by early SPR investigators under the curiously mechanistic title of 'Thought Transference'. At intervals in the history of the Society one distinguished member or another has claimed, on the basis of well-investigated spontaneous cases, and of experimental work of various

---

1. J. Hasted: *The Metal Benders*, London, 1981.

kinds — the keeping of diaries, the 'guessing' of time shown on cardboard clockfaces, the use of cards — that telepathy had been conclusively shown to exist. Maybe it had to the satisfaction of those actually working in the field; but the rest of the world has reserved judgment for a very long while. But the acceptance of radio and still more of television as matters of habitual, everyday experience makes things easier. If these devices can demonstrate what is going on far away at the very moment when it is happening, the idea that this can occur even without them is not impossible, however you may explain it.

Human survival of death, as has been seen, was *not* one of the subjects the Society was set up to investigate *per se*; but, of course, it was very closely linked with its principal themes. Thus, as Mrs Sidgwick wrote: 'If telepathy with the living is possible, I do not see how one can rule out telepathy with the dead.' If some component of the human being is independent of space and maybe of time — as telepathy, retrocognition, precognition and possibly out of the body experiences may show — why should this component not survive the body, which is constricted by these things? If the self, aware of its own identity, knowing that 'I am I', can have this knowledge direct, unmediated by the senses, does this not argue that it may survive after all of them cease to work, just as it survives for instance the loss of sight or hearing *or* of the ability to move or speak.[1] Incidentally, self awareness is not derived from the body image, which changes radically over the years. It can remain as vivid at ninety years old as at four, despite all the changes in that body's shape, capacity and functioning.

These grounds for thinking survival possible have little to do with the voices and the bits of family memories received through mediums, and cannot be destroyed by the curious theory of Super ESP which has grown up over the years. This is, I think, closely connected with the theory of clairvoyance (which tends to be less popular with SPR members in this country than it is abroad, notably in France and the United States). This theory implies that at some level of consciousness certain people can become paranormally aware

---

1. Guy Wint wrote, after recovering from his first stroke, of the extreme impatience he had felt imprisoned as it were incommunicado in his near-useless body. Guy Wint, *The Third Killer*, London, 1965.

of facts – and landscapes – not vividly present to any one individual mind past or present with which they have any link; that they can draw on some kind of universal knowledge; in fact, that they are potentially omniscient. Data put forward to support this theory are often explained in this country as the result of a mixture of precognition and telepathy. To check that the facts obtained by apparent clairvoyance are accurate – and they often are – you have to get into touch with some human mind that will authenticate them. Telepathy may link the perceiver with that mind, and precognition may reveal its future state.

It is hard to say which explanation is less satisfying. That of Super ESP has commended itself to at least two of the Society's Presidents,[1] and has been attacked by other distinguished persons. Plainly, if it holds good, any hope of proving survival on the basis of communication with the spirits of the dead is ruled out.

Theories of temporary survival – for seven years or so, after which 'messages' begin to fade out – have been put forward; these might account for many curious records, including that of a man suddenly killed in an accident who managed soon after dying to draw attention to the fact that his dog, shut up alone at home, would need to be fed. There have also been theories that a person's experiences and memories might continue passively to exist for a while after his death, to be consulted by mediums and others much as a dead writer's books may be.

It seems unlikely that psychical research as such can prove conclusively that the capacity to survive death is a 'faculty of man' real rather than supposed. Its data can be marshalled on this side or on that, but to interpret what they mean in this particular field will depend on how the individual makes up his mind and forms his decision: a decision which may simply be to suspend judgment, as did Professor Broad who thought he might survive death but rather hoped he would not.

Parapsychological findings may however reveal a universe in which survival can be thought possible; a universe in which consciousness is as significant as physical processes, and the individual mind interacts not only with its own body and sometimes with exterior objects, but with other minds near or distant in time and space.

---

1. Professor Gardner Murphy (1945) and Professor H. H. Price (1958).

Here the developing alliance with contemporary physics could be of great importance. This is beginning to revive the dormant sense of mystery, awe and wonder so long inhibited by self-important academics certain that 'what we don't know isn't knowledge'. Its stress on the part played by the observer in perceiving and recording what goes on – a phenomenon known in psychical research as 'experimenter-effect' – is raising the general boggle threshold; as does its acceptance of an intellectual universe of strange concepts which can only be accepted because they have been shown to produce verifiable results.

On the other hand the high arcane language in which these concepts are set forth often irritates – and alienates – those without specialized mathematical training who nevertheless want to understand what is going on. It is difficult to think both in verbal and in mathematical terms and anyone who attempts to do so must be agonizingly well aware of the Italian proverb 'Tradutore traditore; the translator is a traitor'. But it can be done to some extent, as the work of Bertrand Russell shows; he combined philosophy and mathematics with an admirably lucid and trenchant prose style.

Translation of some sort is a *must* in view of one of the imminent dangers threatening the Society; that its researches may in themselves be narrowed down by the use of esoteric language, and that communication between different disciplines, and with the minds of ordinary educated people may break down. The use of acronyms, jargon terms and – worse still – of normal words kidnapped, distorted and sold into slavery to carry different meanings – may of course be justifiable as a shorthand, time saving, way of talking between experts (rather like the Psalmist's 'deep speaketh unto deep through the noise of the waterspouts'.) But it can – and does – serve to conceal meanings (as happened when Edwardian ladies gossiped in French so that the parlourmaid should not understand) to mystify what are called 'laymen', and – as a status symbol – to indicate membership of some important in-group (like children's secret languages at school). It shows, in fact, that a researcher is 'one of the boys', accepted as scientifically respectable.

This deliberate use of gobbledygook is of course often connected with a nervous need to convince *all* scientists that they are wrong in thinking parapsychology an affair of superstition, fraud, inefficient experimental work and general woolly-mindedness. (Why? No one feels urgently compelled to convince members of the Flat Earth Society that they are mistaken.) This need, incidentally, can make experimenters more interested in the techniques of their work than in its object; rather as a man might tinker with his car engine all one fine Saturday afternoon instead of getting in and driving off to explore the terrain.

I have dwelt on the matter of language because a wider development of the habit of 'signalling' solely in technical terms could destroy the multi-disciplinary basis of the Society for Psychical Research in this country and of many more such societies abroad. This would serve to build no source of knowledge, no universality of discussion, argument, cross-fertilization of ideas; only a wide, barren campus surrounded by mini Towers of Babel (constructed of the most expensive modern ivory substitute – sometimes also used to protect the skulls of their administrators). Each would be surrounded by an electric fence to ensure that its inhabitants were kept incommunicado, safe from contamination by the words, thoughts and intellectual assumptions of other groups. Sometimes they might be let out to play basketball together; but talking would be forbidden.

This danger once faced and averted, here's to the next hundred years.

Presidents of the Society

To trace the development of different kinds of research it has been necessary to go scampering up and down the stairs of time. I hope the following sketches of the Society's Presidents, in chronological order, may help to show the fine, mixed, simultaneous way in which its work was carried on by *individuals*, with their ideas, their assumptions, the philosophical or scientific or theological or historical disciplines in which their minds were formed, their personal interactions, and naturally, an undercurrent which no dowser can track with accuracy, their likes and dislikes.

Of course not all such individuals were Presidents; nor did they need to be to get their work recognized. Many of them have been cited in the context of the investigations to which they contributed; but there is not 'world enough or time' to write in detail about each one.

The list of actual Presidents does however show in general how many different sorts of people, how many different points of view have been (and still are) involved in the Society. It includes two Nobel Prize winners and eight Fellows of the Royal Society among various philosophers and physicists, psychologists and psychiatrists, medical men, classicists, civil servants, theologians, astronomers and electrical and electronics experts, not to mention an anthropologist, a marine biologist, a physiologist specializing in visual perception, an educationalist, and a future Prime Minister.

It must be remembered that one can react emotionally to the dead as well as to the living, not from any parapsychological angle, but from feelings about their behaviour, the way they set out their conclusions, even their prose style, pompous or diffuse or over-technical or computerish, or clear, filled with commonsense, touched with humour, shaped by a knowledge of the humanities. So if a certain distaste for any one of these people should emerge from what I have tried to make a fair statement, this may well be the reason why. The reverse holds good too. I know I should have had an especial liking for some of them; F. W. H. Myers, for instance, William Barrett and Andrew Lang, Gilbert Murray and T. W. Mitchell.

Henry Sidgwick, 1838–1900
President 1882–4 and 1888–92

As Henry Sidgwick was one of the founding fathers of the Society and its first President, further details about him will be found in the first chapter of this book.

He went up to Trinity College, Cambridge in 1855, became a Fellow in 1859, resigned in 1869 for religious reasons, was made Praelector in Moral and Political Philosophy in 1875, and served as Knightbridge Professor of Moral Philosophy from 1883 until 1900.

With Frederic Myers, Lord Rayleigh, A. J. Balfour, and Balfour's sister Eleanor (whom he was to marry) he founded a small group to investigate professional mediums, with which he persevered despite 'the persistent and singular frustration' it involved. Heartened by some of W. F. Barrett's work in 'thought transference' he consented to become the SPR's first President in 1882, a decision which encouraged several of his friends – who had been hesitant – to join it. In 1884 he interviewed Madame Blavatsky and other Theosophist leaders; the sub-committee set up as a result recommended – successfully – that Richard Hodgson should be sent to India to investigate the phenomena which had been reported. Sidgwick resigned the Presidency to allow for change but was re-elected in 1888.

He did a great deal of tedious, inconspicuous, necessary work, notably in verifying the ghost stories some of which were used as a basis for his wife's report on *Phantasms of the Dead*; and carrying out, with her, an elaborate series of experiments to test the suggestion made by two Danish psychologists that what looked like telepathy was in fact the effect of involuntary whispering. (They concluded that this did not account for all the results obtained.) More excitingly, he and she went off to a high powered polyglot houseparty – English, French, German and Italian were spoken – at Professor Richet's house in the Ile Rombaut to test the powers of Eusapia Paladino.

In spite of a stammer, he was a lively talker who 'always succeeded in finishing his sentences'. That he had an agreeable sense of humour appears in his lament about 'the unfortunate appearance of the first students of Newnham' (who were all very good looking and presumably likely to distract male undergraduates from their work).

As a final summary Professor Broad's words in his obituary notice cannot be bettered: 'His main contribution to psychical research' lay 'in the weight which his known intelligence and integrity gave to the serious study of the subject, in the tact and patience with which he handled the very difficult team he had to lead rather than to drive', in his 'extremely high standard of evidence' and in 'his courage and persistence'.

Professor Balfour Stewart, FRS, 1828–87
President 1885–7

Professor Balfour Stewart was one of the distinguished physicist members of the Society. Born in Scotland, he worked at the Universities of Edinburgh and St Andrews on 'natural philosophy', the ancient name for science. In 1859 he was made Director of Kew Observatory and in 1862 became a Fellow of the Royal Society in connexion with his research into radiant heat. He was appointed Professor of Physics at Queens College, Manchester in 1870. His published work included studies of physics and of energy; and he was much interested in the curious phenomena of the medium D. D. Home, of whom he is quoted as saying that though 'Mr Home possesses great electrobiological power by which he influences those present . . . however susceptible the persons in the room to that assumed influence, it will hardly be contended that Mr Home biologized the recording instrument'. Sir William Crookes, who recorded this, was not sure what was meant by 'electrobiological power'. Today, equated with psychokinesis, it might very well be suspected of affecting that instrument.

Professor Stewart's Presidential Address emphasized the need to accumulate, to sift and to discuss evidence for the paranormal. Later he set up a Committee to investigate 'alleged Spiritualistic phenomena' and included among such distinguished members as Crookes, Lodge, Myers and Gurney a skilful conjurer named A. J. Lewis.

Henry Sidgwick
President 1888–92
(see page 175)

A. J. Balfour (created in 1922 first Earl of Balfour), KG, OM, 1848–1930
President 1893

One of the most brilliant of all the brilliant Balfour clan – which included Mrs Sidgwick – involved in the early work of the Society, Arthur Balfour was educated at Trinity College, Cambridge. A member of the 'Souls' group, he devoted himself to philosophical and metaphysical studies for several years, and kept up these interests throughout his political career, which began when he went into Parliament in 1876. In 1879 he published a book on *A Defence of Philosophic Doubt*, pleading for individual freedom of thought as against the increasing dogmatism of science.

His refreshingly practical Presidential Address noted that though the progress of psychical research had not kept pace with that of the physical sciences, the facts established 'though they do not easily fit in to the framework of the sciences . . . yet require investigation and explanation' despite the well entrenched opinion that 'because we cannot as it were put our phenomena in a retort, boil them over a spirit lamp and always get the same results – the phenomena themselves are not worth examining'. He was especially interested in telepathy

because it lent itself to experimental work, and he raised three important questions about it; whether it was 'equally diffused in all directions';
if so, why did not 'its effects diminish inversely as the square of the
distance', and how it was 'guided' so that 'X's message reaches Y rather
than the world at large'.

He served as Prime Minister from 1902 to 1905, and yet found time
to accept the Presidency of the British Association in 1904. There is no
need to describe the rest of his outstanding public life. He gave the
Romanes Lectures and the Gifford Lectures: it was when he was
preparing the latter in 1912 that the Palm Sunday case (described in
the chapter on The Cross Correspondences) of which he was the unconscious centre, first began. It is said that when he lay dying eighteen
years later he was heard to remark, 'I am longing to get to the Other
Side to see what it's like'.

William James, 1842–1910
President 1894–5

Although his father was much interested in the ideas of Swedenborg,
William James, earliest of the Society's American Presidents, seems at
first to have accepted the mechanist view of medicine current during
his time as a student at Harvard, where he achieved his MD in 1869,
and later taught physiology and psychology. Only after reading the
French philosopher Renouvier did he accept the idea of free will and
realize that 'the mind does act independently of physical coercion'. In
1887 he was cured of insomnia by a faith healer, and thereafter opposed
the suggestion that such people should only be allowed to practise
under licence.

Five years earlier he had co-operated in the foundation of the Society
and then of its American counterpart.

He worked closely with F. W. H. Myers, whose concept of the
'subliminal mind' he admired. Both were aware of the different functions of the right and left sides of the brain, recently in the limelight
once more.

He investigated various mediums, including that 'white crow' Mrs
Piper. Among his many brilliant contributions to *Proceedings* was a

study of a man who 'spoke with tongues' (in what James called 'a deific style'; this involved a fine confused fluency in 'Jacobethan English'). With a rare and admirable lack of snobbery, cultural, intellectual or academic, he looked for data wherever they seemed to occur and however lacking they were in conventional respectability; but he then tested them all with the utmost care, sometimes involving professional enquiry agencies.

His Presidential Address in 1896 was cautious but hopeful. The hypnotic field had not yet 'yielded an important harvest'. 'Experimental thought transference' seemed to prove Richet mistaken in believing everyone capable of it (one wonders why Rhine came to revive the notion). Experimenters should be on the *qui vive* for cheating. Myers' *Census of Hallucinations* was admirable; but were 17,000 cases enough? Nevertheless, the Society had produced well documented evidence of the paranormal in personal experience, however 'capricious, discontinuous, and not easily controlled' this might be. He made the crucial point that 'science had come to be identified . . . with a certain belief that the deeper order of Nature is exclusively mechanical', but that the Society's work in showing this assumption to be a mistake, had 'restored continuity to history'.

It has been suggested that some of his brother Henry's work, notably *The Turn of the Screw* owes much to William James' thought. His own best known books, *The Varieties of Religious Experience* – much of which applies to parapsychology – and *The Will to Believe* both appeared in London in 1902.

Sir William Crookes, FRS, OM, 1832–1919
President 1896–9

Crookes, originally trained in chemistry, is described in the obituary as 'largely self-educated'; a process which combined accurate observation, fast learning and the invaluable ability to examine possible connexions between the data of different disciplines. In physical science this stood him in good stead. He became an authority on the spectroscope, discovered thallium in 1861 and cathode rays in 1876, invented the radiometer and the spintharoscope (which counted the alpha rays emitted by radium) and was the first man to have his house lit by electricity – he made the bulbs himself.

Much to his surprise his capacity to make and test connexions between different subjects proved less acceptable when he investigated psychical phenomena in terms of physics. His articles on the subject in the *Quarterly Journal of Science* between 1871 and 1874 caused considerable controversy (perhaps such titles as 'Notes on Phenomena called Spiritual' were off-putting) and the British Association flatly refused to publish one of his papers.

He worked with several mediums, among them D. D. Home, observing that the latter's powers were 'very variable', that he had himself seen him 'lying almost fainting on the floor after producing certain phenomena' and that 'psychic force uses up nervous energy'. (Later observations, on 'Stella C' in the 1920s and on one or two Russian sensitives today, record the same thing.) Crookes described various tests he carried out – electrical, mechanical and otherwise – said he had personally seen Home levitate three times, that there were many good witnesses to other instances, and stated categorically that certain occurrences such as the movement of material substances and the production of sounds resembling electrical discharges recur under circumstances in which they cannot be explained by any physical law at present known. 'I am certain. My whole scientific education has been one long lesson in exactness of observation.'

Though, after 1875, he ceased publicly to study possible relationships between physics and the paranormal he stuck to his guns, and said, in his Presidential Address to the British Association in 1898, that he stood by his earlier statements. He was also serving at that time as President of the Society for Psychical Research; where his Presidential Address (*Proceedings* Volume XII, 1896–7) declared characteristically that 'my *vital* knowledge of my own ignorance' had led to the study of D. D. Home and to 'a glimpse of some important laws of matter and energy' and that he was now attempting to clear away 'certain preconceptions . . . which seem to depend on a too hasty assumption that we know more about the universe than we can possibly do at present'.

Hindsighted but interesting criticisms of some of his electrical tests of Home were made by serious investigators in the 1960s. The same decade saw attempts – in the already fusty Victorian-baiting mode – to create a peculiarly unlikely scandal about his work with a female medium, Florence Cook, liked by his wife as well as himself. These attempts, founded on three hearsay, self-contradictory reports by an old gentleman, alleged that the investigations were a cover up for a liaison with Miss Cook (surely some simpler method could have been found than in seances in Crookes' own house, with family and friends around) and that the results were bogus.

The phenomena on record included startling materializations – perhaps hallucinatory – which remain unexplained, though the *New Scientist* at one time suggested that Crookes had been affected by long-term thallium poisoning. That my own boggle threshold sinks against the latter's original interpretation of the evidence shows no more than that it is hard to believe. But the old gentleman's thesis is still harder to accept. It is worth noting that Charles Richet (qv), who had at first ridiculed Crookes, later apologized after certain researches of his own.

Sir William served as President of the Royal Society in 1913. Some of his parapsychological hypotheses and arguments are to be found in the publications of the Society for Psychical Research. Those interested in earlier papers should consult a valuable collection of them (*Crookes and the Spirit World*, London, 1972) edited by M. R. Barrington, K. M. Goldney, and R. G. Medhurst. I have always liked his statement about an event he had observed: 'I did not say it was possible. I said it happened'.

F. W. H. Myers, 1843–1901
President 1900

Si monumentum requiris, circumspice, runs the epitaph to Sir Christopher Wren in St Paul's Cathedral, whose architect he was. Though it is far too sweeping to apply this sentence to Frederic Myers and the Society for Psychical Research, there can be a temptation to do so.

Of all the founder members he had perhaps the liveliest and widest-ranging mind. Even now, the proponent of some 'new' idea may well find it embedded in his work. Thus, he suggested as early as 1887 that telepathic intuition was mediated through the right side of the brain. He observed that in individual experiments 'latent ideas emerge rather

than those which conscious attention is keeping uppermost,' so that
the receiver might come up with an association with a message rather
than the message itself (say, the image of a scarlet shawl rather than the
name of its habitual wearer). He insisted on the need for a glossary of
terms, and contributed to it the words supernormal, telepathy, veridical (of hallucinations) and telekinesis, now replaced by psychokinesis
or PK, and he appealed for studies of the physiological conditions in
which spontaneous psychical experiences tended to come through;
sleep, dreams, trances, epilepsy, dissociation and approaching death,
and also induced hypnotic states.

There is no need to detail here all Myers' multifarious contributions
to psychical research – they appear elsewhere in this book. It should be
said though that long before Kuhn he realized the vital importance of
working out a new pattern of fact and thought into which the findings
of parapsychology could be integrated and that long before Jung he
formulated his concept of the many-levelled mind, whence such a
pattern could develop.

Although he had an unfortunate habit of transferring to the written
word – by way of Significant Capital Letters – the vocal mannerism
known as 'speaking with a plum in one's mouth', he was always lucid,
and could be trenchant. Thus, in his Presidential Address (*Proceedings*
XV, 1900–1) insisting on the importance of a detached and scientific
approach to phenomena, he asked 'What should we have learnt from
the Vedas, the Book of the Dead, – nay, from the Christian records
themselves – had we approached these sacred texts in the spirit alternatively of Simple Simon and of Voltaire?' This same Address stated
his conviction that psychical research had produced satisfactory evidence for clairvoyance and for telepathy, certainly between the living
and perhaps between the living and the dead. He was himself persuaded of survival.

Alas that a message received through a medium that he would die in
1902 led him to plan out his work with reference to that date. In fact he
died of a heart attack in Rome in 1901.

Let William James' obituary have the last word on him, noting his
development from early training in classical literature and philosophy
into 'the wary critic of evidence, the skilful handler of hypotheses, the
learned neurologist and omnivorous reader of biological and cosmolog-
ical matter known to his friends in later years'.

He contributed many papers to the Society's publications, and collaborated with Gurney and Podmore in *Phantasms of the Living*. His most famous work, *Human Personality and its Survival of Bodily Death* (London, 1903), unfinished when he died, was completed by Richard Hodgson and Alice Johnson and hailed as 'a vast but coherent synthesis'. It has aroused enthusiasm and disagreement ever since.

Two other books were *Fragments of Prose and Poetry*, edited by his widow (London, 1904) and *Fragments of Inner Life* brought out by the SPR (London, 1961).

Sir Oliver Lodge, DSc, FRS, 1851–1935
President 1901–3
and again (with Mrs Sidgwick) as President of Honour in 1932

Though he came of a family of clerics, mathematicians and doctors, Oliver Lodge left school at 14 and thereafter educated himself at various classes including one run by Tyndall where he experimented with electricity; a good jumping off place for a man who was to make such important contributions to radio communication. After matriculating in London he left home to live there, supporting himself by coaching while he studied at the Royal College of Science and at University College. He got his DSc in 1877, and by 1881 he was Professor of Physics and Mathematics at Liverpool. In 1884 he joined the Society, not because he liked the subject of psychical research but – as he notes in his autobiography – because he had 'found a series of facts that were unpalatable and mainly neglected by scientific men, and felt them worthy of attention'. He also contributed to *Nature* a paper on some new experiments in telepathy. In 1887 he became a Fellow of the Royal Society.

In 1900 – after stipulating that he must be allowed to continue his work in psychical research – he accepted an offer to become first Principal of Birmingham University, and shaped its course until he retired in 1919. His knighthood came in 1902, when he had already served for a year as President of the SPR. To its work, throughout his membership, he contributed a great deal of time, trouble, energy and thought; and what has been called the 'instrument theory' of the relationship between mind and brain. It is sad that he is now popularly remembered more for his book on the death of his son Raymond, than for his scientific work in both his chosen fields, 'the physical and the psychical', from whose combined study he hoped for so much. It is sad, too, that so many of his findings in the latter sphere, still interesting and important in themselves, were formulated in terms of 'Ether . . . the common factor of the material and spiritual worlds', a concept now as completely discarded as the 18th century 'phlogiston'. In 1913 he was President of the British Association. He spent much time in his later years in writing and lecturing.

He was, and remained all his life a genial, warm-hearted and sympathetic character, with great gusto. Even in his seventies he enjoyed waltzing (though a young partner of his once remarked to Julian Huxley with awed though affectionate amusement that the exercise was rather like dancing with the dome of St Paul's Cathedral). He made lasting friends with people of very different temperaments and views; the shy Scot Andrew Lang, the enthusiastic Frederic Myers, William Crookes (with whose early theory that telepathy was a matter of 'brain waves' he disagreed), Charles Richet (with whose logical French materialism he was at loggerheads, though they worked happily together in observing and trying to evaluate the phenomena of Eusapia Paladino), Arthur and Gerald Balfour, and William James, then Professor of Philosophy at Harvard. Though he deprecated 'the cold blooded manner' in which James 'regarded psychical research as a branch of psychology' it was through him that he first met that remarkable American medium Mrs Piper, whose phenomena convinced him as early as 1889 of human survival and of the possibility of communicating with the dead.

Although he repeatedly affirmed the need to maintain a scientific attitude he seems sometimes to have become rather obscurantist in this particular connexion, and to have felt that it was irreverent to ask some types of question about it. Thus, (even though the famous Mrs Piper had, under the control of Stainton Moses, given advice about investments) in 1913 my father E. S. P. Haynes, a solicitor, was much worried about a client of his, faced with an enormous unexpected claim for arrears of income tax which could have ruined him. They had arisen because the trustees of a marriage settlement had omitted to deduct income tax from the proceeds sent to him. Both trustees – one of whom was my grandfather, also a solicitor – were now dead. My father was certain they had had good reason for acting as they did and wrote to Sir Oliver explaining the position and asking for an introduction to a medium who could put him in touch with them. The reply was that income tax was not a subject suitable for discussion with spirits, and that he could *not* introduce a medium. My father was however referred to the editor of *Light*, who was less than helpful, and seemed to feel that some sort of sacrilege was suggested. All very odd when one reflects on Sir Oliver's later dictum – but perhaps he had had time to change his mind by then – that 'a departed person still has a power to help struggling humanity and can occasionally communicate with those left behind'. Why should agonized strugglers with the Inland Revenue be excepted? Luckily soon after these rebuffs my father woke at one o'clock one morning fully aware of the solution. He concluded either that he had discussed the matter with his father and forgotten it, or that 'subconscious cogitation' had been at work, or that he had received a direct spirit message. He plumped for subconscious cogitation, and was rather relieved that he had not been obliged to ascribe the knowledge to a medium.

Professor Sir William Barrett, FRS, 1844–1925
President 1904

William Barrett has long been honoured among the chief founders of the Society. One of the first of those distinguished physicists who have contributed so much down the years to its work and to its intellectual standing, he combined great vitality with great intellectual gifts, and an insatiable – and wide ranging – scientific curiosity with stubborn perseverance.

He worked as assistant to that passionate sceptic Professor Tyndall at the Royal Institution from 1862 to 1867, and knew Faraday, who had already published the results of an experiment showing that unconscious muscular movement was involved in 'table-turning' (though what initiated that movement was not diagnosed).

He was interested in all varieties of psychical phenomena, and admitted the possibility of 'a magnetic sense' (whose existence in bees, pigeons and snails has been established over the last few years and whose existence in man now seems extremely likely). Perhaps it should be mentioned that some of his professional work dealt with magnetic alloys. His own careful studies of hypnotism, like those of Myers and others, helped to bring about its scientific recognition and therapeutic use in this country; and already at the turn of the century he was urging that its practice (then often to be found in music-hall 'turns') should be restricted by law, and that it should be used 'only under proper medical supervision'. (Despite pressure from members of the Society itself, and from groups dealing with medical and dental hypnosis, nothing of the sort happened until the 1980s.)

'In the autumn of 1881', wrote Mrs Sidgwick in Barrett's obituary, 'he was already discussing with Henry Sidgwick, Myers, and Gurney in Cambridge the formation of the Society.' He had brought with him the large collection of apparently paranormal cases which he had been accumulating and checking for some time. It was he who convened the preliminary conference in January 1882. He was made Vice-President, and Hon. Secretary to the Committee dealing with 'Thought-Reading', and wrote a paper on the subject for the first issue of *Proceedings*. In 1884 he founded the *Journal* (which was then circulated only to members), and edited it for twelve months, despite the fact that he went to Boston that year, stimulated the formation of an American Society, and attended a meeting of the British Association in Montreal; rather magnanimously, in view of a curious experience some eight years previously, when he had read a paper concerned with psychical research at one of its meetings, asking that a scientific committee should be set up to examine the evidence. Though he was supported by Crookes, Rayleigh and others, and though he held the Chair of Physics at the Royal College of Science in Dublin, a violent controversy broke out, no committee was appointed, and his paper was not published in the usual way in the Annual Report.

Barrett became a Fellow of the Royal Society in 1899. One of his liveliest and most lasting contributions to psychical research was his investigation of dowsing, much of it published in the Society's *Proceedings* Vol XV (1900–1). This paper enquired 'whether the claim of the dowser has any basis in fact', and if so whether this comes from conscious or unconscious experience or observation, or whether there is evidence of paranormal perception. It contains an account of how dowsing is carried out in various parts of Europe, the United States, Latin America, South Africa and Australia; a survey of experimental work, including some of his own, with its successes and failures; a discussion of geological data; and a most interesting historical survey citing a report made by Del Rio as early as 1599 on a Spanish group, the Zahoris, and Kircher's observation in 1650 that unconscious muscular action was involved in the movements of the divining rod. Elsewhere he outlined an idea later put forward by the French physicist Yves Rocard in *Le Secret du Sourcier*[1] that 'the dowser may be . . . gifted with a sense affected by any slight interruption in the continuity or modification of one of the lines of terrestrial magnetic or electric force'; but subsequently abandoned it for the theory that dowsing is like clairvoyance, due to 'a transcendental discernment possessed by the dowser's subconscious mind'.

Barrett's Presidential Address in January 1904 noted that prejudice against the Society's work seemed to be dying down except among scientists; 'because the phenomena cannot be repeated at pleasure' (any more than a shower of meteorites can) and 'because physical science excludes . . . the element of personality'. Twenty years later, in 'Some Reminiscences of 50 Years of Psychical Research'[2] he was reiterating Andrew Lang's plea that the Society should investigate history in more detail; noting that his own early impression that 'spiritualistic phenomena, when not fraudulent, were due to the hallucination of the observer' had given place, after further research, to the conviction that they could be objective; and quoting the saying of the 17th century Glanvil, one of the first Fellows of the Royal Society, that 'matters not proved ought not to be denied because we cannot conceive how they could be performed'. He accepted the idea of survival, and believed that telepathy existed both in men and in animals; but was careful to distinguish between its workings and those of radio communication.

He was throughout his life much interested in the experiences of the dying; his fascinating collection of *Death Bed Visions* was posthumously published in 1926, the year after his own death, still in harness.

---

1. Paris, 1964.
2. *Proceedings* 34, 1924.

Professor Charles Richet, 1850–1935
President 1905

Charles Richet, a very distinguished French physiologist (he won the Nobel Prize in 1913 for his discovery of anaphylaxis) whole-heartedly accepted the occurrence of psi phenomena, which he interpreted in a strictly materialist way. 'I shall admit any hypothesis', he wrote towards the end of his long life, 'short of mathematical and physical impossibility, rather than that of an extra-terrene mind.'

He was writing on dual personality as early as 1875, and ten years later, on psychological reflexes. In 1884 he suggested in *La Revue Philosophique* that 'feeble thought-reading powers or slight mental reverberations may possibly be detected in most persons by applying the laws of probability to a great number of guesses made by them at a limited series of objects'; a suggestion carried out by J. B. Rhine some fifty years later. He did many smaller scale experiments of his own and – while Professor of Physiology at the Faculty of Medicine of Paris – wrote a long paper describing and discussing them in the SPR *Proceedings* for 1888–9. Among the subjects investigated were 'thought-transmission', hypnosis, medical diagnosis and psychokinesis (in connexion with table turning). He argued that clairvoyance existed, as well as telepathy; and set out his methods, which involved the use of playing cards, photographs, drawings and dowsing rods.

In 1890 he founded the *Annales des Sciences Psychiques*, whose title was changed in 1920 to *Revue Metapsychique*. He worked alone or with colleagues of different nationalities with various mediums, including Mrs Piper, Eusapia Paladino and Marthe Béraud, and summed up his general conclusions in *Traité de Metapsychique* (Paris 1922) translated into English in 1923 as *Thirty Years of Psychical Research*. Although he ignored the work of Lambertini and dismissed all parapsychological investigation before Mesmer's time as 'mythical' the book is still of lively interest. He divides phenomena into mental and physical. The first category includes what would now be called general extra-sensory perception, here labelled cryptaesthesia or *lucidité*, foreshadowing the controversial modern doctrine of Universal ESP. The second covers all physical manifestations, including psychokinesis (the inexplicable movements of objects) and materialization by means of ectoplasm, a word coined by himself. This, he wrote, seemed to be an unfamiliar kind of matter, produced by 'emanations from the human organism'. These emanations could 'a) affect distant objects, and b) mould themselves into strange simulacra which can for a time be seen, heard, felt and photographed'. Ectoplasm could also take the form of 'fluidic threads', 'rigid rays' or 'pseudo-pods' (imitation limbs). After his death, René Warcollier, another French parapsychologist, noted that Richet and Gustav Geley had mixed cholesterin with the paraffin wax to be used at a seance at the Institut Metapsychique with the materializing medium Kluski, and had later confirmed that the casts of 'spirit hands' obtained there had indeed been made with this wax; whatever else had happened, they had not been previously prepared and smuggled in.

The book reasserted that 'the spiritist hypothesis is absurd' in its assumption that 'human personality survives the destruction of the brain'; and yet Richet's last Professorial lecture in 1926, when he had to retire under an age limit, again proclaimed his conviction that parapsychological phenomena did in fact occur.

A genial man who liked talking, food, wine, poetry and good company, he had many friends in England, including Myers, Gurney, the Sidgwicks and Lodge who took him to task for using the word 'vibration' too loosely, and years later noted when writing his obituary that he had received a letter from him, dated July 1932 saying that 'without being resolutely spiritualist in the manner of Conan Doyle and Allan Kardec, I am insensibly approaching your ideas'.

The Rt Hon Gerald Balfour, PC, LLD, 1854–1945
President 1906–7

Gerald Balfour has been described as 'inclined to be remote, detached and dispassionate' in the tradition of his family. A classical scholar fascinated by philosophy and natural science, he retained these interests all his life. At Trinity College, Cambridge, like his eldest brother

Arthur, he met Henry Sidgwick and other members of the psychical research group and joined the Society in 1883.

Though he was elected to the House of Commons in 1885, and served at different periods as Chief Secretary for Ireland and as President of the Board of Trade he quitted politics after the electoral defeat of 1906, and devoted many years to studying the complicated, interlocking, automatically written scripts known as the Cross Correspondences (about which he contributed a long article to the *Hibbert Journal* in 1909) and he became particularly interested in the development of 'Mrs Willett's' work in this connexion; not only for the data it produced but for the way in which it developed. He wrote in 1935 (*Proceedings* XL) a very long survey of her mediumship, written as a study of the psychological mechanisms involved in the personality of a sensitive who remained awake and aware while writing down her 'messages', now concentrated, now letting 'the pen run free'. He provided an immense museum of data here, too little used; making it clear throughout that though he believed in Mrs Willett's 'supernormal powers' and was inclined to believe in survival, it was not his object to establish evidence for either. What he wished to do was to illuminate the actual process that went on.

Most of his later concepts are already implicit in his Presidential Address (*Proceedings* Vol. XIX, 1905–7). He dismisses Flournoy's idea that telepathy is physical, a matter of 'rays', defining it as 'a universal form of interaction between psychic existences'. He 'cannot understand' Myers' ideas about the subliminal self, preferring Leibnitz' theory that the living creature is 'a hierarchy of monads'. He sees the human individual as 'an ordered association of psychic units, or centres of consciousness, linked by telepathy', and so on. If that telepathy breaks down, presumably multiple personalities emerge.

Though all this seems excessively esoteric, and one is sometimes reminded of the riddle 'What goes ninety nine clunk, ninety nine clunk, ninety nine clunk' (answer, a centipede with a wooden leg), those with world enough and time to read his work may still find much that is rewarding.

Mrs Henry Sidgwick, née Eleanor Mildred Balfour, 1845–1936
President 1908–9
(and again, as President of Honour with Sir Oliver Lodge), 1932

Mrs Sidgwick was the eldest of eight children born to J. M. Balfour and Blanche, daughter of the second Lord Salisbury. Among her brothers were Arthur, who became Prime Minister, Francis, an outstanding biologist who died young in a mountaineering accident, and Gerald, a philosopher. Deeply interested in pure mathematics, which she thought 'specially suited to a disembodied existence', she collaborated with her brother-in-law, Lord Rayleigh in experimental work on electrical standards of measurement, and in three papers published in the *Philosophical Transactions of the Royal Society*. In 1874 she sat with various physical mediums but was not impressed. She married Henry Sidgwick in 1876. Closely connected with Newnham College all her life, she served as its Treasurer for many years, and as its Principal from 1892 to 1910.

She joined the SPR in 1884, edited its *Journal* and *Proceedings* from 1888 to 1897, became a Council member in 1901, and was Honorary Secretary from 1907 to 1932. An admirable administrator, she also contributed many reports to the Society, reports which exemplified her clarity of thought, her energy and her enormous industry. Among them were studies of Mrs Piper's trance phenomena (she thought her 'control' was 'some element of her own consciousness') and of Mrs Leonard's Book Tests, in which she suggested that clairvoyance might be involved; she also wrote on Gilbert Murray's telepathy experiments. She helped to compile *Phantasms of the Living* and the first *Census of Hallucinations*, and wrote many papers for *Proceedings* from one on *Phantasms of the Dead* in 1885 to one on 'The History of the SPR' in 1932.

Mrs Salter, who had known her for many years both at home and at Cambridge said in an article setting out her brilliant, solid work, 'I never remember hearing her make anything that could be called a joke', but paid tribute to her 'twin qualities of intellect and character'.

Arthur Smith, 1848–1922
President 1910

Lawyer, business man and administrator, Arthur Smith's Presidential Address claimed as his only distinction 'that he has worked for the objects which our Society seeks from days even before its foundation, and is determined to go on thus working'. He joined the Society in 1882, became a member of Council in 1883, and served with admirable efficiency as Hon Treasurer (and business adviser) for twenty-nine stressful years, from 1888 to 1917.

He was much interested in the nature of evidence; as the presentation of relevant facts, as personal testimony, and as legal or philosophical proof. On this basis he believed that 'telepathy had been substantiated' but discussed as an open question the evidence for the identity of 'communicators' through mediums.

Andrew Lang, MA, 1844–1912
President 1911

Andrew Lang, born in Scotland, learned to read at four years old, and was further educated at Edinburgh Academy, the University of St Andrews and Balliol College, Oxford. He became a Fellow of Merton College, where the now well known anthropologist Evans-Wentz was among his pupils.

He approached psychical research in the main through his studies of anthropology and folk lore all over the world; and may have taken an especial interest in it because of his own occasional sightings of 'wraiths' both of the living and the dead. He took these with calm interest. He also described in one article published in January 1912, his experience of what he called a 'hereditary hallucination', a phantom cat said to be a family death omen, and noted that it had not coincided with death in his own case. Perhaps, all the same, some physiological premonition was involved; he died, suddenly and unexpectedly six months later.

A scholar of integrity, he wrote with clarity, wit, and an extraordinarily wide range of learning. He was concerned all his life to contrast theory with fact, to disturb the carefree composure of those who accepted say the whole tidy structure of Frazer's *Golden Bough* or Podmore's comforting if strident assertion that all poltergeist phenomena could be ascribed to 'naughty little girls', by adducing worldwide evidence to the contrary, drawn from oral tradition, historical sources and modern contemporary evidence. His studies of firewalking, as practised in Fiji, India, Japan and New Zealand were especially interesting in that they cited, as well as the accounts of reliable Western eyewitnesses, careful medical reports by doctors who had examined the feet of those who had trodden shoeless across beds of red hot embers. He paralleled these events with some of the phenomena of D. D. Home.

Among his sixty published volumes were of course the well known series of Fairy Books collected from so many national sources. The remainder, for full grown readers, included studies of Homer, of St Joan, of the much discussed 18th century London apparition in Cock Lane, of *Magic and Religion*, and of the whole territory of *Dreams and Ghosts*. All were well documented, as were his innumerable articles and papers, contributions to many periodicals, to the *Encyclopedia Britannica*, to his pupil Evans Wentz's work on *Psychical Research and Anthropology in Relation to the Fairy Faith in Ireland*; and of course to the Society's *Proceedings*.

The Rt Reverend William Boyd Carpenter, DD, 1841–1918
President 1912

Described in the Dictionary of National Biography as 'a persuasive advocate of Victorian religious liberalism' and in oral tradition as the Bishop who, to show he was a Modern Churchman, refused to wear gaiters, Dr Boyd Carpenter had a brilliant ecclesiastical career. He became Bishop of Ripon in 1884 and a Vice-President of the Society in 1888. His interest in it had been aroused, he said, by 'the studiously scientific spirit it claimed'. He founded Ripon Hall, a theological college, advocated Old Age Pensions, and, an admirable orator, gave both the Halsean and the Bampton Lectures. After resigning his bishopric in 1911, he became a Canon of Westminster. His Presidential Address the following year stressed that 'the resolution to maintain our power of discrimination in the presence of abnormal phenomena is essential to our mental equilibrium'; a very sensible remark, even if it does sound as though Gibbon had taken to preaching sermons.

Henri Bergson, 1859–1941
President 1913

There is no need to write in detail of one of the greater philosophers of the last hundred years, admired in his own country by the personalist Gabriel Marcel, by the Nobel prize winner Alexis Carrel, and by Pierre Teilhard de Chardin. He held the Chair of the Philosophy of History at the College de France from 1900 to 1921, and was elected to the Academie Française in 1918. Sadly, his death at ninety-one coincided with the last years of the appalling Nazi persecution of his fellow Jews, with whom he strongly identified himself.

He exerted a profound influence on the development of Vitalist philosophy in America and Europe, including Britain, where he aroused the interest of George Bernard Shaw and many others. William James hailed his work as bringing about 'a new Copernican revolution in thought'.

L'Evolution Créatrice (Paris 1909, soon afterwards translated as *Creative Evolution*) is the best known of all his books. Its central idea of *Elan Vital*, or living energy working through all things, helped (as Professor H. H. Price wrote in an obituary) to undermine the materialist basis of the then fashionable Positivism. Some of his physiology is now out of date, notably his attribution to the whole brain (rather than its left hemisphere) of the dominant power to concentrate on immediate action or abstract thought, so inhibiting the emergence of ESP and of much memory, which only surface at times of relaxation.

But the main stream of his thinking is still vividly alive. His Presidential Address praised the Society's methods of research in collecting, studying, verifying and comparing data, examining witnesses, evaluating evidence, 'as historians and lawyers do'; and acknowledged that 'when I note the enormous number of facts on record, their family likeness, the agreement of so many independent witnesses, I am led to believe in telepathy'. The experimental method, he observed, as it dealt solely with measurement, made it possible to study the workings of the brain, but not what it was working on (as it might be philosophy or the football pools, to use a modern instance). He thought the survival of death probable 'since the life of the organism is far wider than cerebral life'.

Among his other books – I cite the English editions – are *Time and Free Will* (London, 1910) and *Matter and Memory* (London, 1911).

Dr F. C. S. Schiller, DSc, 1864–1937
President 1914

Dr Schiller, a philosopher, joined the Society in 1884 and became a member of Council in 1901. He was interested throughout his life in psychical research, though the Dictionary of National Biography says he advocated the curious belief that 'truth can be equated with usefulness, and an opinion can be regarded as true if practically useful'; which does not sound like a good foundation for any kind of research, psychical or otherwise. (One remembers how totalitarian leaders have applied it.)

Nevertheless, his lively Presidential Address honoured earlier philosopher Presidents such as Henry Sidgwick, William James and Henri Bergson; and though much of his published work – including book reviews – combined long-windedness with a high degree of technicality and much conscientious fence-sitting, he could on occasion be trenchant, as when he wrote a splendidly belligerent paper headed 'Boss Locutus Est', attacking an article by one Hugo Munsterberg in the *Atlantic Monthly*. He maintained the balance between statistical and observational methods of research, noting that 'the Pythagorean reverence for number could be carried to a superstitious intensity' and that 'statistics may be made . . . to serve as opiates to the critical faculty and induce a comfortable glow of scientific rectitude'. He also stated plainly, in an article in *Proceedings* on 'Philosophical Assumptions in the Investigation of Future Life', that 'the philosopher can assure the psychical researcher that no *a priori* impossibilities block his way'.

In 1929 he was made Professor of Philosophy at the University of South California.

Professor Gilbert Murray, FBA, OM, 1866–1957
President 1915–16 and 1952

Gilbert Murray, classical scholar and internationalist, a most likeable man of great integrity was born in Australia. He was already interested in the fate of the aborigines when his widowed mother took him to England at eleven. At St John's College, Oxford he achieved a First in classics, was made a Fellow of New College, and later became Regius Professor of Greek. He wrote studies of Greek literature, and translated Greek plays so that they could be part of living English experience. His interest in oppressed peoples and in the cause of peace continued all his life. After World War I he founded the League of Nations Union, and lectured in many countries on the subject.

He was also one of the very few distinguished scholars to possess a remarkable degree of extra sensory perception. His first Presidential Address, in 1915, discussed a number of experiments with various friends – the letters of the young Aldous Huxley, describe an interesting incident – and with members of his family. He would leave the room in which the experimenters sat and go into another; both doors would be shut. In the experiment room a subject would be chosen, and written down word for word. He was then called back, and asked for his impressions, which were remarkably often wholly or partially accurate. The Address discussed the way in which these emerged; sometimes as a feeling of quality or atmosphere, sometimes in visual imagery, sometimes with complete understanding of the subject. For a while he would have liked to attribute them to hyperaesthesia, an extraordinarily acute sense of hearing, of which he was unconscious; but when it was found he had been guessing an unspoken idea in the mind of someone present (a waxed moustache; a kangaroo; a drunken man), he accepted telepathy. In 1919 Mrs Verrall published in Proceedings XXIX a discussion of the 505 experiments (each duly recorded on the spot) carried out between 1910 and 1915. The results were extremely significant.

Gilbert Murray's second Presidential Address in 1952 noted his doubts about spirit photography, haunted houses and 'most poltergeists', and his unease about precognition and psychokinesis; but reaffirmed his belief in telepathy.

L. P. Jacks, LLD, DD, 1860–1955
President 1917–18

A philosopher and a Unitarian clergyman, L. P. Jacks edited the long-famous *Hibbert Journal* for forty-one years, from 1902 to 1943. He was made Professor of Philosophy at Manchester College, Oxford in 1903, and its Principal in 1951, four years before his death.

His Presidential Address discussed 'The Theory of Survival in the Light of Its Context', and makes difficult and somewhat abrasive reading, not only because he rightly – and uncomfortably – calls into question matters of language and assumption, and inaccurate habits of thought, but also because in considering how one might recognize genuine 'communications' from the dead he ignores the very vivid 'sense of presence', the consciousness of an invisible identity, of which there are so many records. 'A man might be able to pick out his wife from 10,000 other women by her face, her voice, her dress', he wrote, 'but not by her moral characteristics', which some had thought to survive death. He suggested however that there might be a multiplicity of worlds in which the living and the dead co-exist simultaneously, presumably on a purely mental level.

John William Strutt, third Baron Rayleigh, OM, FRS, 1842–1919
President 1919

Lord Rayleigh (he succeeded his father in 1873) was an experimental physicist. He had a most distinguished career, beginning—where else? —at Trinity College, Cambridge, of which he became a Fellow in 1866. From 1879 till 1884 he was Cavendish Professor of Physics. In 1884 he was elected President of the British Association for the Advancement of Science. In 1904 he won the Nobel Prize, and in 1905 was awarded the Order of Merit. He discovered the gas argon, worked on electromagnetic phenomena, the wave theory of light and optics, and was interested, says Oliver Lodge, writing his obituary notice (*Proceedings* Vol 51, 1921) in 'the twinkling of the stars, the blue of the sky and the colours of opals'.

While still at Trinity, he joined in some hypnotic experiments with a Madam Card, and though not susceptible himself observed several of his personal friends willy-nilly obeying her commands. Afterwards 'they assured me that they could not help it, and indeed they made such fools of themselves that I had no difficulty in believing them. From that evening I have never felt any doubt of the possibility of influencing unwilling minds by suggestion.' This interested him in the idea that mediums might consciously or unconsciously induce hallucinations in their clients.

He married as it were into psychical research; his wife Evelyn was one of the brilliant Balfour brothers and sisters among whom were Arthur, Gerald, Francis and Eleanor (Sidgwick). He was further interested in the subject by William Crookes' *Early Notes on Phenomena called Spiritual during the years* 1870–73, which stressed the fact that D. D. Home with whom he had worked positively 'objected to darkness during his seances'. Crookes had also worked with a Mrs Jencken (née Fox) whom Rayleigh later asked to stay (together with husband, baby and nurse) at his country house. Though matrimony seems to have dimmed her powers, *some* interesting phenomena were obtained, recorded and evaluated. Later he became interested in Eusapia Paladino and thought her worth investigating despite the fact that she was known to cheat from time to time.

His Presidential Address points out that certain matters – such as globe lighting – are ignored by scientists because they cannot explain them; urges that telepathy should be 'fully established' (some of his predecessors took it for granted that this had already been done) and encourages Gilbert Murray to go on experimenting in this field.

William McDougall, FRS, 1871–1938
President 1920–1

William McDougall was a strong link between psychical research in this country and psychical research, just developing its transatlantic name of parapsychology, in America.

Educated at St John's College, Cambridge, he became Wilde Reader in Mental Psychology at Oxford in 1905, went in 1921 to Harvard as Professor of Psychology, and thence, in the same capacity, to Duke University, in 1927. Here one of his students was J. B. Rhine, from whose work so much has developed. McDougall founded at Duke in 1937 the still flourishing *Journal of Parapsychology*.

His remark on the first page of the first number, that parapsychology is concerned with 'the relations of mind to matter' sums up his convictions. He was what might today be called a dualist. He believed both mind and matter to be real, and he strongly opposed the behaviourism so fashionable in his time, and not quite extinct even now.

His Presidential Address (*Proceedings* XXXI, 1921) is still relevant and stimulating. He records his great admiration for the 'scientific candour and courage' of William James, the only previous President to have been a psychologist; and suggests that the failure of other psychologists and scientists to join the Society may arise not because they are all dogmatic materialists but because of their fear that if they show interest in the subject 'there may be a great outburst of superstition . . . on the part of the public'. (That this has indeed happened is not necessarily the result of psychical research; Chesterton's remark that if people don't believe in religion they'll believe in something else seems quite as likely an explanation.) In any case,

McDougall found 'the policy of sitting on the lid of Pandora's Box' risky and dangerous. It might be empty, he said, but he did not think so.

He valued the diversity of opinions in the Society, noted that he belonged to its right (presumably conservative) wing, and put forward a theory of personality as 'a society of selves . . . of which *I* am the dominant member likely to survive death . . . if the survival of death be true'. A fine provocative remark was that if his brains were to be destroyed 'I should enjoy only imageless thought'.

His books included *Physiological Psychology* (1905), *Body and Mind* (1911), *Outlines of Psychology* (1923), *Abnormal Psychology* (1926) and *The Energies of Man* (1933).

Dr T. W. Mitchell
President 1922

Dr Mitchell was the first practising physician to be elected President. His lively Presidential Address traced the historical connexion between medicine and parapsychology from the shaman of primitive societies to the priest/doctor of ancient Egypt and Greece; and went on to the ideas of Paracelsus and Mesmer. He made three particularly useful points; first, that it was continually necessary to return from neat theories to untidy facts; second, that a phenomenon could be real and objective no matter how idiotic the hypothesis put forward to explain it; third, that he believed many doctors and psychologists were unwilling to take part in psychical research because they feared their careers would be ruined if it were known.

Dr Mitchell served as Hon Secretary of the Medical Section of the Society set up in 1911; this arranged for a special medical issue of *Proceedings* in 1912, and for a special medical supplement to the *Proceedings* published in July 1914. At the end of World War I the Medical Section was discontinued, as the British Psychological Society had formed one of its own, and it seemed unnecessary to have two; a pity, from the psychical research point of view. Mitchell noted, incidentally, that Britain's ability to deal with war neuroses owed much to the pioneer work of men such as Gurney and Myers; and also how useful medical psychology could be in the study of 'mediumistic trances', deep hypnosis, and multiple personality. He published in 1922 a book on *Medical Psychology and Psychical Research* and his Myers Memorial Lecture entitled *Beneath the Threshold* (1931) suggested that the gap was narrowing between the concepts of Myers and of Freud, of whom he was an eclectic and undogmatic follower. He edited for many years the *British Journal of Medical Psychology*. Among his most interesting papers in the Society's *Proceedings* was a study of 'The Appreciation of Time among Somnambules' (*Proceedings*, XXI, 1908–9). Somnambules were hypnotized subjects who had no conscious memory of what had been said during the trance state; and yet punctually carried out post hypnotic suggestions to perform some task at a given future date or even hour.

The distinction between 'physical' and 'mental' was more sharply drawn then than now but though he inclined to the idea that their ability was not 'merely physiological' (how mere is mere?) he linked it with Myers' concept of subliminal consciousness, with Gurney's suggestion that this function could count days, with his own observation that some subjects could carry out mathematical reasoning during their trances, and with the possibility that all this might be connected with the feats of 'calculating prodigies' (and, one might now add, with those of certain autistic children). It remains for some enterprising modern investigator to link the matter with the working of 'biological clocks'. William James' adjuration, 'connect, connect, only connect' is still vital.

Camille Flammarion, 1842–1925
President 1923

One of the Society's eminent foreign Presidents, the French Camille Flammarion was best known as a professional astronomer of the first rank. He founded in 1882 a review, *L'Astronomie*, later became President of the Astronomical Society of France, and published various books on various books on the subject, both scientific and popular. His interest in psychical research began early. At 19 he became a member of the *Societé Parisienne des Etudes Spirites*. His election card was signed by Allan Kardec, founder of the Continental spiritist movement which later spread to Latin America. He was in 1869 in touch with the Dialectical Society – which that year established a Committee to deal with psychical research. This Society had been set up with the help of Alfred Russell Wallace (who formulated the theory of evolution almost simultaneously with Charles Darwin), William Crookes, and others. Later on Flammarion appealed to the readers of various French periodicals to answer a list of queries based on the SPR Census of Hallucinations. In 1900 he published a book, *L'Inconnu et les Problemes Psychiques*, springing from their replies.

His lucid and learned Presidential Address drew both on the humanities and on his own specialized knowledge. He declared that telepathy 'is as much a fact as are London, Sirius and oxygen'; and stressed the fact that Marconi had said at a great public meeting that it did *not* operate through 'physical vibrations' analogous to electrical waves. He discussed the foundation of the *Institut Métaphysique International* in Paris, and its use of statistical methods of investigation; and – with less enthusiasm – a newly published collection of Victor Hugo's mediumistic experiments during the 1850s, which had produced messages not only from various historical figures such as Aeschylus, Moses, Shakespeare and Moliere, but also from Death, the Ideal and – Androcles' Lion. Among his own *quelques principes* he affirms that human beings have faculties, unknown to science, which survive the body, that 'manifestations of the dead' do happen on occasion, and that telepathy occurs not only between the living, but between them and the dead.

J. G. Piddington
President 1924–5

Piddington was unfortunate in substituting his mother's maiden name for his own, which was Smith. He did this to avoid confusion; but ran into an unexpected risk – that of being identified by posterity with 'The Piddingtons' a husband and wife team who carried out well organized music hall 'telepathy acts'.

He joined the Society in 1890, and served as its Hon Secretary from 1899 to 1907 and later as its Treasurer. An admirable administrator, he did much unspectacular but essential work, financial and otherwise.

It was he who established the Society's Research Endowment Fund; and he who devoted a great deal of time, scholarship and ingenuity to interpreting cases of cross correspondence, some of them complex and obscure. Already in 1906 he was encouraging Mrs Verrall to keep up her automatic writing; and in 1923 he was carefully evaluating some of the scripts that had seemed to foretell some of the events of World War I, notably the sinking of the Lusitania.

He had a gift for summing people up well – demonstrated in his obituary of the Australian Richard Hodgson which, after acknowledging the value of his work, presented him as 'a sociable, athletic man', who 'dealt hammer blows in controversy' and 'knew he was right'.

Piddington's Presidential Address (*Proceedings* **XXXIV**, 1924) noted that, though progress had been slow and hesitating, there had been real advance; and that scientists, who were not always good at assessing human testimony, should not be regarded as 'the last court of appeal'. Long-winded as it tends to be, it makes one important point that needs constant reiteration; that of the danger of the Society's lowering its critical standards in order to retain members (and their subscriptions) who were impatient with slow, complex, research procedures. *What would it profit to save the Society and to forfeit the end to which the Society is a means?*, he asked.

Professor Dr Hans Driesch, 1867–1941
President 1926–7

Hans Driesch, biologist and philosopher, when working at the Marine Zoology Station at Naples in the 1890s carried out an odd experiment with a sea-urchin's egg. He killed one half of it; and found that the surviving half produced an embryo perfect except that it was only half the usual size. Concluding that 'the living cell aims at some sort of wholeness', he went on to formulate a theory of what he called 'entelechy'. As briefly set out, many years later, in his fascinating but cautious Presidential Address of 1926, it suggested that the development of organisms was directed by 'a unifying non-material mind-like something . . . an ordering principle which does not add either energy or matter' to what goes on. This principle might exist outside time and space; an idea which recurs in the work of a later President, Sir Alister Hardy (who declared himself an orthodox Darwinian just as Driesch declared *his* viewpoint was compatible with 'a mathematical and materialist approach to biology') and with the recent work of Dr Rupert Sheldrake. Driesch also suggested that 'the mind may carry out a morphogenetic action at a distance'.

Dr Elmar Grüber's able survey of Driesch's work (*Journal*, SPR, September 1978) suggested that he was a Vitalist as early as 1892.

His Gifford Lectures were published in 1907 and 1908. Visiting London in 1913 he met Mrs Sidgwick, and after discussions with her he joined the Society. In 1919 he became Professor of Systematic Philosophy at Cologne University and in 1921 Director of Philosophical Seminars at Leipzig. In May 1922 he gave in Prague the inaugural address to the newly formed Czech Society for Psychical Research. In another inaugural discourse – this time at the Fourth International Congress for Psychical Research (whose *Transactions*, edited by Theodore Besterman appeared in London in 1930)– he put forward the idea that 'the soul, like a monad remains identical with itself after death' but that then the normal channels of communications are those which are paranormal for the living.

He early realized the importance of J. B. Rhine's work, and translated his *New Frontiers of the Mind* into German. Of his own books there were often both English and German versions. *The Science and Philosophy of the Organism*, indeed, was first published in London in 1908; the German edition appeared in 1909. Nineteen fourteen saw *The Philosophy of Vitalism*, and *The Crisis in Psychology* came out in 1925. A monograph on parapsychology was translated by Theodore Besterman as *Psychical Research* in 1933.

Driesch contributed to many periodicals in Europe and America, as to the Society's publications; his paper on *Memory and its Relation to Psychical Research* (*Proceedings* 43, 1935) opened up a field tentatively explored nearly fifty years later by Dr Susan Blackmore.

His work is not easy to read, even in English, partly because his mind worked in accordance with a Germanic pattern of words, thoughts and inferences; but it is of importance, notably for those attempts to link biology and psychical research which are being renewed in our own time.

Sir Lawrence J. Jones, Bt, died 1955
President 1928–9

Sir Lawrence Jones joined the Society in 1888, and though the date of his birth is not recorded, he must have been in his eighties when he died. He had two spontaneous extra-sensory experiences of his own, and engaged in a number of sittings with a non-professional medium, Miss Kate Wingfield, which convinced him that the dead survived and that it was possible to get into touch with them. His Presidential Address described Miss Wingfield's progress (she seems to have been distinctly versatile). 'Clairvoyance and automatic writing (which, assisted by taps and table tilting, had been the means through which communications were received) developed into trance mediumship', in which state she delivered messages from various people including an ancient Egyptian medical man who 'became the family doctor'. Luckily his advice was full of ordinary commonsense. This medium also levitated a table and produced 'apports'. Though she had no Control of her own, she allotted a different Guide – as it were a guardian angel – to each sitter. She also showed what may have been a curious telepathic or precognitive awareness of a murder and its circumstances before anything had been reported.

Sir Lawrence did note however that not all spirit messages were trustworthy, in that Myers for instance (who told him about it) had been informed that he was to die in February 1902 and *actually* died in January 1901, while Richard Hodgson had been misled in the same way.

Dr Walter Franklin Prince, PhD, 1863–1934
President 1930–1

Dr Prince was first drawn to psychical research when, as Rector of All Saints, Pittsburgh, already interested in psychotherapy, he came across 'Doris Fischer', a girl who after much ill-treatment by a drunken father had developed a number of different, sometimes conflicting, personalities (on occasion they left notes for one another!) Dr Prince and his wife adopted her as a daughter in 1908, and by 1914 reintegration was on the way.

His investigations were published by James Hyslop, then Secretary of the American SPR, in its *Journal* and *Proceedings* in 1915 and 1916, and he contributed a paper on the case to the American *Journal of Abnormal Psychology* in 1916.

In that year, he became Hyslop's assistant, and did much research work; remarkable for its 'thoroughness and attention to detail'. After a temporary change of policy at the ASPR he became Research Officer at its Boston counterpart, whose *Journal* he edited. In 1927, during a visit to Europe, he investigated Rudi Schneider.

Attracted by laboratory work, and results that could be interpreted statistically, he found a kindred spirit in the young Joseph Banks Rhine (qv) who later wrote of him as 'my principal teacher in psychical research'. His Presidential Address however, after distinguishing between 'the will to believe' and 'the will to prove', stressed the psychical researcher's continual need for detachment and the danger of 'getting stuck in a working hypothesis'; and maintained the importance of field work and historical and legal investigation as well as that of scientific procedures.

Among his books were *The Psychic in the House* (Boston 1926), *The Case of Patience Worth* (Boston 1927) and *The Enchanted Boundary* (Boston 1930).

Sir Oliver Lodge, DSc, FRS and Mrs Henry Sidgwick
Joint Presidents of Honour 1932
(see pages 183 and 191)

Dame Edith Lyttelton (née Balfour), DBE, GBE, died 1949
President 1933—4

Edith Balfour, of the clan but not the family of the other 'SPR Balfours', married in 1892 a widower of seventeen years standing, Alfred Lyttelton, KC, MP, at one time Colonial Secretary. A woman of great intelligence, ability and enterprise, in touch with most of the social and political activities of her time, she worked in an organization for the relief of refugees, and for the English Speaking Union; and served as an official delegate to the League of Nations.

She joined the Society in 1902, and its Council in 1928. One of her less known services was to recruit Rosalind Heywood as a member after a conversation begun on the spur of the moment in a lift. Rosalind (who died in 1980) later became a Vice-President, and did much valuable work, taking part in various qualitative experiments, carrying out investigations, contributing to the *Journal* and producing two brilliant books, *The Sixth Sense* (London, 1959) and *The Infinite Hive* (London, 1964) which have illuminated the subject matter of parapsychology for thousands of readers inside the Society and beyond.

Edith Lyttelton began, after her husband's death in 1913, to produce automatic writing, first as 'Mrs King' and later under her real name. The scripts of February and May 1914 seem to have foretold the sinking of the *Lusitania* the following year. Later ones produced sinister allusions – meaningless at the time – to Berchtesgaden and Munich. Some of her work tied in with the famous – and extremely complex – Cross Correspondences.

In her Presidential Address Dame Edith observed rather ruefully that she had had no training in science, philosophy or psychology, and that her interest in psychical research arose from a desire to explain her own personal 'perceptions of something unknown to the conscious mind', which came to her in the form of 'an inner voice and imaging'. She believed that these, and other veridical hallucinations were no more than mechanisms for conveying ESP (as were ouija boards etc.) and she stressed that what mattered was the content of the apparent message. She stressed, too, that such perceptions took different forms in different people; thus, in working with J. W. Dunne, she had never achieved a precognitive dream, though when she was awake and her mind still, 'precognitions drop in like snow'. She produced tentative suggestions as to the nature of time, and believed that psi-impressions could come both from what has been called 'Super ESP' and from some 'field of experience' in which living and discarnate minds could interact.

In her youth she wrote several plays, one dealing with the problem of sweated labour; and her books include *Our Superconscious Mind* (London, 1931) and *Some Cases of Prediction* (London, 1936).

Professor C. D. Broad, 1887–1971
President 1935–6 and 1958–60

Charlie Dunbar Broad originally wanted to be an engineer, and continued all his life to be fascinated by model engineering; a taste which probably contributed much to the precision and objectiveness of his thought. A master at Dulwich College however encouraged his interest in science and he won a scholarship in this subject to Trinity College, Cambridge where, after gaining a First Class in the first part of the Natural Science Tripos he decided that he was not mathematical enough to be a physicist, turned to philosophy, and again got a First. Trinity awarded him a Prize Fellowship. He lectured in Logic at the Universities of St Andrews and Dundee, worked for the Ministry of Munitions in World War One, and was appointed Professor of Philosophy at Bristol, whence he returned to Trinity in 1923. In 1926 he became Lecturer in Moral Science, and served as Knightbridge Professor of Moral Philosophy from 1935 to 1953. He had Fellowships and honorary degrees in several countries.

After all this one might have expected, as his Cambridge pupil Henry Coombe Tennant did, 'someone tall, saturnine and remote', only to find him 'mild and cherubic, playing with a yo-yo' in his rooms, which had once belonged to Sir Isaac Newton. He remained all his life a man of immense intellectual ability, unselfconscious candour, and charm of an almost Lewis Carroll quality. I went to tea with him once in those very rooms, and a polite undergraduate offered me anchovy toast from the hearth, only to be met with the gentle rebuke (pointing towards a plate on the table), 'She must eat her bread and butter first'.

Alan Gauld, who wrote a brief biographical sketch in the *Journal* for June 1971 noted that one of Broad's most interesting achievements was to combine 'a humanistic and a scientific turn of mind'. It should be added that in both contexts he thought with strenuous precision, in both he defined his terms and in both he set out his argument clearly in a language not embarnacled with in-group jargon. He used recondite words; but they were all to be found in a good dictionary. His work could be hard to follow, because it involved considerable intellectual exercise, but not because his meaning was in doubt.

He joined a Cambridge psychical research group in 1906, the Society in 1920 and its Council in 1930. His Presidential Address, 'Normal Cognition, Clairvoyance and Telepathy' (*Proceedings* 43, 1935) noted that all perception, sensory or extra sensory, has to be interpreted by the mind; and dealt in detail with telepathy (of whose existence he was certain) suggesting that 'each of us may often or continuously be influenced by other minds without realizing the fact'. He also put forward the concept of 'a common substratum of experience affected by the separate experiences of all human beings, which might affect one another through it', a concept echoing back to Jung and forward to Sir Alister Hardy's suggestion (*Proceedings* 50, May 1935) that there might be 'a general subconscious sharing of a form and behaviour design between members of a species', a design modified by their individual reactions.

Broad's second Presidential Address in 1958 (*Proceedings* 52, Feb, 1959), discussed 'Dreaming and Some of its Implications', observing that dreams can include the process of reasoning (as when he himself dreamed he had been levitated some 8 feet, caught up a heavy glass vase from a shelf high above the fireplace, and swooped down to put it on the floor to prove the levitation had been real and not the result of hypnotic suggestion). He also discussed the nature of perception, and the possible implications of out of the body experiences. He contributed valuable papers to *Proceedings* from time to time. Among his books were *Scientific Thought: The Mind and its Place in Nature: Religion Philosophy and Psychical Research:* and *Induction, Probability and Causation*.

He did not like the idea of surviving death, but came to think it possible.

Robert John Strutt, fourth Baron Rayleigh, FRS, 1875–1947
President 1937–8

Lord Rayleigh, who succeeded his father in 1919, carried on the family tradition both in science and in psychical research. He became a Fellow of the Royal Society in 1905, served as Professor of Physics at Imperial College, London, from 1908 till 1919, and did valuable work on radio activity in rock formations.

His Presidential Address in 1937 dealt with 'The Problem of Physical Phenomena in Psychical Research'. Though 'physical' had by this time been substituted for 'spiritualistic' as applied to such happenings, the subject was still very much under a cloud and he almost apologized for discussing 'a somewhat unfashionable topic from which the Society had turned away', justifying himself only on the grounds that it was the one he knew most about. Like his father eighteen years earlier he noted scientific reluctance to look at the problem of globe lighting because its appearances were spontaneous and therefore not susceptible to experimental tests; and observed that the same difficulty arose with many forms of psi, and that this should not cause incredulity in either case, important as experimental work was wherever it could be carried out.

After summing up various early investigations, experimental and otherwise, and the criticisms they met, he concluded that later failures to repeat what had happened would 'hardly be a disproof where the identical conditions cannot be re-established'; a rare triumph for commonsense in a field where the importance of having so to speak 'the time, the place and the loved one *all together*' is so seldom appreciated.

He mentioned work done with Eusapia Paladino, discussed the contradictory results obtained by two different investigators with a Miss Goligher in Belfast, and surveyed in more detail the studies of Rudi Schneider carried out in Paris by the Osty brothers in 1932, noting the very odd correlation between 'the loud rapid breathings of the medium and the absorptions of the infra-red beam' originally set up to guard some object used as a target for psychokinetic movement.

Aware that the 'trance personality' of certain mediums, all too anxious to deliver the goods, mental or physical, would resort to trickery if paranormal means failed, he suggested that it was a mistake 'to discard all phenomena produced by a medium once discovered in fraud' since records of their results so often yielded 'an appreciable residue . . . not successfully dissolved by the acid of destructive criticism so freely poured over it. The evidence seems to stand, and if we dogmatically reject it we shall be open to the reproach of laying down what *ought* to be the order of nature instead of observing what *is*'; a warning that all psychical researchers should bear in mind.

Henry Habberley Price, MA, BSc, FBA, 1899–
President 1939–41 and again 1960–1

H. H. Price— on no account to be confused with the flamboyant *Harry Price*— was educated at Winchester, and served in the Royal Air Force from 1917 to 1919. Perhaps it was this experience that led him to found the Oxford University and City Gliding Club, an initiative which shows it would be unjust to form a stereotyped image of him as an Absent Minded Professor immersed in abstract thought to the exclusion of all else. There could be grounds for doing so; on one occasion, for instance, he became so much absorbed during a broadcast discussion that a fellow broadcaster had to stop him knocking out his pipe on a microphone.

He went up to Oxford as a scholar of New College, got a First, and then became in his own words, 'a professional philosopher', in various academic posts, among them that of Wykeham Professor of Logic. He lectured at many British universities, at Princeton, and at the University of California at Los Angeles. Among his books were *Perception, Hume's Theory of the External World, Belief* (his Gifford Lectures) and *Essays on the Philosophy of Religion*.

He contributed much valuable material to the *Journal* and *Proceedings*. His Presidential Address noted (as had Prospero Lambertini 200 years before him) the rarity of paranormal experiences among highly educated people, and urged that these should be encouraged to think in images, which were good vehicles for extra sensory perception. He also urged that they should try various physical procedures as means to increasing sensitivity; among these were fasting, yoga exercises, and reduced atmospheric pressure (as on high mountains). He suggested, moreover, that images once made may persist apart from the minds in which they originated, and may generate more; a forward echo, perhaps, of Dr Rupert Sheldrake's 'hypothesis of formative causation'. He believed that the existence of telepathy, clairvoyance and hauntings had been proved, and that this diminished 'the antecedent improbability of survival'. His last remarks, startling in a man accustomed to argue with the closest logical precision, were that in discussing psychical research — whose data differ so much from those of other subjects — the risk of talking apparent nonsense had to be taken, and that 'it will be the timidity of our hypotheses, not their extravagance, which will provoke the derision of posterity'.

It looks as if modern physics may well prove this delightful character to have been quite right.

Robert Henry Thouless, MA, PhD, 1894–
President 1942–4

Educated at Corpus Christi College, Cambridge, where he was awarded his PhD in 1922, Robert Thouless went on to be a Lecturer in Psychology at Manchester, in Glasgow, and again in Cambridge. Here he became the Reader in Educational Psychology. He was President of the British Association's Psychology Section in 1937, and published a number of books connected with this subject, including *Straight and Crooked Thinking* (1953). He also published *Experimental Psychical Research* (1963) and *From Anecdote to Experiment in Psychical Research* (1972).

His Presidential Address 'On the Present Position of Experimental Research into Telepathy and Related Phenomena', detached, judicial — and stimulating — raised many points that are still important. He stressed the fact that though he was an experimental psychologist, and therefore accustomed to experimental methods of study, he considered observational methods equally important in psychical research. He preferred the term _psi phenomena_ (which implied no theory) to _extra-sensory perception_, which assumed that some special _kind_ of perception was at work. He insisted that people should accept the possibility that psi-phenomena are real and objective even though they cannot be explained in terms of physical causation; that is, that they do not necessarily arise _either_ from fraud or illusion, _or_ from a physical cause as yet unknown (as it might be some new form of radiation). Here hindsight, bearing in mind the discovery of a magnetic sense in birds, bees, snails and probably in humans can only remark 'why not both'; a reaction also provoked by his building on Bergson's wider hypotheses to suggest that psi links us with the amoeba rather than, as Myers suggested, with 'the spiritual world'. Again, why not both?

Obviously much of its material has been modified by the later work of Sir Alister Hardy, FRS (in his Presidential Address for 1966, and in his Gifford Lectures, 'The Living Stream' and 'The Divine Flame') but it is well worth reading still, both in itself and for its occasional evidence that dualism was beginning to revive after long dormancy.

G. N. M. Tyrrell, 1879–1952
President 1945–6

George Tyrrell took his degree at the University of London in mathematics and physics. He worked under Marconi on radio communication, and was demonstrating Marconi's techniques to the Mexican government when he joined the Society in 1905. He served as a signals officer with the Royal Artillery in World War I.

In 1921 he first carried out some quantitative experiments with Miss Gertrude Johnson, whom he and his wife had adopted as a daughter. Miss Johnson had marked extrasensory gifts; she produced automatic writing, 'saw' veridical pictures in a crystal, and had occasional flashes of precognition; one proved very useful in a most prosaic way during World War II when a domestic pail wore out and new ones were almost impossible to find. She dreamt she went to a certain shop, found they unexpectedly had some green ones in; went there early next morning— and duly found and bought a green pail. She also had a talent for finding lost objects, which led him to devise a 'pointer apparatus' for use in further experiments some years later, after a great pressure of work had lifted and left him some leisure. It consisted of 'five small boxes with hinged lids mounted behind a board in such a way that a pointer could be thrust through holes in the board into any selected box without the subject being able to see what was being done. 'The subject was required to lift the lid of the box where she thought the pointer had been put.' It was then suggested that the sound made by the pointer might give a clue, and he invented a similar kind of apparatus, in which a tiny electric lamp glowed when the operator pressed a key; the subject had to guess as before, and successes and failures were automatically recorded on tape. Various later improvements included a mechanical selector which determined the operation of the keys in a random order. (This was to rule out the possibility that the experimenter and the subject might have the same favourite numbers.) Miss Johnson was not, of course, the only subject used; I remember taking a seven-year-old boy to play with this apparatus sometime late in the 1930s; he was not very successful. The machine was destroyed in an air raid, and never rebuilt.

Tyrrell's Presidential Address in 1945 pointed out the danger of a split between statistical and qualitative workers which was 'likely to occur because two different types of mind, and two different temperaments, were involved'. He added that psychical research needs both. His two books, *Science and Psychical Phenomena* (London, 1938) and *The Personality of Man* (London, 1946) vividly illustrate the clarity, the ingenuity and the openness of his mind, ready to admit the extreme oddity of the data of psychical research, which did not fit into the current world outlook; and to accept the fact that 'a kind of intellectual revolution was needed to make sense of them'. Professor H. H. Price, who wrote this in an obituary tribute, disagreed with Tyrrell's theory that evolutionary pressures had increasingly adapted man to pay all his attention to his environment here and now, to become *homo faber*, man the maker, rather than man the thinker. He attributed it to a much briefer historical process, the influence of the philosopher Descartes, spreading like a drop of oil through European civilization.

Whatever the origin of the split between the two kinds of knowledge (which had in fact been observed by the Muslim philosopher, Avicenna many centuries ago) Tyrrell's desire to reintegrate them echoes and re-echoes in the work of many of the Society's Presidents before him and after.

W. H. Salter, 1880–1969
President 1947–8

W. H. Salter went up to Trinity College, Cambridge, with a Classical Scholarship in 1899, took a first class degree in 1901, turned to read Law, and was called to the Bar in 1905. 'He was', wrote Professor Broad in his obituary, 'a typical cultured Liberal Nonconformist' who 'exhibited . . . the many virtues and occasional angularities of that once powerful and now almost extinct Victorian species.' He added to great learning, a talent for administration, and a profound – and comforting – self assurance, a very useful gift for getting on with most people (though one must except Miss Moberley and Miss Jourdain of Versailles fame) and considerable *bonhomie*, which once led to his being crowned with flowers from the tables of a Paris *bistro*, by some French students who had seen him keeping his own small party there in explosions of laughter. A man of rocklike integrity, he had, by the time I came to know him, an odd resemblance to an extremely intelligent and respectable white Aberdeen terrier.

He married in 1915 Helen Verrall, daughter of two classical scholars at Cambridge. Like her mother, she produced much automatic writing. In 1916 W. H. Salter joined the Society, to become a member of its Council three years later. From 1920 to 1931, a very difficult financial period, he served as Honorary Treasurer; and from 1924 to 1948 he was Honorary Secretary. The Society owed an enormous amount to his steady, firm, efficient guidance, to his hard and unremitting work, and to the confidence he inspired.

He deposited two collections of SPR material in the Library of Trinity College, Cambridge. The first, handed over in 1956, consisted of his own reminiscences of the Society. It is not to be opened till 1996. The second, handed over in 1963, not to be opened till 1995, is labelled 'Matter of Importance in connexion with the Cross Correspondences', and contains *inter alia*, a number of unpublished scripts, diaries and letters.

He made many contributions to *Journal* and *Proceedings*, and published two admirable books, *Ghosts and Apparitions* (1938) and *Zoar* (1961).

Professor Gardner Murphy, PhD,
1896–1979
President 1949–50

Professor Gardner Murphy's interest in psychical research began when he heard his family discussing Mrs Piper and her phenomena. A student of psychology with a BA from Yale and an MA from Harvard (where he was later a Hodgson Fellow) he served with the American Army in World War I, before gaining a PhD at Colombia, where he worked for many years. In 1940 he became a Professor of the Menninger Foundation. He then served as visiting Professor of Psychology at George Washington University till his retirement in 1973.

All this time he was extending his interest in psychical research, theoretical and practical. A member of the American Association for the Advancement of Science, he spoke at a Symposium on Parapsychology in Washington in 1948 on *The Place of Parapsychology among the Sciences*.

He made a special visit to England to deliver his Presidential Address in person. It is still relevant, valuable and stimulating. Its themes include the value of mass experiments in ESP as contrasted with those exploiting individual talent; the part played by personal needs and purposes in spontaneous paranormal cognition; the 'criss-cross paths' of association; the contribution made by psycho-analysis; and what he called the *tertium quid*, the sudden unexpected invasion of the mind by psi-impressions. Professor Gardner Murphy's continuing emphasis on the idea that psi inheres in relationships between persons rather than in individuals as such is particularly striking in connexion with the growing interest in 'experimenter effect' today.

S. G. Soal DSc 1890–1975
President 1950–1

Soal's education was that of 'a pure mathematician'. At twenty he graduated from London University with first class honours in mathematics, and though his academic career was interrupted by military service he went back to it after being demobilized in 1919, and became Senior Lecturer in Mathematics at Queen Mary College.

His interest in psychical research began when a brother was killed in action in 1918. He sat with various mediums but got little that could not be explained by telepathy till 1921, when a curious, detailed precognitive experience began to develop concerning the house of a friend whom he believed – wrongly – to be dead.

He admired – and lectured on – Rhine's work in the 1930s and undertook a five-year-long series of experiments of his own, involving 160 people and 128,356 'guesses'. Examined for telepathy these showed no significant results and were laid aside. In 1939 Queen Mary College was evacuated to Cambridge where Soal met Whately Carington. At first there was some coldness – Soal's scepticism 'had become a byword', but they became friends, and Carington urged him to re-examine the shelved experiments for possible evidence of 'temporal distraction'. This was done (cf *Proceedings* 46, 1940 – 1941) by Dr Robert Thouless (qv), Mrs Goldney, and Carington himself. Clear evidence of precognition was found.

Soal continued his investigations despite the difficulties of air raids, blackouts and wartime travel. His Presidential Address in 1950 (*Proceedings*) urged that experiments should aim not to reiterate the occurrence of extra sensory perception but to find out how it worked. He stressed that the phenomena of physics were characterized by uniformity and those of psychology by uniqueness and pointed out that the ability to will and to choose were non physical aspects of human personality.

In 1960 he was violently attacked by a Professor Hansel (*Proceedings* 53) who basing himself on 'the hypothesis that precognition does not take place' ascribed the phenomena recorded in *Modern Experiments in Telepathy* (Soal and Bateman, London, 1954) to trickery or error. Soal replied in the same issue that the agents involved were respectable academics, unlikely to be involved either in these or in collusion. In the March 1971 *Journal* R. G. Medhurst attacked him again in a paper 'On the Origin of the Prepared Random Numbers in the Shackleton Experiments'. This was followed in 1974 by a further attack by other writers in *Proceedings* (Volume 56) which also contained a reply by various defenders.

This is only a brief outline of events described at greater length in Chapter Nine, to which readers are referred for more detail.

Professor Gilbert Murray, FBA, OM.
President 1952
(see page 196)

Professor F. J. M. Stratton DSO, FRS
1881–1961
President 1953–5

F. J. M. Stratton was Professor of Astrophysics, and Director of the Solar Physics Observatory, at Cambridge from 1928 to 1947, and President of Gonville and Caius College there from 1945 to 1948.

As an undergraduate he went to Cambridge with an introduction from Oliver Lodge to Mrs Sidgwick, met her brothers Arthur and Gerald Balfour, and developed a lifelong interest in psychical research, undiminished by his own lack of success in experimental work. He joined the Society in 1902, became a member of Council in 1947, and kept up for many years the file recording the protracted Haunting of Abbey House in Cambridge on which Dr Alan Gauld based his fascinating and baffling article in the *Journal* for September 1972.

Professor Stratton's Presidential Address traced the ancestry of the

Society back to the Cambridge Ghost Club of the 1850s and its development onwards until his own time, noting how many phenomena formerly rejected by dogmatic scientists – meteorites and hypnotism among them – were now accepted. He pointed out the limitations of laboratory experiment, urged that members should report contemporary spontaneous cases, and suggested that it was the job of philosophers to think out 'a reconciling conceptual framework' to include both activities. After recording the increasing recognition of psychical research by British, Dutch and American universities, he quoted with approval Sir William Crookes' remarks in his Presidential Address to the British Association that 'to stop short in research . . . to recoil from fear of difficulty or adverse criticism, is to bring reproach to Science'.

G. W. Lambert, BA, CB, 1889–
President 1955–8

Educated at Cheltenham College, where he came across the work of a former pupil, F. W. H. Myers, Guy Lambert had a distinguished career as a Civil Servant, culminating in his appointment as Assistant Under-Secretary of State for War.

He contributed to Volume 36 of *Proceedings* (1928) a fascinating *Study of the Psychology of Plotinus*, whose views on parapsychology he showed as still lively and relevant. He later worked on the background of various pieces of automatic writing – those of Bligh Bond at Glastonbury, for instance, and above all Mrs Verrall's scripts – tracing names, relationships, places and references with the utmost scholarly accuracy and industry. He discussed the Versailles experiences of Miss Jourdain and Miss Moberly in connection with a plan for the gardens made – but never carried out – some years before the time of Marie-Antoinette with which the two percipients had associated what they saw.

His Presidential Address on 'The Use of Evidence in Psychical Research' (*Proceedings* 50, 1956) distinguished between telepathic hallucinations, which might be seen by several people at once, and subjective hallucinations, which were, he argued, projected for themselves alone by individuals under the stress of anxiety and fear. This Address also outlined the geophysical theory of poltergeist outbreaks which came to dominate his later thought, and is examined in the text of this book.

The Society owes him a great debt of gratitude for research that has involved an enormous amount of very detailed work.

Professor C. D. Broad
President 1958–60
(see page 208)

Henry Habberley Price, MA, BSc, FBA
President 1960–1
(see page 211)

Professor E. R. Dodds, FBA, 1893–1979
President 1961–3

A learned and lively classical scholar, and an Oxford man who later became Regius Professor of Greek, Eric Dodds was co-opted to the SPR Council in 1927. His autobiography, *Missing Persons* (1977) shows his deep interest, from his undergraduate years onwards, in 'that vast range of phenomena which occupy the disputed territory between science and superstition'. He worked for a while on the subject with Professor Schiller; he compared Myers' and Freud's concepts of the unconscious mind; he succeeded in getting telepathic responses from hypnotized subjects; and he came to accept telepathy as a fact of life. He attended experiments with those 'physical' mediums, the Schneider brothers. He investigated 'mental' mediums, and in a proxy sitting with the well known Mrs Leonard, elicited a long string of facts later verified but then unknown to the experimenters, about a dead man of whom she knew nothing but his name. As he could not believe in survival, he was, he said, 'inclined to explain' what had happened as the effect of very complex telepathy.

Among his more general studies *The Greeks and the Irrational* (1951) touched on the paranormal. His contributions to *Proceedings* included 'Why I do not Believe in Survival' (1934), 'Supernormal Phenomena in Classical Antiquity' (1972) and in that same year 'Gilbert Murray's Last Experiments'. His Presidential Address (*Proceedings* 1962) discussed 'Experimental Research at the Universities and at the Society'.

Professor D. J. West, MD, PhD, LittD, MRCPsych, 1924–
President 1963–5

Professor West's main career has lain in the medical, legal and psychological study of crime. He is the Director of the Institute of Criminology, and Professor of Clinical Criminology at Cambridge, where he is a Fellow of Darwin College. He has written eleven books on various aspects of this subject and contributed to many specialized periodicals and symposia.

Between 1947 and 1950, he served as Research Officer to the Society. Numerous *Journal* articles record his energetic careful work, including reports on Mass Observation's study of hallucinations; on the fable that a well known medium had once disclosed to the Home Office the identity of Jack the Ripper; on some Proxy Sittings; and on a supposed case of xenoglossy in which two mediums claimed to have spoken in trance the languages of their Chinese and African 'spirit guides'. At a subsequent meeting experts in both languages said only that the mediums had produced 'sounds no one could understand'. One African tribal language was however unknown to them. West found a man who could speak it and organized another seance at which the latter addressed the medium involved but elicited no more than 'long, voluble, unintelligible replies'. West commented that this did not necessarily involve bad faith on the medium's part. He also investigated a 'haunted' dance hall, spent a night there listening to a tap dripping, floors creaking, and doors rattling in the wind; found a disused sewer which was 'a runway for rats'; interviewed the three main witnesses to the haunting; and found nothing necessarily paranormal. His report on the year's work in 1948 made some interesting suggestions for further study, notably of physiological changes in mediums (now being investigated by Dr Peter Fenwick and others), of extra sensory perception in animals, and of folklore.

Later, he contributed papers on ESP tests with psychotics (outlining his own experiments at three different hospitals, and surveying the results obtained by other psychiatrists) and on a series of long distance clock-card guessing experiments on volunteers, carried out with G. W. Fisk. This yielded evidence of what is called 'experimenter effect' (the idea that subjects score more successfully with one experimenter than with another); a theme taken up again in West's Presidential Address. Here, while dismissing the idea that psi is 'an illusion founded on a mixture of careless experiment, fraud and statistical artefacts', he suggests that 'a high degree of elusiveness is almost the only recognizable characteristic of ESP', and that 'if resistance to progress may lie partly in our own unconscious reluctance to face the phenomena squarely' this should not be impossible to overcome.

He obtained in 1958 the McDougall Award for distinguished work in parapsychology. He is Chairman of the Society's Research Grants Fund.

His books on parapsychological topics include *Psychical Research Today* (London, 1954 – a revised paperback edition 1962) and *Eleven Lourdes Miracles* (London, 1957).

Professor Sir Alister Hardy FRS, 1896–
President 1965–9

Alister Hardy, who has so significantly and so fruitfully linked biology with psychical research, was educated at Exeter College, Oxford, and was for a time one of Julian Huxley's students. He specialized in marine biology and explored on long voyages the ecology of sea creatures. Professor of Zoology at Hull University from 1928 to 1942, he returned to Oxford as Linacre Professor of Zoology from 1946 to 1961, and as Professor of Zoological Field Studies from 1961 to 1963. Gifford Lecturer from 1963–5, he founded (and directed till 1976) the Religious Experience Research Unit at Manchester College, Oxford.

In 1949 he suggested in his presidential address to the Zoological section of the British Association for the Advancement of Science that telepathy was relevant to biological studies. In the SPR *Journal* (May/June 1950) he wrote 'assuming the reality of telepathy . . . the discovery that individual organisms are somehow in psychical connexion across space is of course one of the most revolutionary . . . ever made' adding that 'if we admit telepathy in man . . . we must expect something akin to it to mould the patterns of behaviour among members of a species'. In *Proceedings* (Vol. 50, 1953) he worked out the hypothesis that 'there is a general subconscious sharing of a form and behaviour design, a sort of psychic blue-print between members of a species' adding that 'the mathematical plans of growth seem . . . to have all the appearance of . . . a pattern outside the physical world which has served as a plan for selective action by way of changing combinations of genes'.

Sir Alister's Presidential Address to the SPR (*Proceedings* Vol. 55, 1966) declared him to be a Darwinian and a Mendelian, accepting the evidence for the DNA chemical genetic code; but stressed the importance of adaptation, habit and behaviour as a source of evolutionary change, noting for instance that an animal species does not by chance develop webbed feet and take to the water to use them; but that members of that species which begins to dive after fish produce the most successful generations of offspring when their genes favour the development of such feet. No less did he emphasize the importance of dualism as opposed to monism of either sort; and of realizing that consciouness is a given, primary experience, not a by-product of the body's mechanisms.

The first volume of his Gifford Lectures, *The Living Stream* (London, 1966) related these conclusions to contemporary neo-Darwinianism; the second, *The Divine Flame* (London, 1967) surveyed the possible relationship between extra sensory perception and religious experience.

Among his other books are *The Open Sea* (London, 2 vols., 1956 and 1958); *The Biology of God* (London, 1975); *The Spiritual Nature of Man* (London, 1979) and, with Robert Harvie and Arthur Koestler, *The Challenge of Chance* (London, 1973).

Professor W. A. H. Rushton, FRS, ScD, MRCS, LRCP, 1901–80
President 1969–71

A distinguished physiologist primarily concerned with the field of nerve excitation and vision, William Rushton contributed much to psychical research by putting forward natural explanations for phenomena presented as paranormal; by suggesting possibilities for experiment; and by asking awkward questions. Thus, he showed how the device called a 'gismo' employed by the American Ted Serios in producing his 'psychic photographs' *could* have been made to do so in a perfectly ordinary way; though, as a lively controversy later brought out, there was no hard evidence that it had actually been used in this manner.

Dr Bernard Carr observes how stimulating his conversation was, and that 'it was through talking to him about colour vision that I was prompted to investigate the relative roles played by telepathy and clairvoyance in extra sensory perception by using colour-blind Eeste cards'.

Some of the awkward questions (based on the fundamental assumption that *all* perception, sensory or extra sensory, must take place through a physiological mechanism) were trenchantly asked in his short, clear Presidential Address, which he called 'First Sight Second Sight'. Where, he enquired, was the 'eye' of second sight; with what organ in the brain could its functioning be linked; how could information be passed from one brain to another by telepathy when, in split-brain cases, it cannot even pass from one side to another of the *same* brain? And so on. He recognized clearly that for himself 'the trouble with parapsychology is that it is nearly impossible to believe it true, and nearly impossible to believe it false'. Such a rare and admirable openmindedness is most uncomfortable and extremely difficult to maintain. That he did so maintain it shows his lasting and uncompromising desire for truth.

An academic, he was connected with Trinity College, Cambridge, for some thirty years, and for many of them − and until he died − a Vice-President of the very active Cambridge Society for Psychical Research; as well as the main body. He was very kind and very good company; both his talk and his letters were alive with humour.

Professor C. W. K. Mundle, 1920−
President 1971−4

Clement Mundle, one of the Society's philosopher presidents, was brought up in the Scottish tradition, and gained his First in Philosophy, Logic and Metaphysics at the University of St Andrews in 1939. After serving in the RAF from 1940 to 1945 he took another first class degree in 1947, at Oxford. He became Head of the Philosophy Department at Dundee (1947−55) and of the Philosophy Department of the University College of North Wales, Bangor (1955−76). He joined the Society in 1948.

Among his books are *A Critique of Linguistic Philosophy* and *Perception − Facts and Theories*. He has contributed to various symposia, and to many philosophical and parapsychological periodicals in Britain and abroad, among them the Society's *Journal* and *Proceedings*. His Presidential Address, 'Strange Facts in Search of a Theory' surveys with detachment the interaction between the ideas of researchers, the facts they accumulate, and the theories they work out. He looks at the gaps between dualism and monist materialism, and examines various explanations of data so far established; from Hans Berger's ideas of the transformation of electrical brain rhythms into 'psychic energy' and back again, to Ninian Marshall's concept of 'resonance between similar objects' (hardly applicable to experimental work by humans with cards or even with woodlice), Whately Carington's theories of telepathy, Bergson's linkage of memory and clairvoyance in some universal mind, and Dunne's work on precognition which, he suggests, may arise either from inference, possibly based on telepathy, or on psychokinesis.

His final conclusion is that psychical research has established the occurrence of phenomena not yet understood, which can be interpreted either in dualistic or in materialistic terms; but that in order to make verifiable hypotheses we should 'ascertain more facts.'

Dr John Beloff, BA, PhD, 1920–
President 1974–6

John Beloff studied philosophy and psychology at the University of London. He became Research Assistant at the University of Illinois in 1952, and Lecturer in Psychology at the Queen's University, Belfast the following year. In 1956 he was appointed Senior Lecturer in Psychology at the University of Edinburgh. Here, acting as Supervisor, he has encouraged post-graduate studies in psychical research, and various promising parapsychologists have emerged.

Dr Beloff was elected President of the American-based International Parapsychological Association in 1972 and again for 1982, when he was to preside, at Trinity College, Cambridge, over the Centenary Conference of the Society for Psychical Research, concelebrated with the Silver Jubilee of the Parapsychological Association.

Among his books are the trenchant *The Existence of Mind* (1962) and *Psychological Sciences* (1963). He edited *New Directions in Parapsychology* (1974) and has contributed to various symposia (including *Brain and Mind* (1966), *Astride the Two Cultures* (1976), *Parapsychology and Philosophy* (1977) and an *Encyclopaedia of Parapsychology* (1978)); and to many periodicals, among them *Theoria to*

Theory, the *British Journal for the Philosophy of Science*, and *Encounter*, as well as specialist parapsychological journals in Britain – including the Society's publications – Europe and the United States.

In his Presidential Address, published in *Proceedings* in 1975, John Beloff surveyed the vast field of psychical phenomena, and the spectrum of belief in its observers from total sceptics to those who seek confirmation, from those who only trust in the results of laboratory work to the all too credulous. He suggested both that a multiplicity of view points should be encouraged and that in many cases judgment should be suspended. He also declared himself a dualist, convinced of the existence of both mind and body, and that paranormal phenomena 'make sense' only in the context of their interaction.

Professor A. J. Ellison DScEng, FIMechEng, FIEE, Senior Member SEM, Member IEE, 1920
President 1976–9 and 1981–2

After gaining a first class degree at the University of London, Arthur Ellison worked for some years in industry. From 1958 until 1972 – with a period as Visiting Professor at the Massachusetts Institute of Technology in 1959 – he served as Lecturer, and then as Senior Lecturer, at Queen Mary College. Since 1972 he has been Head of the Department of Electrical and Electronic Engineering at the City University, London.

Author of much work on his own special subjects, he published in the *Journal of the Institution of Electrical Engineers, Electronics and Power* (1979) a short survey of Recent Developments in Psychical Research. He has contributed some interesting papers to the Society's publications, and is part-author of two symposia, *Psychism and the Unconscious Mind* (London, 1968) and *Intelligence came First* (London, 1975).

His first Presidential Address, 'Mind Belief and Psychical Research' was printed in *Proceedings* for 1978. His second, delivered at the Royal Society in 1982 celebrates the centenary of the Society by enquiring what we really know after a hundred years of investigation.

Dr J. B. Rhine, PhD, 1895–1980
President 1980

Joseph Banks Rhine was educated in Ohio. With his fellow student and future wife, Louisa Ella Weckesser, he gained a doctorate in biology at the University of Chicago, where for a time he worked on plant physiology. In 1927 husband and wife turned to explore psychical research under Professor William McDougall (q.v.) at the newly formed Department of Psychology at Duke University, North Carolina. He investigated the well known 'Margery' whom he had previously assumed genuine, and found '6 possibilities and 4 positive instances of fraud', plus 19 'suspicious circumstances'. A subsequent study of 'Lady the mind-reading horse' showed that if she could not see the tiny unconscious movements of her trainer, her powers failed.

Convinced that the only way to prove extra sensory perception was 'to evaluate data in mathematical terms' Rhine began his now famous mass experiments with volunteer students. Their results formed the basis of his book, *Extra Sensory Perception* in 1934, which aroused shocked fury, especially in the United States, and brought out the usual accusations of carelessness, statistical inaccuracy and/or fraud. Soon afterwards he was given leave to found a separate Parapsychology Laboratory at Duke, did so and ran it till 1965; when, discovering it would not survive his retirement, he set up the Foundation for Research into the Nature of Man (FRNM) to raise funds, reconstituted the Parapsychology Laboratory as the Institute for Parapsychology and rehoused it outside the University Campus.

Rhine independently discovered phenomena previously observed by members of the Society for Psychical Research, notably the 'decline effect', in which a run of early successful scoring changed after a while into no more than could be expected in accordance with probability theory.

Particularly interesting is his discussion of 'psi-missing', in which scorers guessed significantly below the chance level, as if they unconsciously recognized and avoided the right answers. He devised many ingenious methods of experiment using the Zener cards, which bear five different symbols rather than numbers. With these he tested telepathy, clairvoyance and precognition. In 1943 he and his wife began psychokinetic tests with dice.

Although, as Brian MacKenzie of the University of Tasmania wrote (*Journal of Parapsychology* FRNM March 1980), many of his ideas are also to be found in early SPR *Proceedings*, he discovered them on his own account, gave them a mathematical foundation, publicized them on a large scale, and, to quote John Randall (SPR *Journal*, June 1980) probably 'did more than anyone else to make parapsychology acceptable to the 20th century mind'.

Among his books not yet mentioned are *New Frontiers of the Mind* (1937), *The Reach of the Mind* (1947) and *The New World of the Mind* (1953). He also contributed many papers to specialist periodicals, and his *Myers Memorial Lecture* (*Telepathy and Personality* 1950) concluded that the question of survival could not be answered by parapsychological methods.

The SPR, honoured by his acceptance of the Presidency for 1980, was deeply grieved by his death in harness, and most grateful when his widow, Dr Louisa Rhine, who had long and devotedly shared his work agreed to serve as President for the remainder of his term.

Dr Louisa E. Rhine, PhD
President 1980

Much of Dr Louisa Rhine's lifelong work has been inextricably blended with that of her husband, Professor J. B. Rhine (q.v.). Together they experimented, discussed, planned and carried out new methods – with all the careful detailed work that this entailed – together surveyed and considered the results obtained. It is impossible to assess her contribution separately; possible only to guess at its immense supportive value. It is characteristic that, on her husband's death, she should have accepted the Society's invitation to take over the Presidency for the remainder of his term of office. Her individual achievement has been to go through the great number of spontaneous cases sent in to them from widely different sources and places; to assign these to various categories – telepathy, clairvoyance, precognition, psychokinesis – and to see whether they fell into recognizable patterns,' in which the same contributory causes seemed to be involved. Particularly interesting is her study of ESP in childhood and old age.

Her first book, *Hidden Channels of the Mind* (London, 1961) dealt with cases received from 1948 onwards, examined these matters, and cited many individual instances to illustrate the general argument. A second, *The Invisible Picture* (Jefferson, USA 1981) analysed another 150 cases out of a total of 10,000 received. Her Presidential Address surveyed her husband's long, determined, persevering and successful life and work.

Professor A. J. Ellison, DSc Eng, FI Mech Eng, FIEE, Senior Member SEM, Member IEE, 1920–
President 1981–2
(see page 227)

Appendix I

The Perrott-Warrick Studentship

in psychical research at Trinity College, Cambridge (originally the Perrott Studentship)

This was set up in 1940 as a memorial to F. W. H. Myers, in accordance with the terms of a bequest made by F. D. Perrott. The Warrick contribution came in later. Myers had of course been a Fellow of the College.

Psychical research is defined in this connexion as 'The investigation of mental or physical phenomena which seem *prima facie* to suggest a) the existence of supernormal powers of cognition or of action in human beings in their present life or b) the persistence of the human mind after bodily death.'

The Studentship is tenable for one year, and may be extended for another, but no more. The Fund whose proceeds support it has also provided grants for *ad hoc* expenses, projects and lectures.

Among the Students have been Whately Carington (1940) whose valuable large-scale book on *Telepathy* appeared five years later; Celia Green (1958); Anita Gregory (1965); George Zorab (1967); D. J. Ellis, (1970); Adrian Parker (1972); Brian Miller (1973); Carl Sargent (1974); Richard Broughton (1975) and Susan J. Blackmore (1981).

Three of these, Celia Green, Adrian Parker and Carl Sargent, obtained higher degrees on the basis of their work as Perrott-Warrick Students. Celia Green, now Director of the Institute of Psychophysical Research at Oxford, has amassed and investigated much new material, and has written various books, notably on *Out of the Body Experiences*, *Lucid Dreams*, and *Apparitions*. Anita Gregory (Honorary Secretary to the Society 1980 onwards) has published and collaborated in a number of volumes and is presently bringing out a study of Rudi Schneider, about whose phenomena her Perrott-Warrick thesis was written. She has worked for some twenty years with the North London Polytechnic, and has succeeded in getting a course on parapsychology introduced there. David Ellis has issued a fascinating report on what are known as 'The Raudive Voices' 'heard' or 'overheard' on tape recordings. Brian Miller and Richard Broughton have worked with Dr John Beloff at the Psychology Department of Edinburgh University, carried out experiments, lectured and contributed papers to various parapsychological journals in Europe and America, including of course that of the SPR. Carl Sargent, of the Psychology Laboratory in Cambridge, operating on similar lines, has a good deal of published work to his credit – much, again, in the SPR *Journal*. He has also produced No 17 of the Parapsychology Monographs published by the Parapsychology Foundation in New York. It deals with *Exploring Psi in the Ganzfeld*.

Appendix II

The Ghost Detector

Mr John Cutten, former Secretary of the Society, has very kindly given me particulars of his ingenious invention, 'The Ghost Detector'. The various components, he writes, are as follows:

'The main control box containing the electronics
Camera loaded with infra-red film
Wind vane
Ordinary camera controlling flash unit
Flash unit with infra-red filter
Tape recorder
Flash unit
Vibrator under wind vane
Triggering apparatus for infra-red camera
Bulb for remote control of camera
Photoelectric cell
Microphone
Pilot light
Thermostatic control

'Equipment of this kind was used in a house in Primrose Hill where I spent a night in a bedroom reputed to be haunted. Three people had claimed "experiences" there, but always on the first Monday of the month, and only then.

'In such cases, it is frequently claimed that ghostly visitations are accompanied by: draughts of air, vibrations, changes in the illumination of the room, noises, changes in temperature, or physical disturbances.

'If any such change takes place in the "haunted" room the apparatus is operated automatically and the first camera takes a photograph with the infra-red film. At the same time a buzzer is sounded to awaken the investigator if asleep, and the tape recorder is automatically switched on. The investigator can then press the bulb to take an ordinary photograph with the standard film unit.

A thin wire is trained around the room which, if touched, also triggers off the equipment.

'The main idea is to try and photograph any occurrence so that there is some evidence of what actually caused it. I had no expectation of getting a photograph of a ghost but of detecting by some remote chance whatever physical event might have caused the disturbances in Primrose Hill.

'So far my apparatus has been triggered once only when a vase was found broken on the floor, presumably knocked off the shelf by the cat, which was also in the room.

'It is of course a matter of guesswork where to place the cameras or any other part of the equipment. The Ghost Detector has, incidentally, been featured on BBC television, Scottish Television, ITV and television networks in the United States and Spain.'

Index

This index deals for the most part with people, names and books, because the themes of the Society's work recur in so many connexions and in so many places that to index them all would be to write another volume. Paranormal cognition, psi, extra-sensory perception, whatever you like to call it, appears throughout the book in its four main forms; telepathy (earlier known as 'thought transference'), an inexplicable awareness of what goes on in other people's minds and feelings, sometimes at a great distance; clairvoyance, an inexplicable awareness of what is going on, far away or near at hand, but does not seem to be vividly mirrored in any other human mind at the relevant time; precognition, an inexplicable awareness of some future event; and retrocognition, an apparently direct impression of some happening in the past. Psychokinesis or PK — the effect of the mind or of the psyche not only on its own particular body but on exterior objects — is also fairly widely distributed, but is discussed in detail in the chapters entitled WILDFIRE, and PHYSICAL MEDIUMS.

The Proceedings of the Society were indicated in Roman numerals until 1926, and thereafter in the usual Arabic ones.

The only names indexed from that section of the book dealing with the Presidents of the Society (pages 174–230) are those of the Presidents themselves, and the relevant page numbers are shown in bold print for easy reference.